Practical & Foundational Economics

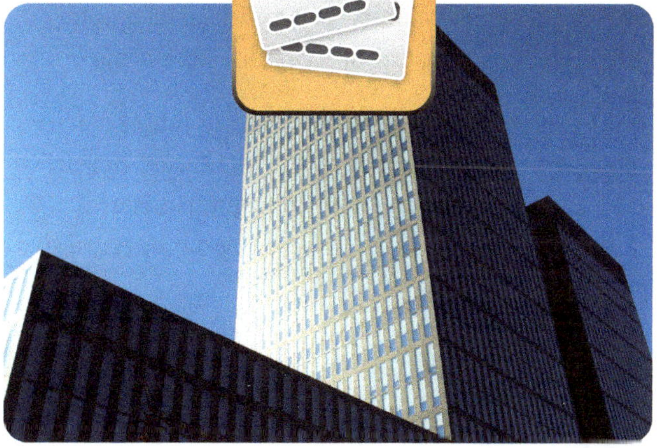

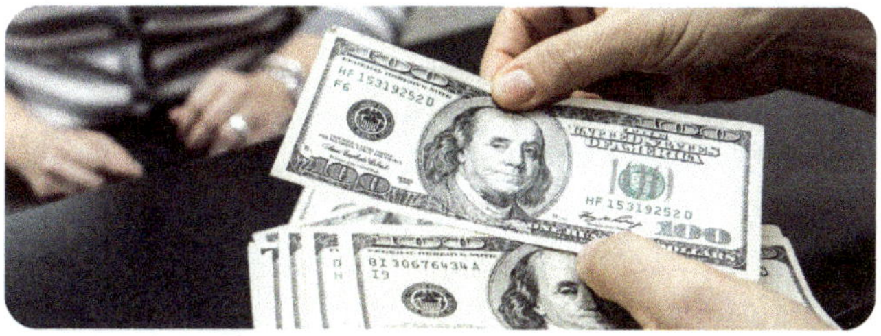

Zeezok™ PUBLISHING

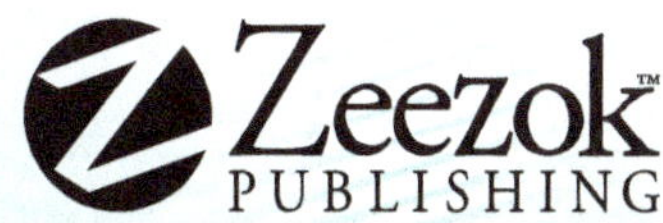

Timothy Spickler, M.Ed.
Kevin Vanderground, J.D.

Practical & Foundational Economics

by Timothy Spickler, M.Ed.
Kevin Vanderground, J.D., Editor

ISBN 978-1-61006-105-6

August, 2018 Edition

Printed in the United States of America

Zeezok Publishing, LLC
PO Box 1960 • Elyria, OH 44036
info@Zeezok.com

www.Zeezok.com

Table of Contents

Assessments Section

General Introduction

Welcome to Zeezok Publishing's *Practical & Foundational Economics* high school economics course. We're thrilled that you've chosen to study this important topic using our curriculum. Designed to teach basic economic principles with practical application to the student's real-life situation, *Practical & Foundational Economics* covers all the national standards as determined by the Council for Economic Education. We unapologetically affirm that capitalism is the best economic model devised by the mind of man. It works because its foundation rests squarely on the economic principles found in God's Word. It fails when sinful human beings misuse the system for their benefit without proper consequences. The solution to our economic problems is not greater government control over the economy. Rather, we need a restoration of biblical authority in our nation and constant reminding of biblical economic principles: "defraud not the poor of his living" (Ecclesiastes 4:1), "visit the fatherless and the widows in their affliction" (James 1:27), "the borrower is servant to the lender" (Proverbs 22:7), "labor not to be rich" (Proverbs 23:4), and "provide things honest in the sight of all men" (Romans 12:17). It is our prayer that *Practical & Foundational Economics* will train succeeding generations to look at this life, not from the perspective of what they can acquire, but how they can use the resources God gives them to serve Him.

To the Student

You are about to embark upon a one-semester study of economics that we've entitled *Practical & Foundational Economics.* This title reminds us that the economic principles of capitalism have a practical daily application. During the dozens of economic decisions you make every day, you probably don't preface your decisions by stating that "value exists in the mind, and value changes with time, place, and circumstances." You may not verbalize this economic principle, but your actions verify it multiple times throughout the day. *Practical & Foundational Economics* is not boring memorization of economic terminology but learning how to use these principles in real-life situations.

Practical & Foundational Economics provides the ultimate in scheduling flexibility. You need to complete two lessons per week throughout the semester. Consult with your home school supervisor on an acceptable timetable to complete the assignments. The multipart teaching lessons are broken down into shorter reading sections followed by a set of review questions. These teaching lessons can be completed in one long session or finished over a period of two or three days. The review lessons prior to the quizzes and tests give you several days to prepare for the assessments. These review lessons contain a "Concepts to Review" section to guide your preparation for the quiz or test, but be sure to study all of the information and review questions prior to taking the assessment. For an overview of the course content, read the table of contents on page iii. The topic index on page xiii lists the national content standards for economics and the specific lessons covering those standards. The scope and sequence on page ix lists which lessons need to be completed each week.

To the Parent

Thank you for choosing Zeezok Publishing's *Practical & Foundational Economics* for your high school economics requirement. We trust that it will challenge you and your student as you work your way through the course.

As we did with its predecessor, *A Noble Experiment* high school government course, we've tried to simplify your workload as a home schooling parent. The student workbook contains everything needed to complete the course. The answer keys and assessments can be easily removed from the back of the student workbook before the student begins the course. The included grade book provides a convenient means of recording the student's score for each graded assignment.

Sample answers given for the short-answer questions summarize a correct response for each question. Accept any reasonable answer related to the answers provided.

For your convenience, we have provided periodic assessments in the form of quizzes and tests, as well as a two-part final exam. Answers to these assessments are included in the answer keys. Feel free to alter the testing materials to accommodate your student's strengths or to use alternative means of evaluation.

The *Imprimis* articles (reprinted with the gracious permission of Hillsdale College) provide a great opportunity for economic interaction with your student. We at Zeezok Publishing encourage everyone in your family old enough to comprehend the information to get involved in the discussion. These articles contain much food for thought about what is right and wrong with the American economy.

The only significant writing assignment in *Practical & Foundational Economics* is the paper on the history of a business. The short, paragraph-length responses on several of the assessments should be used to practice good writing techniques and improve the student's writing style. Parents desiring their child to do more extensive writing could have the student write an extended response to the four *Imprimis* articles or add their own essays to the assessments.

Thank you for purchasing our product; we hope it will meet and exceed your expectations.

Student Course Syllabus

Week 1

- Read "To the Student"
- Read Lesson 1, complete Lesson 1 Review Questions
- Complete Lesson 1 Practical Application Activity
- Read Lesson 2, complete Lesson 2 Review Questions

Week 2

- Read Lesson 3, complete Lesson 3 Review Questions
- Complete Proverbs Crossword Puzzle
- Use Lesson 4 Quiz Study Guide / Scripture Memorization Verse 1 to prepare for the Lesson 4 Quiz
- Complete Lesson 4 Practical Application Activity
- Complete Lesson 4 Quiz
- Read Imprimis Article #1 and complete the article's discussion assignment

Week 3

- Complete Lesson 5 Oral History Project: History of a Business, Part I (compose a series of interview questions)
- Read Lesson 6, complete Lesson 6 Review Questions
- Complete the Lesson 6D Marxism assignment

Week 4

- Use the Lesson 7 study information to prepare for the test in Lesson 8
- Complete Lesson 7 Practical Application Activity
- Complete Lesson 8 (Test)

Week 5

- Read Lesson 9, complete Lesson 9 Review Questions
- Complete Lesson 9 Practical Application Activity
- Read Lesson 10, complete Lesson 10 Review Questions
- Complete Lesson 10 Practical Application Activity

Week 6

- Read Lesson 11, complete Lesson 11 Review Questions
- Use Lesson 12 Quiz Study Guide / Scripture Memorization Verse 2 to prepare for the Lesson 12 Quiz
- Complete Lesson 12 Practical Application Activity
- Complete Lesson 12 Quiz
- Read Imprimis Article #2 and complete the article's discussion assignment

Week 7

- Complete Lesson 13 Oral History Project: History of a Business, Part II (conduct interview with selected business professional and type a transcript of the interview)
- Read Lesson 14, complete Lesson 14 Review Questions

Week 8

- Read Lesson 15, complete Lesson 15 Review Questions
- Complete Lesson 15 Practical Application Activity
- Use the Lesson 16 study information to prepare for the test in Lesson 17
- Complete Lesson 16 Practical Application Activity

Week 9

- Complete Lesson 17 (Test)
- Read Lesson 18, complete Lesson 18 Review Questions
- Complete Lesson 18 Practical Application Activity

Week 10

- Read Lesson 19, complete Lesson 19 Review Questions
- Complete Lesson 19 Practical Application Activity
- Complete Lesson 19 Transfer Earnings Case Study
- Read Lesson 20, complete Lesson 20 Review Questions

Week 11

- Use Lesson 21 Quiz Study Guide / Scripture Memorization Verse 3 to prepare for the Lesson 21 Quiz
- Complete Lesson 21 Quiz
- Read Imprimis Article #3 and complete the article's discussion assignment
- Read Lesson 22, complete Lesson 22 Review Questions

Week 12

- Read Lesson 23, complete Lesson 23 Review Questions
- Use the Lesson 24 study information to prepare for the test in Lesson 25
- Complete Lesson 24 Practical Application Activity

Week 13

- Complete Lesson 25 (Test)
- Complete Lesson 26 Oral History Project: History of a Business, Part III (write paper and turn it in to home school supervisor for grading)

Week 14

- Read Lesson 27, complete Lesson 27 Review Questions
- Complete Lesson 27 Practical Application Activity
- Read Lesson 28, complete Lesson 28 Review Questions
- Complete Lesson 28 Practical Application Activity

Week 15

- Use Lesson 29 Quiz Study Guide / Scripture Memorization Verse 4 to prepare for the Lesson 29 Quiz
- Complete Lesson 29 Quiz
- Read Imprimis Article #4 and complete the article's discussion assignment
- Read Lesson 30, complete Lesson 30 Review Questions

Week 16

- Read Lesson 31, complete Lesson 31 Review Questions
- Use the Lesson 32 study information to prepare for the test in Lesson 33
- Complete Lesson 32 Practical Application Test Section

Week 17

- Complete Lesson 33 (Test)
- Use the Lesson 34 review information to prepare for Final Exam Parts 1 and 2

Week 18

- Complete Final Exam Parts 1 and 2

Grade Book

Assignment	Points	Cumulative Points	Letter Grade
Lesson 1A—Review Questions	/20		
Lesson 1B—Review Questions	/15		
Lesson 1—Practical Application Activity: My Personal Stewardship Responsibility	/100		
Lesson 2A—Review Questions	/18		
Lesson 2B—Review Questions	/7		
Lesson 2C—Review Questions	/8		
Lesson 3A—Review Questions	/14		
Lesson 3—Proverbs Crossword Puzzle	/20		
Lesson 3B—Review Questions	/10		
Lesson 4—Quiz	/30		
Lesson 4—*Imprimis* Article #1 Discussion Activity	/50		
Lesson 5—History of a Business, Part I	/50		
Lesson 6A—Review Questions	/11		
Lesson 6B—Review Questions	/9		
Lesson 6C—Review Questions	/28		
Lesson 6D—Marxism	/10		
Lesson 8—Test	/76		
Lesson 9A—Review Questions	/10		
Lesson 9B—Review Questions	/5		
Lesson 9—Practical Application Activity: Value of a 1985 Mercury Grand Marquis	/15		
Lesson 10A—Review Questions	/11		
Lesson 10B—Review Questions	/27		
Lesson 10—Practical Application Activity: Choice and Opportunity Cost	/20		
Lesson 11A—Review Questions	/10		
Lesson 11B—Review Questions	/13		
Lesson 12—Quiz	/33		
Lesson 12—*Imprimis* Article #2 Discussion Activity	/50		
Lesson 13—History of a Business, Part II	/100		
Lesson 14A—Review Questions	/15		
Lesson 14B—Review Questions	/18		
Lesson 15A—Review Questions	/6		
Lesson 15B—Review Questions	/11		
Lesson 15—Practical Application Activity: Competition	/20		
Lesson 17—Test	/66		
Lesson 18A—Review Questions	/9		
Lesson 18B—Review Questions	/11		
Lesson 18C—Review Questions	/12		
Lesson 18—Practical Application Activity: Cost Schedule	/18		
Lesson 19A—Review Questions	/15		

Assignment	Points	Cumulative Points	Letter Grade
Lesson 19—Practical Application Activity: Transfer Earnings and Economic Rent	/13		
Lesson 19—Transfer Earnings Case Study	/18		
Lesson 20A—Review Questions	/12		
Lesson 20B—Review Questions	/18		
Lesson 20C—Review Questions	/6		
Lesson 20D—Review Questions	/10		
Lesson 20E—Review Questions	/8		
Lesson 21—Quiz	/30		
Lesson 21—*Imprimis* Article #3 Discussion Activity	/50		
Lesson 22A—Review Questions	/8		
Lesson 22B—Review Questions	/19		
Lesson 22C—Review Questions	/45		
Lesson 23A—Review Questions	/4		
Lesson 23B—Review Questions	/7		
Lesson 23C—Review Questions	/5		
Lesson 23D—Review Questions	/5		
Lesson 25—Test	/69		
Lesson 26—History of a Business, Part III	/100		
Lesson 27A—Review Questions	/14		
Lesson 27B—Review Questions	/6		
Lesson 27C—Review Questions	/21		
Lesson 27—Practical Application Activity: An Unprofitable Restaurant	/20		
Lesson 28A—Review Questions	/23		
Lesson 28B—Review Questions	/9		
Lesson 28C—Review Questions	/18		
Lesson 28—Practical Application Activity: Health Care Reform	/50		
Lesson 29—Quiz	/30		
Lesson 29—*Imprimis* Article #4 Discussion Activity	/50		
Lesson 30A—Review Questions	/18		
Lesson 30B—Review Questions	/18		
Lesson 30C—Review Questions	/12		
Lesson 31A—Review Questions	/56		
Lesson 33—Test	/73		
Lesson 35—Final Exam, Part I	/79		
Lesson 36—Final Exam, Part II	/75		

TOTAL POINTS: ________ /1,970

FINAL LETTER GRADE: ________

Topic Index

Council for Economic Education National Standard	Lesson #
Scarcity	3, 9, 10, 11, 14, 18, 19, 23
Decision Making	1, 2, 3, 6, 9, 11, 14, 18, 19, 20, 23
Allocation	2, 3, 6, 11, 18, 19, 23
Incentives	2, 3, 6, 9, 11, 15, 18, 19, 20, 23
Trade	30
Specialization	1, 18, 20, 23, 30
Markets and Prices	2, 6, 11, 15, 23
Role of Prices	2, 11, 15, 19, 23
Competition and Market Structure	6, 11, 15, 22
Institutions	2, 15, 22, 27
Money and Inflation	28, 30
Interest Rates	28, 30
Income	1, 18, 20, 23
Entrepreneurship	10, 18, 27
Economic Growth	6, 22, 23, 27
Role of Government and Market Failure	2, 6, 20, 22, 27, 31
Government Failure	6, 20, 22, 27, 31
Economic Fluctuations	14, 20, 22, 30, 31
Unemployment and Inflation	28, 30
Fiscal and Monetary Policy	28, 30, 31

LESSON 1

NAME DATE

/35 Score

God, Man, & a Proper Economics Foundation

Objective

The student will discuss economic ramifications of God's existence and ownership of the earth. The student will explain economic realities based on the fact that man was made in the image of God.

Lesson 1A Reading

"The heavens declare the glory of God, and the firmament showeth His handiwork." (Psalm 19:1) As a boy growing up in rural Pennsylvania, I used to lie on the ground staring up at the star-filled nighttime sky. How could anyone view this stunning solar display and believe that it all happened by chance or because of a cataclysmic catastrophe? Genesis, Chapter 1, tells us that the eternally existing God spoke the worlds into existence. He created the earth and all its inhabitants. We cannot study economics and arrive at proper conclusions concerning our subject matter without a better understanding of who God is and who we are. Let's begin by looking at God as the Creator.

"In the beginning, God created the heavens and the earth." (Genesis 1:1) John 1:3 tells us that "all things were made by him [Jesus Christ]; and without him was not any thing made that was made." Psalm 24:1 says, "The earth is the Lord's, and the fullness thereof; the world, and they that dwell therein." God, as the Creator, owns everything. Based on this thought, can human beings really "own" anything? The Christian understands that his personal property actually belongs to God. God allows us to acquire certain material possessions to use for His glory, but as the Creator, He owns it all. Who gave the inventor a mind capable of envisioning new products? Who gave the musician the talent to write and perform music? Unsaved men and women don't recognize God's ownership of their life and possessions, but failure or refusal to acknowledge His right of ownership does not alter its reality. Even some Christians have a problem with giving to God what is rightfully His. He (God) owns it all, but He made mankind stewards of His creation.

As part of His divine plan, God gave man dominion (control) over His creation. "And God said, Let us make man in our image, after our likeness: and let them have dominion over the fish of the sea, and over the fowl of the air, and over the cattle, and over all the earth, and over every creeping thing that creepeth upon the earth." (Genesis 1:26) God repeats this responsibility in His charge to Adam in Genesis 1:28. God gave man control over the rest of His creation, knowing full well that after sin entered the world some men would neglect or fail this stewardship responsibility. The omniscient God lets men abuse His creation through wars, irresponsible mining or forestry practices, oil spills, and other activities detrimental to other human beings or the environment. These renegade stewards forget that we are accountable to the One who made us a trustee of His creation. A trustee is someone who manages a resource on behalf of someone else. Dominion over God's creation does not give us the right to torture animals, poison the soil, or waste earth's resources. The 19th-century hunters who decimated the bison herds for sport, thus threatening the welfare of the Native Americans living on the Great Plains, ignored their God-given role as trustees of creation. Every human being needs constant reminders of their biblical stewardship responsibilities.

The 19th-century hunters who decimated the bison herds for sport…ignored their God-given role as trustees of creation.

God the Creator also sustains His creation. "For by him [Jesus Christ] were all things created, that are in heaven, and that are in earth, visible and invisible, whether they be thrones, or dominions, or principalities, or powers: all things were created by him, and for him. And he is before all things, and by him all things consist." (Colossians 1:16-17) Notice the phrase "and by him all things consist" in the last part of verse 17. The Greek word translated as "consist" (*synistēmi) means* "to place together, to set in the same place, to bring or band together, to put together by way of composition or combination, to put together or unite parts into one whole."[1] Jesus Christ holds His creation together. Do I need to worry about the world running out of fossil fuels, the destruction of the rainforest, damage to the ozone layer, or global warming? No, because God is in control of His creation. Men's actions may harm the earth, but God manages to maintain human life upon our planet in spite of these and other environmental threats. As mentioned in the previous paragraph, God's ability to preserve and sustain His creation does not justify deliberate abuse of the earth or its inhabitants. This sin-scarred earth will last until its future destruction by fire (see 2 Peter 3:10). Until that time, the One powerful enough to create it out of nothing certainly has the ability to sustain it in spite of man's harmful practices.

Review Questions

Directions: *Answer the following questions based on the Lesson 1A reading.*

1. How can you prove God's ownership of the earth? *(2 points)*

____

____

____

2. As a follower of Christ, should you have a problem with tithing on your income? Explain your answer. *(3 points)*

____

____

____

3. How does God demonstrate that He has not surrendered all of creation's stewardship to mankind? *(5 points)*

____

____

____

____

4. Is leaving the lights on in your room when you're not in it a violation of your stewardship responsibility? Why or why not? *(2 points)*

____

____

____

[1] http://www.blueletterbible.org/lang/lexicon/lexicon.cfm?Strongs=G4921&t=KJV)

5. How does this photo of an overgrown parking lot disprove the idea of irreparable damage from slash-and-burn agriculture?" *(3 points)*

____

____

____

____

____

____

6. Since God sustains His creation, could mankind permanently destroy it prior to God's destruction of the earth as foretold in 2 Peter 3:10? *(2 points)*

____

____

____

____

7. How can a Christian find balance between the environmentalist extreme of "worshipping Mother Earth" and the opposite pendulum of abusing the earth based on our dominion over God's creation? *(3 points)*

____

____

____

____

____

Lesson 1B Reading

In this section of Lesson 1, we'll evaluate our view of mankind. The Holy Scriptures tell us that we are made in the image of God. (Genesis 1:26) This fact has three important economic ramifications.

God gives each of us talents and abilities in order that we might also be creative. This creativity enables us to provide for our economic needs. In Genesis 4:20-22, we read about three individuals with creative abilities.

> And Adah bare Jabal: he was the father of such as dwell in tents, and of such as have cattle. And his brother's name was Jubal: he was the father of all such as handle the harp and organ. And Zillah, she also bare Tubalcain, an instructer of every artificer in brass and iron.

Jabal excelled at animal husbandry, Jubal invented musical instruments, and Tubalcain specialized in metallurgy. They could supplement their subsistence farming efforts with these God-given creative abilities, or they could make a living through specialization (trading goods or services produced with their talents for food, clothing, shelter, etc.). God gifts every human being with creative talents to use for their economic well-being. Individuals who find employment utilizing these creative abilities experience happiness and fulfillment in their daily work. People laboring at jobs where they cannot use their God-given talents will feel frustrated and unfulfilled. We need to discover and develop our talents and use them for our livelihood.[2]

> *Man, like God, has the ability to think, reason, and make choices.*

Another economic characteristic mankind possesses because of being made in the image of God is a rational mind and a free will. Man, like God, has the ability to think, reason, and make choices. These abilities allow us to distinguish between alternatives and make wise decisions (decisions that will better our economic well-being). With a family depending on me to provide for their needs, I willingly get out of bed and go to work. Our God-given reasoning powers enable us to distinguish between good food and poisonous plants. Interestingly, our free will enables us to do things harmful to our economic success. I could stay in bed without good reason and skip work. I could ruin my mind with illegal drugs or gamble away my paycheck. I can choose to harm my body by eating unhealthy foods and refusing to exercise. Without the God-given qualities of a rational mind and a free will, we wouldn't be able to make both good and bad economic choices. The capacity to make choices affects our life here on earth and our future destiny.

The third economic principle that emanates from being made in God's image is the eternality of our existence. We will either live with God or apart from God forever based on our personal relationship with His Son. Jesus said, "I am the Way, the Truth, and the Life; no man cometh unto the Father but by Me." (John 14:6) Are you ready to meet your Maker? The decision to trust Christ as your Savior from sin is far more important than any economic success you might achieve in this life. "For what shall it profit a man, if he shall gain the whole world, and lose his own soul?" (Mark 8:36) The Christian should invest in things of eternal value. We cannot take a huge bank account, a fancy automobile, or a nice home with us into the next life. Matthew 6:19-21 reminds us to lay up our treasures in heaven rather than here on the earth. Heavenly investments offer a far greater and guaranteed rate of return than the stock market or real estate on this earth ever could. Are you living with eternity's values in view?

A final economic principle about man, although not related to his bearing the image of God, is man's sinfulness. This will manifest itself in selfishness, covetousness, and greed (among other vices). Given the opportunity and incentive, people will take advantage of other people. This is why governmental and economic systems based

[2] For assistance in this area, see Crown Financial Ministries and the CareerDirect© program available at http://www.careerdirectonline.org/.

on the perceived goodness of man will always fail. Communism and socialism fail (as do all utopian societies) because humans will never be content making the same amount of money as everyone else. Those with the means to do so (in a communist or socialist system, those working for the government) will find a way to get more money than their neighbor. As a result, the economic system with the most individual freedom and responsibility works best for everyone because we share equal opportunity to both earn for ourselves and protect ourselves from foolish decisions.

Review Questions

Directions: *Answer the following questions based on the Lesson 1B reading.*

1. List the three economic principles relevant to man because he is made in the image of God. *(3 points)*

2. Identify the creative abilities God has given you that will be a part of your economic future. *(5 points)*

3. How does God get greater glory from giving human beings a free will? *(2 points)*

4. List three **observable** decisions you made this week that illustrate your God-given rational abilities and capability for making choices. *(3 points)*

5. How will the reality of eternity impact your future economic decisions? *(2 points)*

NAME ______ DATE ______

Score

Practical Application Activity:

My Personal Stewardship Responsibility

Directions: *This activity will help you solidify your personal beliefs about specific aspects of stewardship. Before selecting your answers, search the Scriptures and discuss your beliefs with your parents. You may also wish to seek godly counsel from other adults. After completing the chart, give it to your home school supervisor for grading. Be prepared to give a valid reason for your choices.*

Specific Aspect of Stewardship	Yes	No	Points Awarded
Recycling of paper, plastic, and metal			
Driving fuel-efficient vehicles			
Proper disposal of contaminants (motor oil, refrigerants, etc.)			
Use of "green" cleaning agents instead of chemicals			
Buying items only from environmentally responsible corporations			
Growing as much of my own food as possible			
Eliminating unhealthy food from my diet			
Carpooling to work			
Utilizing public transportation whenever possible			
Planting trees or getting involved in reforestation efforts			
Raise my stewardship awareness through periodic self-education on environmental issues			
Recycling of old technology (TVs, computers, cell phones, etc.)			
Reduce my carbon footprint through use of solar or wind energy			
Using recycled materials when building or remodeling a home			
Go off-grid to meet my energy needs			
Run errands on my bicycle rather than use a fossil-fuel vehicle			
Mow the grass without using an internal-combustion-engine mower			
Buy organically grown food			
Tell others about ways to improve their stewardship of God's creation			
Eliminate chemical pesticides and fertilizers from my garden/lawn			

Total Points: ________/100

Grader: Award up to five points for each aspect based on the student's preparation and response as to why they will or will not practice or participate in each specific activity.

LESSON 2

NAME DATE

Score

Introduction: The Definition, Basic Principles, & Terminology of Economics

Objective

The student will define economics. The student will explain the "pure science" limitations of economics, and identify problems of logic for economists. The student will define the Latin term ceteris paribus *and discuss its application to the study of economics.*

Lesson 2A Reading

What is economics? The ancient Greeks and Romans used the term to refer to wise management of a single household. Today's use of the term has a much broader meaning. Economics is "the science that deals with the production, distribution, and consumption of goods and services, or the material welfare of humankind."[3] Economists make a distinction between microeconomics and macroeconomics. Microeconomics, from the Greek prefix meaning small, is "economic analysis of particular components of the economy, such as the growth of a single industry or demand for a single product."[4] You will delve into microeconomics as you complete the "history of a business" paper that is part of this course and in the lesson on supply and demand. Microeconomics also deals with individual consumer decision-making and spending habits. Macroeconomics, on the other hand, deals with "the broad and general

[3] economics. (n.d.). *Dictionary.com Unabridged.* Retrieved March 22, 2011, from Dictionary.com website: http://dictionary.reference.com/browse/economics

[4] microeconomics. (n.d.). *The American Heritage® New Dictionary of Cultural Literacy*, Third Edition. Retrieved March 10, 2011, from Dictionary.com website: http://dictionary.reference.com/browse/microeconomics

aspects of an economy, as the relationship between the income and investments of a country as a whole."[5] Macroeconomics considers those factors contributing to an entire nation's economy or the global economy. Some economists consider international economics or global economics as a third subcategory of study under the umbrella of economics, while others consider international economics to be part of macroeconomics. Global economics is "the interdependent economies of the world's nations, regarded as a single economic system."[6] International trade agreements and foreign financial investments in developing nations are just two examples of global economics in action. Now let's take a closer look at our definition of economics. By examining the component parts of this definition, we can understand some of the challenges facing economists.

As stated previously, economics is a science dealing with the production, distribution, and consumption of goods and services. More specifically, economics is a social science. Notice first of all that economics is a science. Economists (those who specialize in the study of economics) can be classified as scientists, more specifically, social scientists. Unlike their laboratory colleagues, however, these social scientists labor under a different set of circumstances with greater limitations.

The Scientific Method

- Collect data
- Study data
- Form hypothesis
- Test hypothesis
- Make prediction

Economists face unique challenges when trying to utilize the scientific method in their discipline. Suppose, for instance, that an economist who believes that cutting taxes results in greater government revenue wants to test his hypothesis. He convinces the city council members of a medium-sized city to reduce property taxes, personal income taxes, and business taxes, while offering tax abatement for existing and new businesses for one year. The city stands to lose $500,000 if the economist's theory is wrong. At the end of one year, the mayor and council members meet to discuss the results. The budget numbers show that city revenue was $2,000 less than the previous year. The council members unanimously conclude that the economist's theory contains fatal flaws and end the experiment. City taxes return to their pre-experiment levels, and our discouraged economist seeks someplace else to test his theory. From this one experiment, can we confidently predict that cutting taxes does not result in increased government revenue? Of course not! This example proves the limitations of economics as a pure science. The economist used the scientific method—he formed a hypothesis and tested his hypothesis in the real world. He collected data during the year-long experiment, and the data shows that city revenues actually increased by $498,000. So cutting taxes did result in increased government revenues, but not in

---

[5] macroeconomics. (n.d.). *Dictionary.com Unabridged.* Retrieved March 10, 2011, from Dictionary.com website: http://dictionary.reference.com/browse/macroeconomics

[6] http://schumpeter2006.org/blog/2006/12/20/definition-of-global-economics

an increase large enough to cover the initial lost revenue. So what limitations of economics as a pure science does our hypothetical situation point out?

The first limitation is the problem of objectivity. The city council members rejected the economist's findings because the city budget faced a $2,000 deficit after the experiment. With their political careers at stake, they didn't want to continue an experiment that might jeopardize their re-election campaigns. The economist cannot totally divorce himself from pre-existing prejudices. His conclusions reflect value judgments formed from personal life experiences and religious or philosophical beliefs.

A second factor separating economics from the pure sciences is the impossibility of isolating and controlling all of the variables. The chemist in a laboratory carefully manipulates a single variable in order to replicate his experiment and prove or disprove his hypothesis. The economist cannot control all the variables vital to the success of his experiment. In our cutting-taxes experiment, did the city actively promote its lower-taxes policy? Is one year long enough to obtain accurate results? Did businesses outside the area know about the tax abatement and notify city officials of their intention to relocate shortly after the one-year time period? Were the property tax savings offset by rising utility rates, leaving city residents with no additional income to spend locally on consumer goods with sales tax revenue for the city? The economist, unlike the chemist, must deal with unknown variables or variables he cannot control.

A third factor limiting the economist is the nature of his subject matter. Unlike the scientist mixing chemicals or compounds, the economist faces the moral and ethical restraints involved in dealing with people. Human beings are made in the image of God, and His Word provides specific guidelines for the way we ought to treat one another. During World War II, the Nazis used POWs for various medical experiments—a clear violation of the scriptural command to "love our neighbors as we love ourselves." The frustrated economist in our illustration cannot demand that city officials jeopardize people's lives in order to make his theory work (i.e., not plow the snow off city streets in the winter to reduce the city's budget need below the income level of his cutting-taxes program). Economics is largely about choice.[7] Theories are hard to test and data hard to evaluate because we are dealing with humans who face a seemingly infinite

Female prisoners in Ravensbrück during World War II

[7] Nobel Prize winner Gary Becker and Judge Richard Posner have been the most distinguished advocates of viewing economics as a science of choice.

number of choices in a single day, most of which are barely recognized as choices by the people making them. People make those choices for different reasons in different contexts. The test of a theory is whether it can predict the result (i.e., the future). As previously mentioned, there are so many variables in a single choice that predicting behavior becomes dangerous in the absence of a large amount of data spanning a wide variety of people and contexts.[8]

The second part of our economics definition talks about production, distribution, and consumption of goods and services. Economic goods are man-made things that consumers value highly enough to purchase or acquire through other means. Economic goods cost something, even if acquired illegally (a thief risks getting caught in the process of stealing economic goods and going to jail or making restitution). Services are the product of human labor with an associated cost. A math teacher imparting knowledge to her students is providing a service (education). A technician repairing a computer is not manufacturing the device but restoring its operating ability. Both goods and services command a price in the market.

Review Questions

Directions: *Answer the following questions based on the information and principles in the Lesson 2A reading.*

1. Define economics. *(1 point)*

____

____

____

2. Explain the difference between microeconomics and macroeconomics. *(2 points)*

____

____

____

____

3. List the three limitations of economics compared to the "pure" sciences. *(3 points)*

____

____

____

4. How might a consumer acquire an economic good without purchasing the desired object? *(2 points)*

____

____

____

____

[8] Thus the importance of studying economic history.

5. Explain the difference between an economic good and a service. *(1 point)*

6. In 2 Thessalonians 3:10, the Apostle Paul wrote, "For even when we were with you, this we commanded you, that if any would not work, neither should he eat." Why might a person who believes this biblical admonition have a problem with government welfare programs? *(1 point)*

7. List three variables the person in question #6 might overlook or fail to consider concerning those receiving government assistance. *(3 points)*

8. If your grandfather drove a truck in the 1920s for $1.25 an hour, do you believe that was a fair wage for that time period? What limitation(s) of economics as a pure science presented in the reading does this question illustrate? *(5 points)*

Lesson 2B Reading

In addition to its limitations as a social science, economics can be susceptible to problems of logic. Using our example of cutting taxes to increase government revenue from the previous reading section, let's examine four of these potential problems of logic.

If we try to prove from just one example that cutting taxes does not result in greater government revenue, we are guilty of *generalizing from small samples*. To get accurate results, we would need to implement this policy in many towns and cities, while controlling all the variables that might inherently cause our experiment to fail, such as community leaders' resisting efforts to attract new business.

If we try to prove that every city would experience the same results if they cut taxes, we commit the *fallacy of composition* (what is true of a part is true of the whole). Our experiment might yield successful results in small towns and large cities, just not in medium-sized cities.

If the city council members try to convince the citizens that the lower tax rates were the sole cause of last year's lost tax revenue, they would be guilty of a *post hoc fallacy*. This problem of logic presupposes a wrong cause in a cause-effect relationship. The $2,000 shortfall in the city budget might be the result of lost sales tax revenue due to the city residents' making Internet purchases instead of buying from the local department stores, or any number of other income-reducing factors.

If our economist's program was highly popular with the people, and the city council members want to avoid a political backlash from stopping the experiment, they might use the *appeal to pity fallacy* or the *appeal to fear fallacy*. By arguing that cutting taxes hurts senior citizens and the poorer city residents, the council members play on their citizens' sympathies or fears. How could anyone support something that harms the city's elderly and disadvantaged?

Economic decision making and evaluation are subject to these and other problems of logic. When government implements economic policies, every citizen is affected. If those policies are flawed due to problems of logic, they adversely impact the region's or the nation's economy. Knowing how to spot erroneous economic information is the starting point in preventing government policies based on faulty reasoning.

Review Questions

Directions: *Answer the following questions based on the Lesson 2B reading.*

1. Define the fallacy of composition. Give a sports-related illustration of the fallacy of composition. *(2 points)*

2. What is the *post hoc* fallacy? *(1 point)*

3. Is the following statement an example of the *post hoc* fallacy? Why or why not? *(2 points)*

   The reason the baseball team has a nine-game losing streak is that the team has a combined .250 batting average.

4. The following statements may or may not be true, but you cannot be sure without additional information. Identify the potential problem of logic in the following statements and write a question that could be used to obtain more information in evaluating each statement. *(2 points each)*

   Mayor Knowitall—"We need to build a new fire station on the south side of the city. Response times from the existing stations are too slow."

   Governor Imforit—"Automobile emissions testing in two neighboring states has improved their air quality 69 percent. Our state legislature needs to enact similar requirements for our state."

Lesson 2C Reading

The final concept in this lesson is *ceteris paribus* (key-te-rees pah-ri-boo s)—a Latin phrase meaning "other things being equal." Economic decisions involving choices reflect this concept. We always choose the alternative we perceive to be in our own best interest. That "best interest" may not be from a purely financial perspective. If your gasoline purchases reflect brand loyalty over the lower price at the station across the street, something in your subjective (mental) valuation process trumps saving a few cents more per gallon. Economists and advertisers would be interested in learning about your reason(s) for passing up the cheaper gasoline. Could you be persuaded to drop your brand loyalty? What must competitors do to win your business? Some U.S. consumers prefer to buy "Made in America" products, even if foreign-made similar items cost significantly less. Keeping Americans employed means more to them than saving money every time they go shopping. Charitable giving is a good example of people ignoring their own financial best interest because they perceive giving to be in their overall best interest. Scripture tells us that giving is in our own best interest. The rewards may not be seen in this life, but if you perceive generosity to be in your best interest, you will still give. Or you may simply enjoy giving more than keeping your personal resources—the subjective joy of giving means more to you than the objective value of the material goods you give away. You'll learn more about subjective value and objective value in Lesson 9.

Review Questions

Directions: *Answer the following questions based on the Lesson 2C reading.*

1. Define *ceteris paribus.* *(1 point)*

   ____

   ____

2. Why is *ceteris paribus* an important concept in economics? *(2 points)*

   ____

   ____

   ____

3. Bob, a professional truck driver, has been offered a job by two different companies. List five reasons why he might turn down the job paying 75 cents per mile to accept the job paying 50 cents per mile. *(5 points)*

   ____

   ____

   ____

   ____

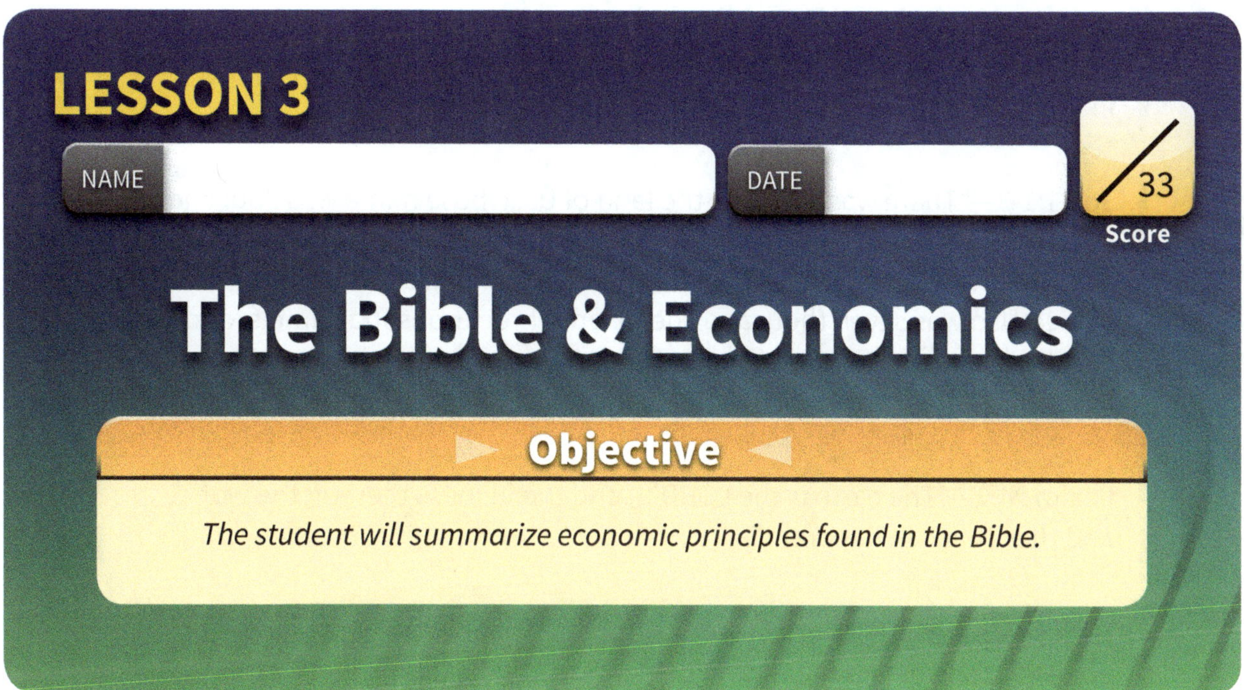

Lesson 3A Reading

As you probably surmised from Lesson 1, the Bible has a lot to say about economics. This lesson deals with various economic principles found throughout the Holy Scriptures. Read the following verses from the Old Testament.

> Genesis 1:28—"And God blessed them, and God said unto them, Be fruitful, and multiply, and replenish the earth, and subdue it: and have dominion over the fish of the sea, and over the fowl of the air, and over every living thing that moveth upon the earth."

> Genesis 2:15—"And the LORD God took the man, and put him into the garden of Eden to dress it and to keep it."

> Genesis 3:17-19—"And unto Adam he said, Because thou hast hearkened unto the voice of thy wife, and hast eaten of the tree, of which I commanded thee, saying, Thou shalt not eat of it: cursed is the ground for thy sake; in sorrow shalt thou eat of it all the days of thy life; Thorns also and thistles shall it bring forth to thee; and thou shalt eat the herb of the field; In the sweat of thy face shalt thou eat bread, till thou return unto the ground; for out of it wast thou taken: for dust thou art, and unto dust shalt thou return."

> Leviticus 19:13—"Thou shalt not defraud thy neighbour, neither rob him: the wages of him that is hired shall not abide with thee all night until the morning."

Deuteronomy 19:14—"Thou shalt not remove thy neighbour's landmark, which they of old time have set in thine inheritance, which thou shalt inherit in the land that the LORD thy God giveth thee to possess it."

Job 1:1-3—"There was a man in the land of Uz, whose name was Job; and that man was perfect and upright, and one that feared God, and eschewed evil. And there were born unto him seven sons and three daughters. His substance also was seven thousand sheep, and three thousand camels, and five hundred yoke of oxen, and five hundred she asses, and a very great household; so that this man was the greatest of all the men of the east."

Psalm 24:1—"The earth is the LORD'S, and the fullness thereof; the world, and they that dwell therein."

Ecclesiastes 5:10—" He that loveth silver shall not be satisfied with silver; nor he that loveth abundance with increase: this is also vanity."

Ecclesiastes 5:19—"Every man also to whom God hath given riches and wealth, and hath given him power to eat thereof, and to take his portion, and to rejoice in his labour; this is the gift of God."

Review Questions

Directions: *Answer the following questions based on the Lesson 3A reading.*

1. What is the meaning of the word "dress" in Genesis 2:15? *(2 points)*

2. Adam's other responsibility was to "keep" (*sha-mar'*) the Garden of Eden. What does the Hebrew word *shamar* mean? *(2 points)*

3. How did Adam's work change after the Fall? *(2 points)*

4. Which Scripture verse promotes the sanctity of private property? *(2 points)*

5. Is there anything inherently wrong with material wealth? *(2 points)*

6. In what way can wealth be a problem? *(2 points)*

7. How should the wealthy view their wealth, according to Ecclesiastes 5:19? *(2 points)*

Proverbs Crossword Puzzle

Directions: *Look up the following verses in the book of Proverbs to complete the crossword puzzle. Write the economic principles from the verses in the corresponding spot on the puzzle.* (20 points)

Across

4 Proverbs 18:16
7 Proverbs 16:8
8 Proverbs 20:17
9 Proverbs 19:5 (NIV)
10 Proverbs 14:23
13 Proverbs 4:7
16 Proverbs 6:6-11
17 Proverbs 15:6
18 Proverbs 10:4
19 Proverbs 8:11

Down

1 Proverbs 13:11
2 Proverbs 1:19
3 Proverbs 12:11
5 Proverbs 2:1-5
6 Proverbs 11:4
8 Proverbs 17:16 (NIV)
11 Proverbs 7:25-26 (NIV)
12 Proverbs 5:1
14 Proverbs 27:18
15 Proverbs 3:9-10

Lesson 3B Reading

The New Testament gives us additional economic insights. Read the following verses from the New Testament.

> Matthew 6:19-21—"Lay not up for yourselves treasures upon earth, where moth and rust doth corrupt, and where thieves break through and steal: But lay up for yourselves treasures in heaven, where neither moth nor rust doth corrupt, and where thieves do not break through nor steal: For where your treasure is, there will your heart be also."

> Matthew 6:24-33—"No man can serve two masters: for either he will hate the one, and love the other; or else he will hold to the one, and despise the other. Ye cannot serve God and mammon. Therefore I say unto you, Take no thought for your life, what ye shall eat, or what ye shall drink; nor yet for your body, what ye shall put on. Is not the life more than meat, and the body than raiment? Behold the fowls of the air: for they sow not, neither do they reap, nor gather into barns; yet your heavenly Father feedeth them. Are ye not much better than they? Which of you by taking thought can add one cubit unto his stature? And why take ye thought for raiment? Consider the lilies of the field, how they grow; they toil not, neither do they spin: And yet I say unto you, That even Solomon in all his glory was not arrayed like one of these. Wherefore, if God so clothe the grass of the field, which to day is, and to morrow is cast into the oven, shall he not much more clothe you, O ye of little faith? Therefore take no thought, saying, What shall we eat? or, What shall we drink? or, Wherewithal shall we be clothed? (For after all these things do the Gentiles seek:) for your heavenly Father knoweth that ye have need of all these things. But seek ye first the kingdom of God, and his righteousness; and all these things shall be added unto you."

Acts 4:32-Acts 5:5—"And the multitude of them that believed were of one heart and of one soul: neither said any of them that ought of the things which he possessed was his own; but they had all things common. And with great power gave the apostles witness of the resurrection of the Lord Jesus: and great grace was upon them all. Neither was there any among them that lacked: for as many as were possessors of lands or houses sold them, and brought the prices of the things that were sold, And laid them down at the apostles' feet: and distribution was made unto every man according as he had need. And Joses, who by the apostles was surnamed Barnabas, (which is, being interpreted, The son of consolation,) a Levite, and of the country of Cyprus, Having land, sold it, and brought the money, and laid it at the apostles' feet. But a certain man named Ananias, with Sapphira his wife, sold a possession, And kept back part of the price, his wife also being privy to it, and brought a certain part, and laid it at the apostles' feet. But Peter said, Ananias, why hath Satan filled thine heart to lie to the Holy Ghost, and to keep back part of the price of the land? Whiles it remained, was it not thine own? and after it was sold, was it not in thine own power? why hast thou conceived this thing in thine heart? thou hast not lied unto men, but unto God. And Ananias hearing these words fell down, and gave up the ghost: and great fear came on all them that heard these things."

2 Thessalonians 3:7-12—"For yourselves know how ye ought to follow us: for we behaved not ourselves disorderly among you; Neither did we eat any man's bread for nought; but wrought with labour and travail night and day, that we might not be chargeable to any of you: Not because we have not power, but to make ourselves an ensample unto you to follow us. For even when we were with you, this we commanded you, that if any would not work, neither should he eat. For we hear that there are some which walk among you disorderly, working not at all, but are busybodies. Now them that are such we command and exhort by our Lord Jesus Christ, that with quietness they work, and eat their own bread."

Review Questions

Directions: *Answer the following questions based on the Lesson 3B reading.*

1. According to Matthew 6:19-21, list three reasons why we should lay up treasures in heaven rather than here on earth. *(3 points)*

2. Why shouldn't Christians worry about material possessions and physical provision? *(1 point)*

3. What evidence do you see in Acts, Chapters 4 and 5, that the Christians were practicing communism? How does this passage refute the communist belief that man can create a class-less society in which all individuals share equally? *(4 points)*

4. According to 2 Thessalonians 3:7-12, some of the believers at Thessalonica were "busybodies." The Greek word translated as busybodies is *periergazomai* (per-ee-er-gad'-zom-ahee), referring to an individual who takes an interest in trivial, useless matters or hustles about uselessly. In the context of the passage, what message was the Apostle Paul trying to communicate to the Thessalonians? *(2 points)*

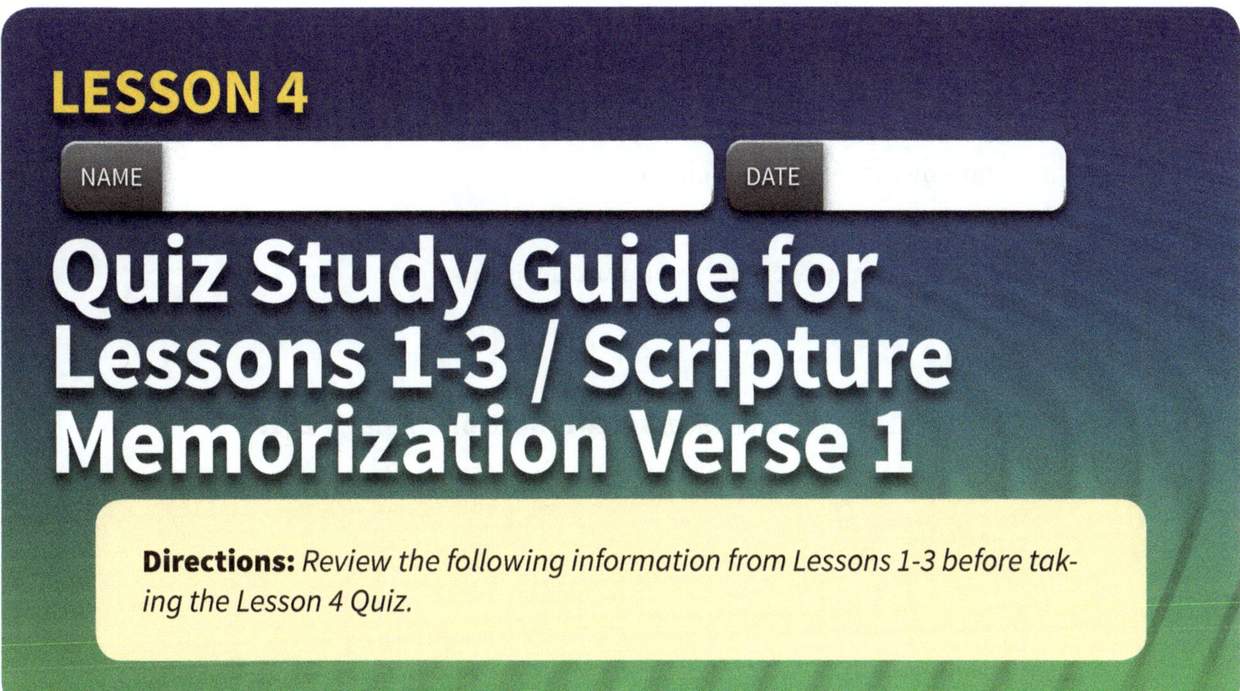

LESSON 4

NAME

DATE

Quiz Study Guide for Lessons 1-3 / Scripture Memorization Verse 1

Directions: *Review the following information from Lessons 1-3 before taking the Lesson 4 Quiz.*

Scripture Memory

- **Proverbs 14:34—**Righteousness exalteth a nation, but sin is a reproach to any people.

Concepts to Review

- God owns the earth because He created it and He sustains it.
- God gave man dominion over His creation. Man will answer to God for his role as a trustee of God's creation.
- Having been made in the image of God, man has creative abilities, a rational mind and a free will that enable him to make choices, and a conscious eternal existence in either heaven or hell.
- Economics is a science, but there are major differences between economics and the "pure" sciences.
- Microeconomics and macroeconomics are the two main branches of economics.
- Economic goods are man-produced goods that have value. Services are the product of man's labor with an associated cost.
- Economics is subject to various problems of logic.
- *Ceteris paribus* affects most economic decisions.
- Review all of the Lesson 3 Bible passages except the Proverbs crossword puzzle.

Practical Application

- Explain how economic decisions made by nonbelievers illustrate that we are made in the image of God.
- Discuss why economics is not a pure science.
- Identify an example of an economic decision not based on *ceteris paribus*.
- Apply scriptural principles to everyday economic decisions.

The Lesson 4 Quiz is located in the assessments section on page 211.

NAME DATE

Imprimis Article #1

Dinner Table Discussion/Co-op Class Discussion

Directions: *Read the following article and prepare a list of five discussion questions based on the reading. Have your parents and any siblings old enough to engage in the conversation read the article, then schedule a mealtime to discuss the article as a family, using your discussion questions. You will be graded on your understanding of the article (10 points), list of discussion questions (10 points), and participation in the discussion (30 points). If doing this assignment as part of a co-op class, your supervisor will ask you to write five discussion questions prior to the class discussion. Grading will be the same as if doing the assignment in a family setting.*

Imprimis article— What Kind of Society is Good for Business and Investing?

Foster S. Friess

The following is adapted from a speech delivered on May 11, 2002, on the Hillsdale College campus, upon Mr. Friess receiving Hillsdale College's Adam Smith Award.

In thinking about what kind of society is good for business and investing, we need to remember two things. First, enlightened self-interest is a powerful and positive force for good in a free society. As Adam Smith said, "It is not from the benevolence of the butcher, the brewer, or the baker, that we expect our dinner, but from their regard to their own interest." In this light, it is a worrisome fact that Americans are becoming increasingly dependent when it comes to making the decisions that most affect their interests—e.g., decisions about caring for their health, educating their children and spending their earnings. If we are to keep America and its economy on the right track, we must find a way to return to our citizens more control over their lives.

Second, love of neighbor is the *most* powerful means of changing things for the good. It was with this in mind that President George W. Bush asked each of us in his 2001 inaugural address "to do small things with great love." Too often we create and depend on grandiose bureaucratic programs to address social problems, and in the meantime allow ourselves to forget about real people. For those of us with faith, it is enough to remember that we are called on by the Lord not to eradicate poverty, but to help our neighbor. For all of us, it should be clear enough by now that bureaucratic programs, such as the 40-year-old War on Poverty, tend to be counterproductive, whereas one-on-one efforts and private and local efforts—what I call lighthouse missions—bear real fruit.

Let me tell you a story to explain what I mean by lighthouse missions: An elderly couple living in a small coastal village approached the lighthouse keeper one day and said, "We are out of oil for our home, and it is cold." He gave them oil. The next day, a young couple petitioned for oil for their lamps so their children could study after dark. He gave them oil as well. But as a result of these and other well-meaning deeds, he ran out of oil, and without the light that it was his duty to provide, two ships crashed on the rocks killing hundreds of sailors.

It is not good or productive to allow ourselves to lose focus on our individual lighthouse missions, no matter how well meaning the thing that distracts us. And the same general principle adheres politically: Our local, state and national governments have lighthouse missions—responsibilities or duties that they are best suited to perform, and on which they should focus. In the case of the national government, these responsibilities are assigned by the Constitution. For instance, it is charged with providing the whole people a defense against foreign threats, for which it is uniquely suited. It is not, on the other hand, tasked with providing individuals with their various unique needs. And when it attempts to do the latter, it usually makes things worse.

Let me speak of just two examples of this—healthcare and education—before returning to the idea of individual responsibilities.

Healthcare Common Sense

Our current healthcare system is neither efficient nor cost-effective. To fix it, we must cease to treat patients and potential patients as captive victims. Instead we must allow them to be informed and independent consumers.

The first step toward this goal is to restore the direct connection between the recipient of healthcare and the doctors and hospitals delivering the service. Doctors should not receive payment from an agent who did not receive the service. Nor should recipients of service be limited in selecting where or from whom they receive it.

Second, the idea of health insurance must be divorced from the idea of prepaid healthcare. Think about this: If car insurance operated on the same basis as health insurance, we would be reimbursed for windshield wiper blades, headlights, oil changes, tires and gas.

Not surprisingly, we find that the source of much of the difficulty with healthcare reform exists at the national level, where individual needs are not and cannot be best understood. Changing a single line in the Internal Revenue Service code would allow the needed reform to proceed. That one line would allow individuals, rather than employers, to deduct health care benefits. Instead of sending money to HMOs, employers would deposit money into employees' individual healthcare accounts, where it would be non-taxable and portable from one job to another.

These accounts could be called "Spend-It-or-Keep-It" (SIKI) accounts to emphasize their key feature: They allow individuals to capitalize on healthcare savings generated through increased exercise, healthier diets, etc. The SIKI would be similar to an Individual Retirement Account, providing a means for tax-free investment and becoming part of an individual's estate. Once a certain level of healthcare security is reached, the excess could be spent for any purpose. Shifting control of healthcare spending to the consumer in this way would create millions of cost control centers—individuals in charge of themselves and their healthcare accounts. At the same time it would increase productivity by freeing companies to focus on their own lighthouse missions: producing goods and providing services.

With a SIKI system in place, voluntary healthcare cooperatives could be formed to negotiate pricing, monitor outcomes and educate members about health issues. These cooperatives could be organized within companies, through fraternal organizations, or in several other ways. Catastrophic polices with high deductibles could be purchased with a portion of the SIKI accounts, with balances to be used for direct payment to providers or for purchasing a prepaid healthcare plan. Uninsurable neighbors could be assigned to these cooperatives or, if necessary, placed in special pools that receive subsidization from local or state governments, ensuring that none go without care.

Another major problem with healthcare today is that doctors practice "defensive medicine" to avoid the overbearing consequences of malpractice suits. Along the same lines, more than 20 obstetricians in the Las Vegas area have announced that they may have to close or move their practices to another state to avoid excessive lawsuits and increasingly unaffordable insurance premiums. A survey taken by the Nevada State Medical Association revealed that 28 percent of physicians have already closed their Nevada practices due to high liability costs.

This is a nationwide problem and extends into many other areas besides healthcare. What is needed to solve it is tort reform that revives the idea of real responsibility and ensures reasonable awards when fault is found. This requires legislation. But in keeping with our principle of lighthouse missions, one would hope that state governments—which are perfectly capable—would address this problem before the national government finds it necessary to intervene. As Dwight Eisenhower once said, "Our best protection against bigger government in Washington is better government in the states." And few things could do more for economic productivity than swift state action in this area.

Education Common Sense

Friends of mine who home school their five kids, ages 7 to 15 years, told me the following story: At one point Dad suggested issuing report cards like other schools. Mom replied, "Fine, but they'd get all As." Classic maternal favoritism, the dad thought at first—then was astounded when Mom added, "Because we don't move them on until they get it." Consider this mother's radical common sense: If our entire education system were converted to learning levels based on real progress rather than grade levels determined by age—and if the pernicious concept of social promotion were eliminated—the door would be open to significant achievement in our educational system.

Under this "radical" policy, a student would go over the multiplication tables or the important dates in U.S. history until he knows them. Age would be irrelevant. A ten-year-old could be at level three in math, level six in history and level eight in science. No child would be left behind because no child would advance before he is ready. But in order for this policy to get off the ground, we must break the current and disastrous public school monopoly.

Charter schools and vouchers are mechanisms that are gaining ground as a way of giving the children of poor and middle class parents the same education opportunities as the wealthy. But why is it like pulling teeth to extend such opportunities? Why do so many parts of the government oppose it with such vengeance? Would we tolerate being told where to buy our groceries, our gas or our clothing? Yet, by and large, we tolerate this command-and-control system for the education of our children.

And returning to the individual level, one of the greatest educational advances we can make in the next two decades will come through one-on-one volunteer mentoring efforts. These efforts are expanding all across America, and everyone who is able should consider taking part.

Independence and Responsibility

In conclusion, we Americans today cede too much power to our elected representatives, and we need to take that power back. Let me give you an example. Our legislators find increasingly creative ways to misappropriate the hard-earned money of American workers. Consider $50,000 procured by Congresswoman Lois Capps to cover the costs of tattoo removal for her constituents in and around Santa Barbara, California. This immoral misuse of the American worker's earnings must be stopped. American taxpayers should determine tax rates, e.g. , by demanding of their elected officials that those rates be capped at no more than 25 percent. At that point we can hold our legislators responsible, not for being less wasteful than their colleagues, but for setting the right priorities with limited resources

But to regain this authority over our own lives in such a way as to be able to keep it—in other words, to remain free—we will need to become individually responsible as I discussed at the beginning; helping our neighbors and not demanding special treatment for ourselves.

On the first point, I like to contrast churches that define their success by the beauty of their physical facilities and the size of their congregations and financial budgets with those that define it by the percentage of their members who have lighthouse ministries of their own outside the church. A church with 100 members, of whom 90 perform some kind of service in their community, is more successful than 8,000-member churches with what Mike Regele has called "ingrown congregations which exist to minister to their own needs."

On the second point I like to quote Winston Churchill: "The inherent vice of capitalism is the unequal sharing of blessings; the inherent virtue of socialism is the equal sharing of misery." A free society mandates that constituents know how to live free and not as slaves to their passions.

Contrasted to Adam Smith's insight that free people in pursuit of their own self-interest will, in the process, fulfill the needs of others, there was a humble carpenter 2000 years ago who encouraged us to give selflessly of ourselves to others. The economic success of our country depends, in a sense, on our ability to attend simultaneously to both of these ideas.

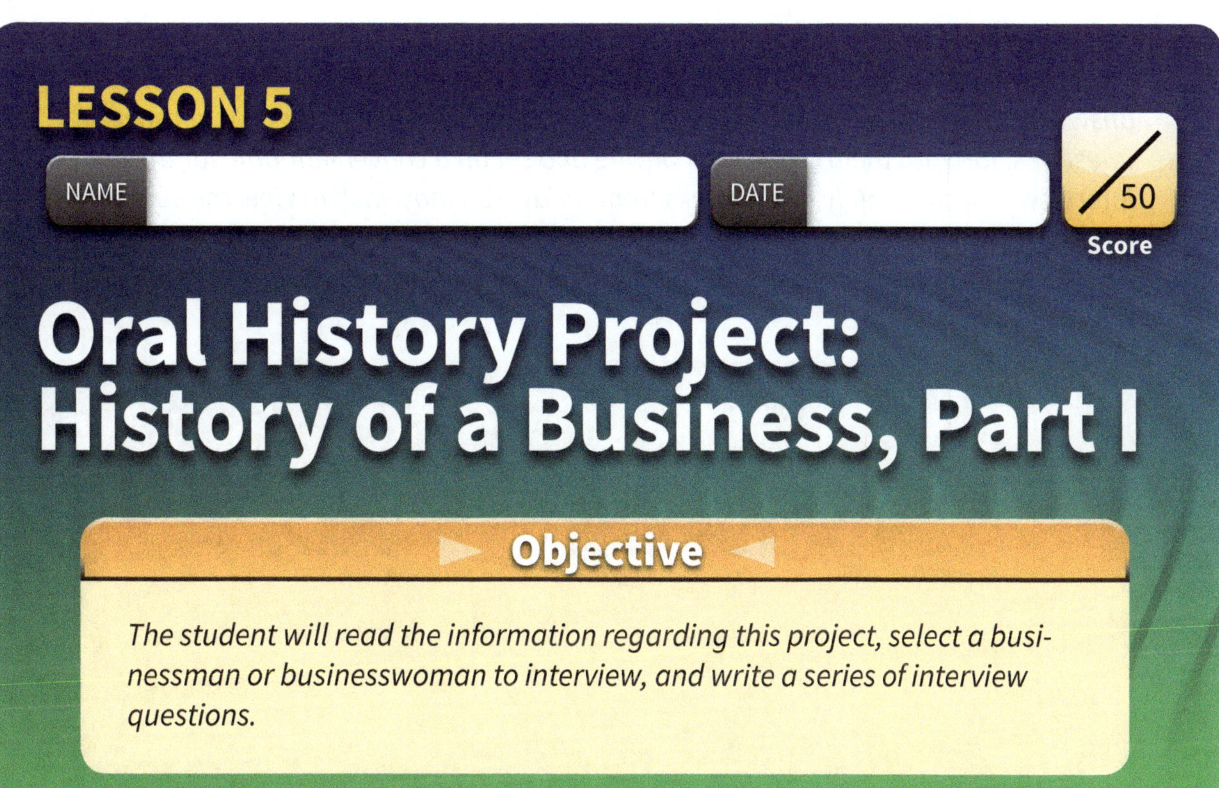

For this assignment, the student will write a brief (two to three pages) paper on the history of a business. This three-step oral history project begins with today's selection of a successful entrepreneur to interview for this project. After selecting the business and obtaining the owner's permission regarding the project, the student will write a series of open-ended interview questions to give to the entrepreneur prior to the actual interview. At a later date, the student will meet with the entrepreneur and record the interview. The student will produce a written transcript of the recorded interview and write the finished paper near the conclusion of the course.

Directions: *Write the entrepreneur's name, the name of the business, and the contact information on the following lines.*

Grading: *See answer key for grading rubric.*

Entrepreneur's Name:

____

Business:

____

Contact Information (phone number, e-mail address, etc.):

____

____

____

Directions: *On a separate sheet of paper, write or type a set of open-ended interview questions to ask the interviewee. Remember, you need enough information from the answers to write a two- to three-page paper. After your school supervisor approves the questions, forward them to the interviewee and set up a convenient time for the actual interview, approximately three weeks from today. You may wish to view the sample interview questions below for the fictitious woodworking business, Willie's Whirly-Gigs, for ideas prior to writing your own questions. Answers to these sample questions can be found in Lesson 13.*

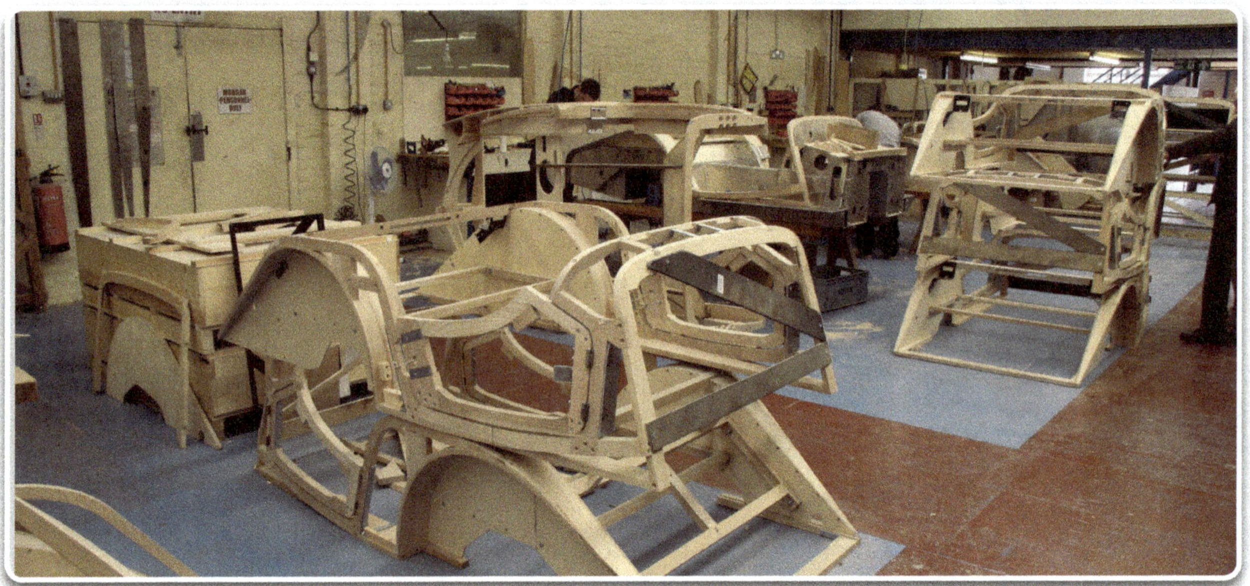

Sample interview questions for Willie's Whirly-Gigs woodworking business:

1. What is your name and the name of your business?
2. How long have you been in business?
3. You are a skilled woodworker. Tell us how you got started in this craft.
4. Why did you start Willie's Whirly-Gigs?
5. How did you acquire the capital needed to start Willie's Whirly-Gigs?
6. What kinds of products does Willie's Whirly-Gigs specialize in?
7. What are some of your favorite projects from past years?
8. What challenges have you had to overcome in your business?
9. What makes Willie's Whirly-Gigs unique or different from other woodworking shops?
10. How has your business changed in the last two years?
11. What are your plans for the future?

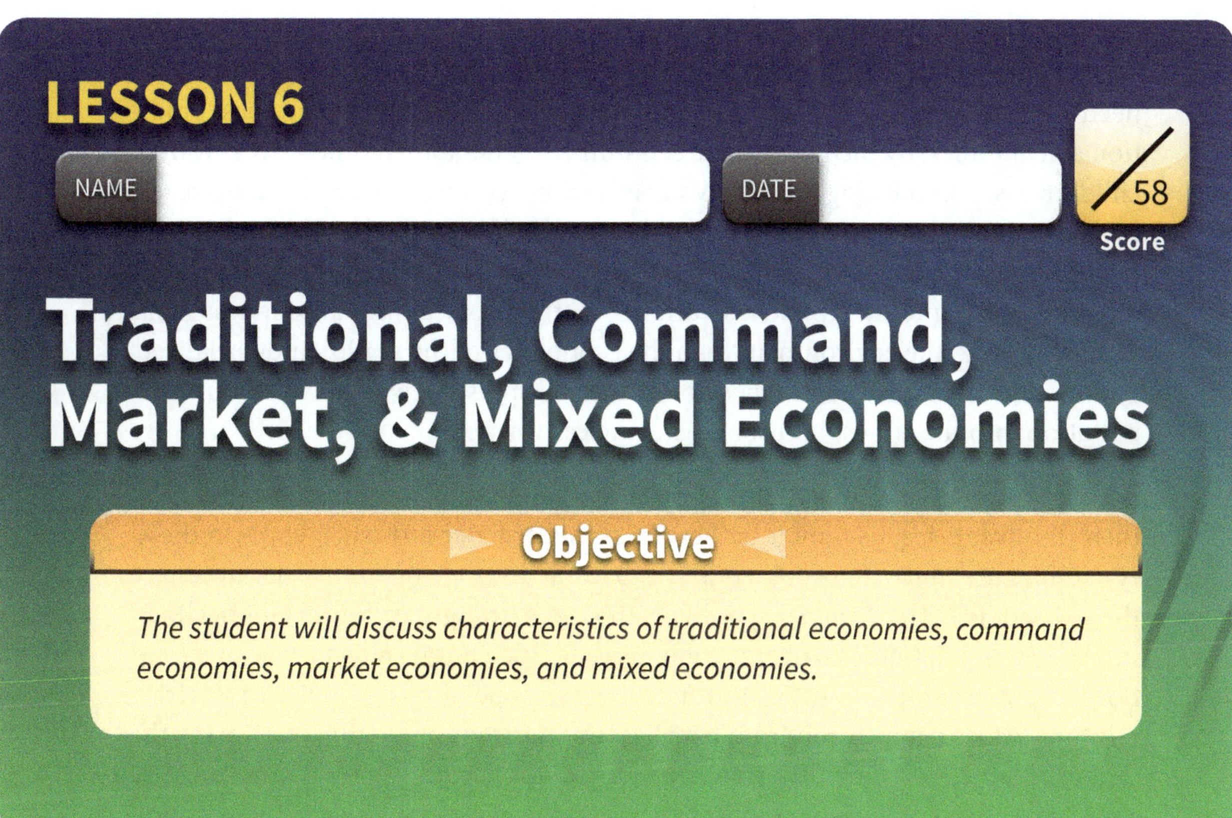

LESSON 6

NAME

DATE

/58 Score

Traditional, Command, Market, & Mixed Economies

Objective

The student will discuss characteristics of traditional economies, command economies, market economies, and mixed economies.

Lesson 6A Reading

In a world full of information and technological advances, traditional economies still exist. Various people-groups throughout the world continue to live as their ancestors did hundreds of years ago. Let's examine some of the characteristics of traditional economies.

As the name implies, traditional economies are based on traditions. Cultural mores dictate economic decisions. "That's the way we've always done it" could be the motto of traditional economies. Parents teach their children the skills necessary for survival. The children, in turn, will teach their children these same skills. Economic activity revolves around the family, clan, or tribal unit. Men and women have different, distinct economic responsibilities in a traditional economy.

Traditional economies have some advantages over command and market economies. Traditional economies rarely have to deal with surplus inventory. They produce only what they need, so traditional economies don't experience unemployment due to overproduction. Since these economies don't rely on technology, grandparents never become useless due to lack of knowledge about the new gadgetry, and future generations need not fear unemployment due to automated manufacturing techniques. Traditional economies, by their very nature, minimize generational differences. Young children assist in meeting the family's needs while learning the life skills necessary to survive, and grandparents never get put on a shelf because they have nothing to contribute. Intergenerational dependence makes for a tight-knit family unit. Hunting, gathering, and the subsistence farming methods of traditional economies may do less harm to the environment than the economies of the world's industrialized nations do. Traditional economies don't cause oil spills, spew massive amounts of pollution into the atmosphere, or create nuclear waste.

Before you get an idealized view of traditional economies, let's look at some of their disadvantages. As hunter-gatherers and subsistence farmers, people in these economies are much more susceptible to natural disasters or similar disruptions to their way of life. They could starve to death due to drought or significant declines in wildlife populations. Environmental disasters such as oil spills or volcanic eruptions might harm their hunting grounds. Pygmy populations in the central African rainforests face competition from tribal groups desirous of logging or clearing the rainforest for cash crop cultivation. Outside groups desirous of obtaining tribal lands could endanger a traditional economy's way of life. Numerous examples of exploitation of Native American tribes in this manner can be found in U.S. history. The Native Americans living on the Great Plains fought to protect their hunting grounds from encroaching settlement. One can easily sympathize with the Native Americans' plight when whites began indiscriminately destroying the animals upon which the Indians depended for survival.

We must note that not all traditional economies remain in technological isolation. Some Canadian Inuit, for example, use snowmobiles for transportation or radios for communication with the outside world. In these situations, the traditional economy embraces technology that makes life easier without sacrificing the values of their traditional way of life. Technology is their servant rather than their master.

Review Questions

Directions: *Answer the following questions based on the Lesson 6A reading.*

1. How do traditional economies foster family unity? *(2 points)*

____

____

2. List two advantages that traditional economies have over capitalist and command economies. *(2 points)*

____

____

____

____

3. Why are subsistence-level traditional economies more vulnerable than capitalist and command economies? *(2 points)*

4. Would you classify the Amish as a traditional economy? Why or why not? *(5 points)*

Lesson 6B Reading

In command economies, also known as planned economies, the central government controls the means of production and decides what will be produced. Command economies emphasize the collective good over individual profits. Central planners develop a macroeconomic model for their command economy and work to implement these goals. To avoid the economic peaks and valleys of market economies, command economies try to limit the sometimes wild upturns and downswings of market economies by keeping their people in perpetual poverty. This dangerous course makes command economies subject to political unrest as the "have-nots" in society try to overthrow the "haves" in power. Such political disturbances lead to violent put-downs of the protestors by the command economy's security forces. If the underlying causes that led to the uprising in the first place are not resolved, the masses need only a charismatic leader to stir up new demonstrations against a repressive regime.

Command economies will ultimately fail because they create a system that destroys man's incentive to work. The author remembers reading a story about a collective apple orchard in the former Soviet Union. Army units had to come in and pick the apples because the farm residents quickly learned that they would get paid even if they didn't work in the orchard. Perfectly healthy workers pretended to be sick in order to skip work, but they still got paid the same wages as those who toiled tending the apple trees. Without a profit incentive, work came to a standstill in the orchard, and soldiers who had to obey orders from their superior officers were brought in to salvage the crop. While command economies may pride themselves on "solving" the problem of capitalist greed, they fail to fulfill Christ's admonition to "remove the beam from your own eye before dealing with the splinter that is in your neighbor's eye." In a command economy, wealthy industrialists get replaced by corrupt government leaders who profit from their leadership positions. The fundamental problem with communism, socialism, and other command economies is that they fail to recognize the fallen, sinful nature of man. Command economies rail against capitalist greed but forget that they too are greedy. No one is exempt from sin. People will always seek to maximize their perceived well-being. In a planned economy, the only people with the means to do so work for the government.

Command economies should not be confused with economic planning. Various levels of government in traditional and market economies may from time to time engage in economic planning. During World Wars I and II, for instance, the United States used economic planning to produce the military hardware and foodstuffs necessary to win those wars. Urban revitalization may involve economic planning without a government takeover of resources and the means of production, but the economic planning could be necessary as a result of a failure to recognize market forces at work. For example, a city or region dependent on auto manufacturing may suffer tremendous job loss due to foreign competition from better-quality cars. Without knowing the real reason(s) why consumers stopped purchasing American-made automobiles, government policies could prop up the American automobile industry without fixing the real cause of the decline in sales. As another example, if city residents are leaving town because of crime, high property taxes, pollution, lack of jobs, and noise, economic planning will not revitalize the city without addressing these causes of the exodus.

Review Questions

Directions: *Answer the following questions based on the Lesson 6B reading.*

1. How do command economies take away an individual's incentive to work? *(2 points)*

2. Who determines what is produced in a command economy? *(1 point)*

3. Why are entrepreneurs a threat to a command economy? *(2 points)*

4. How is economic planning different from a planned (command) economy? *(4 points)*

Lesson 6C Reading

Market economies, also known as capitalist economies, free markets, or the free-enterprise system, allow the interactions of individuals and businesses to determine production, distribution, and consumption, with little or no central government planning or intervention in the economy. A true market economy even excludes government taxation and regulation because these policies remove economic decision-making power from consumers and businesses. Of course, no totally free-market economy exists anywhere in the world, but the theoretical ideal provides a scale on which to evaluate a nation's propensity toward a command or free-market economy.

Supply and demand for various goods and services determine the price levels at which exchanges take place in a market economy. A market economy allocates resources based on consumer wants and desires. One advantage of a market economy is that it produces the goods and services consumers want at prices they are willing to pay. Consumers reward businesses that meet their wants and needs with profits, while businesses unable to meet consumer wants and needs, at prices they can afford, fail. Market economies prosper because of competition (resulting in lower prices and quality products), tangible incentives for hard work, acquisition and protection of private property, freedom from government interference, innovation and technology, and encouragement of entrepreneurs.

Market economies typically provide a greater variety and more abundant supply of goods and services than a command economy does. Critics of market economies, however, are quick to point out the sometimes severe problems of a market economy—market fluctuations with periodic downturns in the economy, inflation (a period of rising prices), and the competitive nature of a market economy that can result in greed. Recessions and depressions are a normal part of free-market economies. Economists and historians sometimes have a hard time pinpointing the exact cause or causes of these declines in a market economy. The Panic of 1893, perhaps the most severe depression in the United States before the Great Depression, came about as a result of railroad speculation, the bankruptcies of several railroad companies, bank failures, currency problems, the Sherman Silver Purchase Act of 1890, protective tariffs, and a severe drought. The depression came to an end in 1897, and the United States began a period of rapid economic growth that lasted until the Panic of 1907. Triggered by a stock manipulation scheme to corner the United Copper Company stock, this financial crisis, which caused several prominent banks and trusts to fail, required emergency meetings of New York City bankers, the U.S. Secretary of the Treasury, and J.P. Morgan to restore the public's confidence and avert a national financial disaster. President Theodore Roosevelt had to okay a last-minute takeover of the Tennessee Coal, Iron, and Railroad Company (TCI) by J.P. Morgan's U.S. Steel Corporation (a clear violation of the Sherman Antitrust Act) to avoid a complete collapse of the New York Stock Exchange. Our nation's centralized banking system, the Federal Reserve, came about as a result of the Panic of 1907. Greedy men took advantage of the system to increase their wealth at the expense of the nation's financial health. Their unscrupulous competitiveness led to the financial ruin of a great number of unknown average Americans.

Should these real or potential problems with market economies force us to abandon the free market in favor of a command economy? Absolutely not! You don't throw the baby out with the bathwater. Severe punishment of those individuals guilty of wrongdoing would curtail the criminal activity that led to these meltdowns of the American economy. All of the individuals involved in illegal activity with the U.S. financial and foreclosure crisis in the first decade of the 21st century should be indicted and prosecuted for their part in this crisis—a free market disturbance that required a government bailout to prevent a complete collapse of the world's financial markets. Many of those involved in the savings and loans scandals in the 1990s went to jail for illegal activity. We have laws on the books to prevent financial criminal activity—we just need to enforce these existing laws when necessary. It is also important to understand that the most recent market collapse should not be viewed as a market failure. Simply because the market goes down does not mean that it failed. On the contrary, the market did exactly what we expect it to do. The market rewards good behavior and punishes bad behavior. Those who recognized that banks had too much debt and that many were holding "assets" that were really worthless made a lot of money. Those who made bad investments or entrusted their money to people who made bad investments lost a lot of money. In other words, the market-based economy worked like it was supposed to work.

Let's conclude this reading section by noting that market economies and command economies are idealized types that don't exist in the real world. Nations that we categorize as market (capitalist) economies or command economies are really mixed economies, blending elements of both but tending toward one or the other, based on the degree of government involvement in the economy. If consumers wield a great deal of control in economic decision making, the mixed economy tends toward capitalism. If government controls industry and agriculture but allows the individuals working on collective farms to sell excess produce over and above the farm quotas for their own profit, then the mixed economy leans toward a command economy. Taxpayer-funded schools and government-run health care are obvious elements of a command economy in the United States.

Review Questions

Directions: *Answer the following questions based on the Lesson 6C reading.*

1. List a major criticism of market economies. *(1 point)*

____

____

____

____

2. Identify four command economy elements in the U. S. free-market economy. *(4 points)*

____

____

____

____

____

3. Place an X on the economic spectrum provided here, identifying the location of the U.S. economy relative to command and free-market economies. List five reasons for your choice. *(10 points)*

Command Economy ▪▪▪▪▪▪▪▪▪▪▪▪▪▪▪▪▪▪▪▪▪▪▪▪▪▪▪▪▪▪▪▪ **Free-Market Economy**

4. Would environmental regulations exist in a true free-market economy? Why or why not? *(3 points)*

5. At what point in history did the United States become a mixed economy rather than a capitalist economy? Give historical examples to defend your answer. *(10 points)*

NAME

DATE

/10
Score

Lesson 6D Marxism

"A spectre is haunting Europe—the spectre of Communism."
Karl Marx, *The Communist Manifesto,* 1848

Karl Marx was born in 1818 in Trier, Prussia. His father was a respected lawyer and a member of the German aristocracy. His early education included the study of the French political philosopher Voltaire, the English political philosopher John Locke, and the French philosopher and writer Diderot. At the universities of Bonn and Berlin, Marx was influenced by the teachings of the German philosopher Georg Wilhelm Friedrich Hegel. Hegel believed that change is inevitable; that throughout history the dominant idea (what Hegel called the ***thesis***) is opposed by an opposite idea called the **antithesis**. These opposing ideas will eventually produce a compromise idea called the ***synthesis***, which becomes the new thesis, only to be challenged by a new antithesis. This cycle will continue until man reaches perfection (Utopia). Much of what Marx wrote about in *The Communist Manifesto* and *Das Kapital*—that history is the record of economic conflict and the struggle between the proletariat (the wage-earning class) and the bourgeoisie (the property class)—can be traced to Hegel's influence.

Directions: *Using the word list, complete the following activity on Marxism.* *(1 point each)*

Word List

God's	bank
property	inheritance
capitalism	confiscation
income	urban
economy	transportation

The 10 Tenets of Marxism*

1. Expropriation of landed ________________, with land rents used for public purposes
2. A graduated or progressive ________________ tax
3. No ____________________ rights
4. ____________________ of rebels' property
5. State control of finances: a national ____________ and a monopoly on credit
6. Centralized communication and ____________________ controlled by the state
7. A planned ________________—national factories, more cultivated land, and planned production and agriculture
8. Universal and equal work using "industrial armies"
9. Elimination of rural and ____________ distinctions
10. Free public education, abolition of factory work for children, and combining education with material production

*taken from *The Communist Manifesto*

Criticisms of Marxism

1. Advocates violent overthrow of the existing social order
2. Fails to recognize that ________________ could correct its problems
3. Goes against ____________ social order

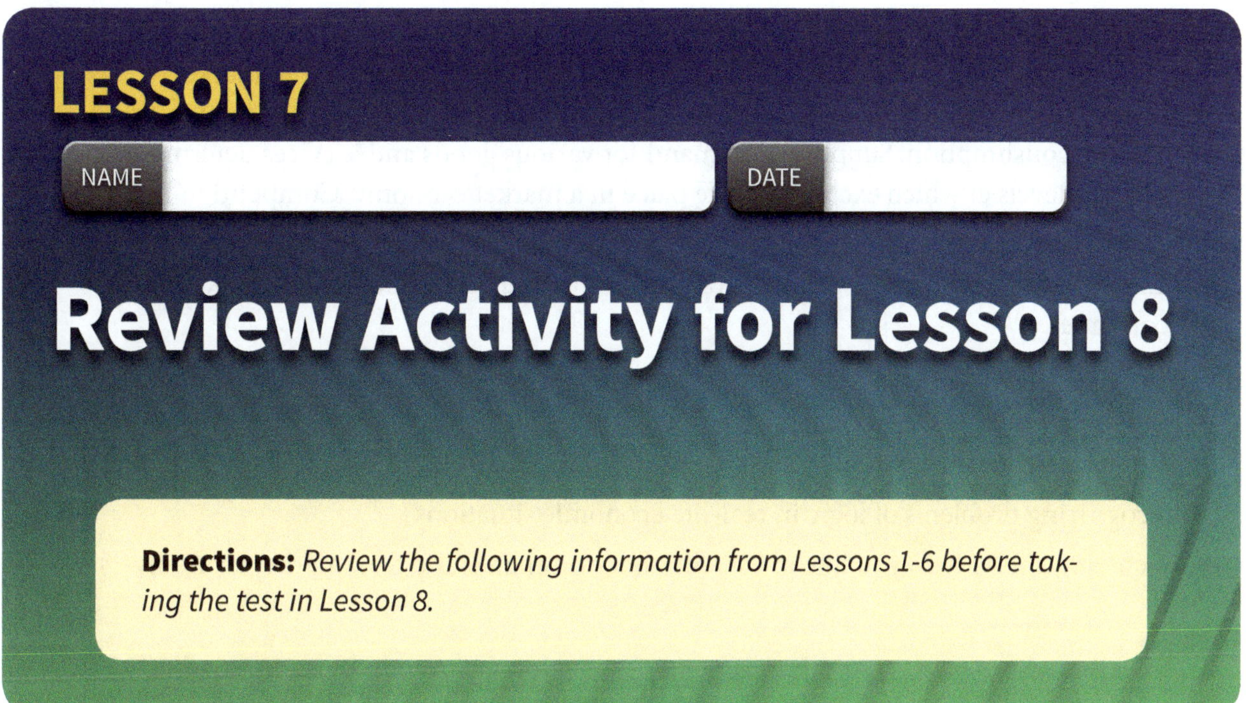

Directions: *Review the following information from Lessons 1-6 before taking the test in Lesson 8.*

Scripture Memory

- **Proverbs 14:34—**Righteousness exalteth a nation, but sin is a reproach to any people.

Concepts to Review

- God owns the earth because He created it and He sustains it.
- God gave man dominion over His creation. Man will answer to God for his role as a trustee of God's creation.
- Having been made in the image of God, man has creative abilities, a rational mind and a free will that enable him to make choices, and a conscious eternal existence in either heaven or hell.
- Economics is a science, but there are key differences between economics and the "pure" sciences.
- Microeconomics and macroeconomics are the two main branches of economics.
- Economic goods are man-produced goods that have value. Services are the product of man's labor with an associated cost.
- Economics is subject to various problems of logic.
- *Ceteris paribus* affects most economic decisions.
- Review all of the Lesson 3 Bible passages except the Proverbs crossword puzzle.
- Traditional economies rarely suffer from overproduction. They pass down their way of life/survival skills to the next generation. They foster unity among the family, clan, or tribal unit. Their subsistence way of life makes them vulnerable to natural or man-made disasters.
- By removing the profit motivation, command economies destroy man's incentive to work.

- Memorize the 10 principles of Marxism.
- Consumers decide what will be produced in free-market economies. Free-market economies suffer from periodic recessions and depressions due to overproduction or too little consumption. Supply and demand for various goods and services determine the price levels at which exchanges take place in a market economy. Competition in a market economy results in lower prices and better-quality merchandise.
- Mixed economies combine elements of both command economies and free-market economies.

Practical Application

- Can you really own a home?
- Recognizing problems of logic in real-life economic situations
- Acquiring a food item you like in a traditional, command, and free-market economy

The test for Lesson 8 is located in the assessments section on page 215.

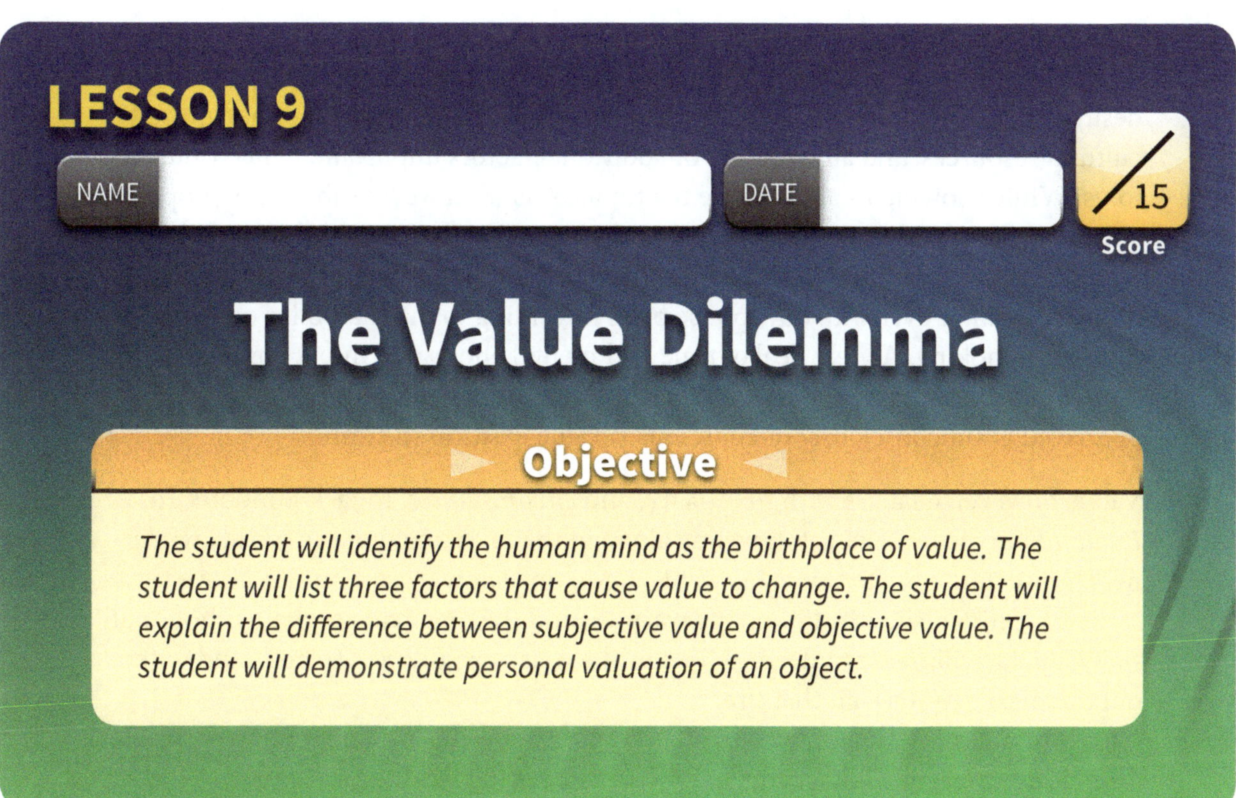

LESSON 9

NAME DATE /15 Score

The Value Dilemma

Objective

The student will identify the human mind as the birthplace of value. The student will list three factors that cause value to change. The student will explain the difference between subjective value and objective value. The student will demonstrate personal valuation of an object.

Lesson 9A Reading

In order to make choices, individuals must first determine the value of various objects. In the Garden of Eden, during Satan's temptation, Eve saw that the fruit from the tree of knowledge was good for food and was something that would make her "wise." She mentally placed a higher value on the forbidden fruit than on God's commandment not to eat the fruit of that particular tree. We use our God-given reasoning powers to rank any number of items as more or less valuable. We do this *subconsciously* when we impulsively buy something that is on the dollar menu at the fast-food restaurant. Our hunger pangs or taste cravings at that moment outweigh the value of saving the individual dollar or putting it to another use. We *consciously*

place value when we mentally labor over a decision such as purchasing a home. Before setting out with a real estate agent, we narrow down our search based on the desired size and location of our home, the community's educational opportunities or cultural resources, and any number of additional factors important, hence valuable, to us. While showing us around, the realtor asks us what we like about the property, and we make comments about the size of the rooms or the huge backyard with plenty of space for entertaining and a garden. After the tour, we think about the home and talk it over with our spouse before deciding to make an offer on the house or to keep looking. A great deal of time and mental effort goes into a home-buying decision, including rational reasons for our choice over all the other options. Whether arrived at subconsciously or consciously, value exists in the mind.

Value, however, changes with *time*, *place*, and *circumstances*. In Jack London's *To Build a Fire*, the protagonist, traveling alone in the severe cold of the Alaska wilderness, must start a fire to warm his wet feet. Melting snow from a branch above the campfire extinguishes the life-giving warmth, and the man realizes that without outside help, he will freeze to death. Alone in the Alaska wilderness (place), and without the means to start another fire (circumstances), the victim would give his every earthly possession for another pack of matches. The mental will to live alters the normal value of matches in the dying man's mind. Would the Russians have sold Alaska in 1867 if they knew about the underground gold deposits and oil reserves? Without definite knowledge of these valuable natural resources, and fearing British or American annexation of the land in the foreseeable future, Tsar Alexander II sold the Alaska Territory to the United States for $7.2 million—a real bargain at about two cents an acre.

Alaska Purchase Check

Fortunately, most mental rearrangements of value don't have such dire or drastic consequences. When you decide to trade in your 10-year-old vehicle for a newer model, it's probably not a life-or-death situation. Nevertheless, you mentally decrease the trade-in car's value enough to part with it for something different.

Review Questions

Directions: *Answer the following questions based on the Lesson 9A reading.*

1. Where does value exist? *(1 point)*

____

2. What three factors cause value to fluctuate? *(3 points)*

____

____

3. How might a video game aficionado demonstrate mental revaluation after conquering all of a game's levels? *(2 points)*

____

____

____

4. When the author was a child, he and his friends bought packs of baseball cards for the stick of gum they contained. Without understanding how collectibles increase in value, they used clothespins to attach the baseball cards to their bike frames. The cards made a cool, whirring sound slapping against the spokes of their bike wheels as they rode down the street. Why shouldn't you attach baseball cards to your bicycle? *(2 points)*

____

____

5. Why do many elderly couples decide to downsize after their children leave home? *(2 points)*

____

____

____

____

____

____

Lesson 9B Reading

Subjective, or psychological, value consists of non-measurable variables, including, but not limited to, a person's likes and dislikes, what a person's friends might think, or the perceived quality of an item. Notice that all of these value judgments take place in an individual's mind. These judgments may or may not be based on concrete experiences. A young man may convince himself he doesn't like lima beans, even if he's never tasted them. If my parents taught me that rock music is wrong, and I believe what I was taught, then I won't purchase or listen to that type of music.

Unlike its subjective cousin, objective value can be measured. You might love broccoli (subjective value), but in order to quantify your love of *brassica oleracea,* you would need to examine your grocery bill receipts. By doing so, you note that last year you bought 500 bunches of broccoli at an average cost of $1.00 per bunch (objective value). With this information, you can objectively declare that you love broccoli to the tune of $500. What a person pays for a good or service is an objective measurement of the value they place on that item.

Review Questions

Directions: *Answer the following questions based on the Lesson 9B reading.*

1. Explain the difference between subjective value and objective value. *(1 point)*

2. What can you learn about subjective value and objective value from the following scenario? *(2 points)*

   On a Friday night shopping spree, you pass up a $35.00 long-sleeve dress shirt at an upscale retail shop. At a chain department store, you look at but don't buy a $5.00 short-sleeve dress shirt. At a close-out store, you buy a $6.00 long-sleeve dress shirt.

3. Suppose you like burgers from two competing fast-food chains. If both franchises charge the same amount for the burgers, what subjective values might factor into your purchase decision? *(2 points)*

NAME DATE

Practical Application Activity:
Value of a 1985 Mercury Grand Marquis

This 1985 Mercury Grand Marquis has been in the author's family for most of its life, having been previously owned by his uncle, grandfather, and father. Do you like this car? Do you value it enough to want to own it or another vehicle just like it? Some teenage drivers wouldn't consider this a "cool" car, but others might desire it for its fantastic ride, roomy trunk and interior, V-8 power, or safety, due to its sturdy frame. So, what's a car like this worth? Would you pay $500 for it? If the owner wanted to sell it, could he get $1,000 for it? Before answering that question, you need more information than the photo can provide. The vehicle has been mechanically well maintained, but the odometer is rapidly approaching 200,000 miles. It uses some oil, and the vinyl top is cracking. The photo angle doesn't show you the rust on the driver's door and left front fender. You also can't see that the back bumper is rusted out, the interior head-liner is down, the rear windshield defroster is defective, the cruise control no longer works, and the dash-mounted speakers were removed for use elsewhere. Two of the power windows don't work on this four-door sedan. The photo doesn't reveal that the left rear axle, the gas tank, and the oil pump have been recently replaced. Now, armed with this additional information, do you like this car? Did the non-photo information make you change your mind?

Directions: *Answer the following questions about the 1985 Mercury Grand Marquis.*

1. After viewing the photograph, did you like this car? *(1 point)* **Yes** **No**

2. Based solely on the photograph, what factor(s) influenced your decision? (Circle all that apply.) *(1 point)*
   - **Body style**
   - **Appearance/Condition**
   - **Size of vehicle**
   - **Four-door vs. two-door**
   - **Perceived quality of vehicle based on previous knowledge**
   - **Powerful engine**
   - **Roominess**
   - **Other factor(s):** ____________________

3. Did you change your mind after reading the additional vehicle information provided in the paragraph? *(1 point)* **Yes** **No**

4. If you answered "yes" to question #3, what factor(s) made you change your mind? (Circle all that apply.) *(1 point)*
   - Vehicle's age
   - High mileage
   - Uses oil
   - Deterioration of the vehicle's body and bumper
   - Maintenance history
   - Missing speakers
   - Non-working electrical components
   - Smooth ride
   - Vehicle's roominess
   - V-8 engine
   - Safety
   - Other factor(s): ____

5. What would you offer for a vehicle in this condition? $________.00 Is your offer based on subjective or objective valuation? *(1 point)*

   ____
   ____
   ____
   ____

6. Match the following individuals with the reason they might value this vehicle. Answers are used only once. *(1 point each)*

   A. I could restore this vehicle and take it to car shows.
   B. There are plenty of useful parts left on this vehicle.
   C. I need a reliable work vehicle.
   D. Insurance will be cheap on this vehicle.
   E. I could learn a lot about older vehicles from this automobile.

   ________ Parents with teenage drivers
   ________ A classic car buff
   ________ The owner of an auto salvage yard
   ________ An auto mechanic
   ________ A two-income family

Directions: *Write a three- to five-sentence response to the following question.* *(5 points)*

7. Why do some cars increase in value as they get older?

   ____
   ____
   ____
   ____

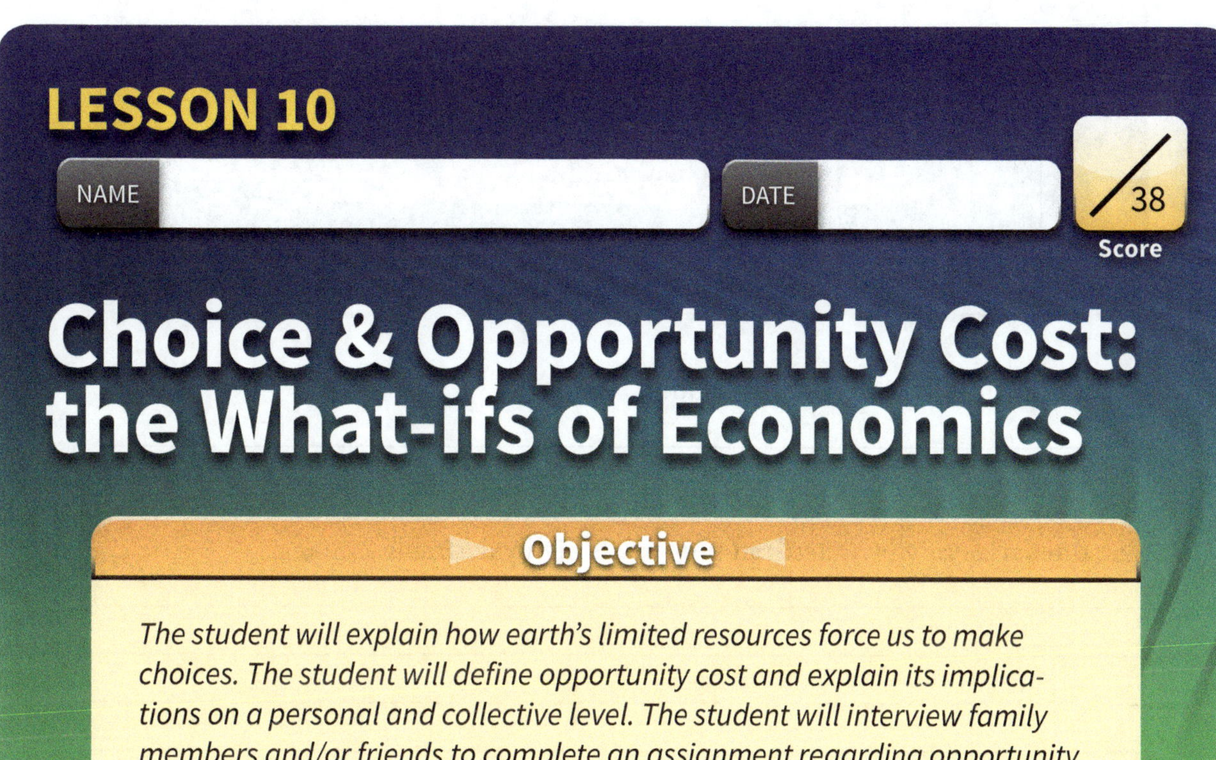

LESSON 10

NAME ______ DATE ______ /38 Score

Choice & Opportunity Cost: the What-ifs of Economics

Objective

The student will explain how earth's limited resources force us to make choices. The student will define opportunity cost and explain its implications on a personal and collective level. The student will interview family members and/or friends to complete an assignment regarding opportunity cost.

Lesson 10A Reading

Bobby wants a boat. Bill covets a fancy sports car. Karen lives for exotic vacations, and Nancy loves her fantastic wardrobe full of designer fashions. Our unique wants and desires demonstrate the greatness of our Creator. Unfortunately, we live in a world with limited resources. Everyone cannot have everything they want. Earth's limited resources must be rationed, forcing individuals to make choices. How are these resources rationed? In a command and control economy such as North Korea, the central government makes the rationing decisions, resulting in extreme poverty for much of its population. In a market-based economy, where people are free to make their own choices about what they consume and how they spend their resources, price serves as the rationing agent.

Review Questions

Directions: *Answer the following questions based on the Lesson 10A reading.*

1. What is mankind's basic economic problem? *(1 point)*

______

______

______

2. What does this problem force us to do? *(1 point)*

3. List three reasons why waterfront property is highly desirable. *(3 points)*

4. How do we ration this desirable resource? *(1 point)*

5. How could you enjoy the pleasures of waterfront property without purchasing it? *(2 points)*

6. If you really want to own waterfront property, what might you need to do, or give up, in order to purchase the desired piece of property? *(2 points)*

7. In your opinion, is this view worth a multimillion-dollar price tag? Support your answer with subjective or objective reasons. *(1 point)*

Lesson 10B Reading

Since limited resources force us to make choices, we must consider opportunity costs. **Opportunity cost** is the next best alternative based on the choice actually made. In any given situation, you might be choosing from multiple rather than either-or options, but only your second choice falls into the category of opportunity cost.

Consider briefly how your day begins. If you set your alarm for 6:30 a.m., but turn it off and sleep until 7:30 a.m., you are choosing an extra hour of sleep over a multitude of other options (having your devotions, exercising, studying for a test, doing chores around the house, checking Facebook, etc.). You cannot do all of these activities at once, so opportunity cost is concerned only with the alternative you actually rejected for additional sleep. If you normally get up early and exercise before starting school, exercise becomes the opportunity cost of hitting the snooze button.

Since you slept in, you don't have time to prepare your regular breakfast of bacon, eggs, toast, and orange juice, so you grab a bowl of cereal before starting your schoolwork. The hot, nutritious breakfast becomes the opportunity cost to a soggy bowl of cereal.As a home schooled senior, you have the privilege of choosing the order in which you complete your school assignments. You don't like British Literature, so you normally put that off until after lunch. Today you decide to get it out of the way first thing in the morning, moving your beloved math to the end of the day. The pleasure of doing math is the opportunity cost of enduring your least-favorite subject at the start of your school day.

Opportunity costs don't always involve dissimilar choices. Every year the author receives six or eight catalogs from nurseries and seed companies. Although he purchases plants from the same company year after year, the other companies try to entice him with their colorful catalogs and coupons for 50 percent off certain-size orders. One particular company in 2011 offered him some terrific bargains and products not available from his regular supplier. However, higher prices for most plants compared to his favorite supplier and more expensive shipping kept this company as opportunity cost for him for at least another year. If this company finds a way to reduce its retail prices and shipping costs, he might give them his business in the future.

We experience opportunity costs with our work, time, money, leisure activities, resources, and every other decision-making process. We subjectively value the choice actually made over the next best alternative. If the choice involves an objective element, such as spending money, we know that the price of the alternative purchase contributes in some way to its being opportunity cost. In the catalog illustration from the previous paragraph, the author either didn't have enough money to purchase from the supplier with the greater inventory, as he had already placed an order with his regular company, or he wasn't willing to spend more just to get a few items not available from his regular supplier. Stated another way, he didn't value the new items enough to place an order with the other company.

So why is opportunity cost a big deal in economics? To understand its importance, think about not just its individual impact but its collective consequences. Millions of individuals, as well as businesses, local governments, states, and even nations make choices that incur opportunity costs. If a business pays its stockholders dividends rather than investing in new technology, the company may lose its competitive edge, resulting in lower profits. If a cash-strapped community votes to raise property taxes rather than increase city revenue by attracting new business, every property owner will have less income to spend on other items. A state that sets aside 3,000 acres of land for a wildlife refuge cannot use that land for an amusement park (a much more lucrative use of the property). An oil-rich Middle Eastern nation that spends its money on military technology cannot use that revenue on public works projects that would benefit its citizens in other ways besides national security. Every opportunity cost (choice not made) means lost income to someone. From the reading, you know that there is at least one plant supplier anxious for my yearly business. One grower (my current supplier) may fear losing my business if it cannot keep expanding its product line and selling plants for less than its competitors. Since I spend very little every year, compared to their entire customer base, losing my business may not hurt them financially, but if thousands of customers switch to other suppliers, the company could be in jeopardy.

Review Questions

Directions: *Answer the following questions based on the Lesson 10B reading.*

1. Define **opportunity cost.** *(2 points)*

____

____

____

2. If you choose to spend the money you got for your birthday rather than save it, how does your bank experience opportunity cost? *(2 points)*

____

____

____

3. If the current furnace is working fine, would insulation or a geothermal heating system be the opportunity cost for a Minnesota home built in 1920? *(2 points)*

___

4. Why is buying a more fuel-efficient car perhaps not your best response to rising fuel prices? *(2 points)*

___

5. How are free samples given to you by warehouse clubs and mall food-court restaurants a recognition of opportunity cost? *(2 points)*

___

6. Explain the symbiotic relationship between opportunity cost and advertising. *(2 points)*

___

7. How does a product registration website create additional opportunity cost for the respondent? *(2 points)*

___

8. Which product line experiences greater opportunity costs—cruise lines or fast-food restaurants? Why? *(2 points)*

___

9. The Federal-Aid Highway Act of 1956 initiated construction of a national system of interstate highways. According to the U.S. Department of Transportation Federal Highway Administration website, there are 46,876 miles of interstate highways.[9] List three benefits of interstate highways. *(3 points)*

10. What is the opportunity cost of building interstate highways? *(2 points)*

11. Interstate highways occupy a large amount of land—some of which (the medians) could be used for farming. Farmers currently bale hay from the medians in some states, but more could be done, including growing grains or fruit and nut trees. This looks like a win-win situation. States would save money on mowing costs and bring in additional revenue by renting out the medians to farmers. The governor of your state wants the state legislature to act on this idea immediately, but you have serious doubts about this proposal. List four potential problems with this expanded use of the land between your state's interstate highways. *(4 points)*

12. Based on your responses to the previous question, do you believe farming is a legitimate opportunity cost for interstate medians? Why or why not? *(2 points)*

[9] www.fhwa.dot.gov

NAME

DATE

Practical Application Activity: *Choice and Opportunity Cost*

Directions: *Interview two family members or friends concerning choices and opportunity costs in the following areas: food, time, education, clothing, and leisure activities. For each category, the interviewee should give you a specific choice made and the next best alternative they gave up. You may need to explain opportunity cost to an interviewee unfamiliar with the concept.*

Interview #1 *(10 Points)*		
Interviewee's Name:		
Relationship to the Interviewer :		Date:
Food	Choice	
	Opportunity Cost	
Time	Choice	
	Opportunity Cost	
Education	Choice	
	Opportunity Cost	
Clothing	Choice	
	Opportunity Cost	
Leisure Activity	Choice	
	Opportunity Cost	

Interview #2 *(10 Points)*		
Interviewee's Name:		
Relationship to the Interviewer :		Date:
Food	Choice	
	Opportunity Cost	
Time	Choice	
	Opportunity Cost	
Education	Choice	
	Opportunity Cost	
Clothing	Choice	
	Opportunity Cost	
Leisure Activity	Choice	
	Opportunity Cost	

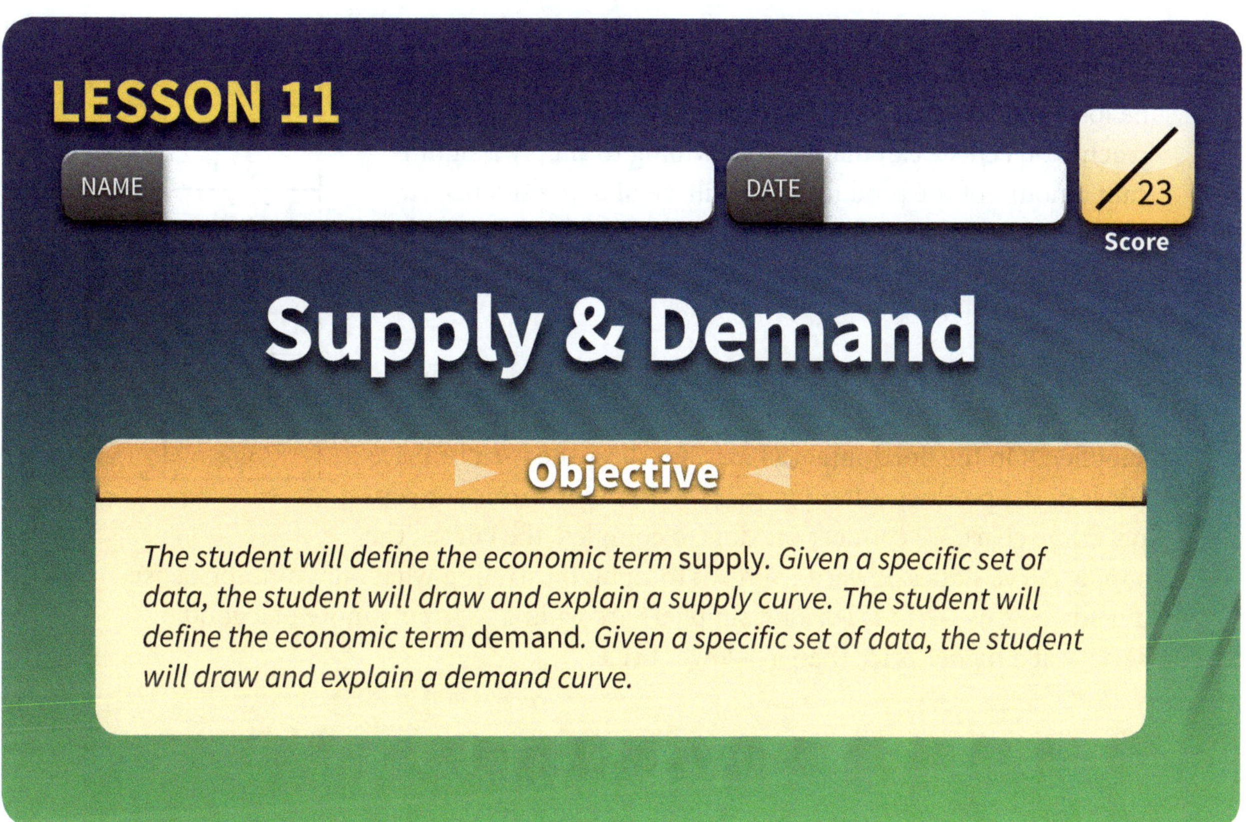

Lesson 11A Reading

God has abundantly blessed our nation. Store shelves contain a plethora of consumer goods. Did you ever stop to consider how those goods got there? If you have, then you've expressed an interest in the concept of **supply**.

For the economist, supply deals with the willingness and the ability of individuals to produce a product or provide a service. Suppliers must have both the desire and the capability of making the product or providing the service. Tom wants to make money by putting in vegetable and flower gardens for his neighbors, but without gardening tools, he cannot provide these services. If Tom has the proper tools, but a bad back prevents him from shoveling, his neighbors cannot hire him to put in a garden. Suppliers must be willing and able to supply the market with a good or service.

So how do suppliers know how much to produce? One of the major factors involved in this decision is the selling price of the good or service. Our God-given rational powers tell us that suppliers will produce more at a higher price than a lower price—the greater the profit margin, the more they will produce. Let's examine a supply schedule to visualize how the supply concept works.

Mark Me Up, founder of the Happy Cola Company, has both the willingness and the capability to produce his carbonated beverage. With bottling plants throughout the United States, he holds a small but significant share of the U.S. cola market. The chart illustrates Mark's willingness and ability to supply his hometown of Liquidity with soda pop each week.

Price	Supply
$0.00	0
$0.05	0
$0.10	1
$0.15	2
$0.20	7
$0.25	11
$0.40	23
$0.50	49
$0.75	105
$1.00	212

Notice that if the product is free or selling for 5 cents, Mark cannot produce the beverage with the smiley-face label because he loses money at those price levels. It's not until the price reaches 50 cents a can that Mark is willing to supply a significant amount of the product to his village of 500 residents. At one dollar per can, Mark is willing to keep the Liquidity Village Market and the Petrol Palace gas station well stocked with his cola.

We can graph this information to better understand Mark's supply decision. On the vertical (Y) axis, we show the quantity supplied. On the horizontal (X) axis, we show the various price levels of the product. After plotting the 10 points from our supply curve chart, we connect the dots to complete the curve. The supply curve slopes upward from left to right, illustrating what our common sense already tells us—*ceteris paribus*, suppliers are willing to supply more of a good or service at a higher price than at a lower price.

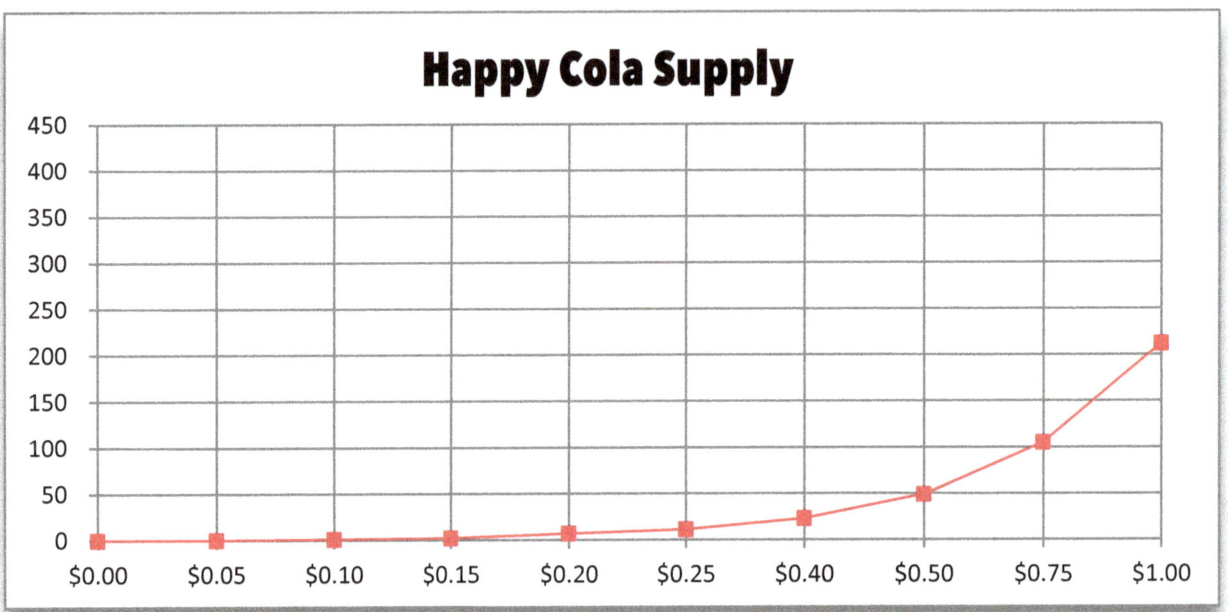

Many other factors besides price impact the supply side of the market. Natural disasters or wars may impede the ability of suppliers to obtain the raw materials needed to manufacture their product. Rising oil prices means higher energy costs, which impact production and distribution costs. Unnecessary government regulation or intervention in the market can upset the supply chain. For instance, if government attempts to control inflation by arbitrarily setting prices below production costs, suppliers will have to cease manufacturing or lose money on the finished product. **Speculation** (engagement in business transactions involving considerable risk but offering the chance of large gains, especially trading in commodities, stocks, etc., in the hope of profit from changes in the market price[10]) could impact supply. If a con-

[10] Speculation. (n.d.). *Dictionary.com Unabridged.* Retrieved March 15, 2011, from Dictionary.com website: http://dictionary.reference.com/browse/speculation

tractor buys up all the foreclosed homes in your town and keeps them off the market until the economy recovers to sell them at a huge profit, your town may experience a housing shortage. The supply side of the market can be quite fragile.

Review Questions

Directions: *Answer the following questions based on the Lesson 11A reading.*

1. What two concepts are inherent in the definition of supply? *(1 point)*

____

____

2. Why does a typical supply curve slope upward from left to right? *(1 point)*

____

____

3. Tom wants to become a garden designer. His dad bought him a rotary tiller and garden tools so he can gain some practical experience while still in high school. After putting in a vegetable garden on his property and redoing the family flower gardens, Tom feels confident enough to charge others for his services. Graph the following chart showing Tom's willingness to put in a 5′ x 15′ flower garden for his neighbors at various price levels. His service includes tilling the garden location, amending the soil with compost or fertilizer, purchasing the plants, and mulching the finished flower garden. *(5 points)*

Price Per Flower Garden	No. of 5' x 15' Flower Gardens Supplied
$0	0
$100	1
$200	2
$300	4
$400	6
$500	8
$600	12
$700	20
$800	24
$900	22

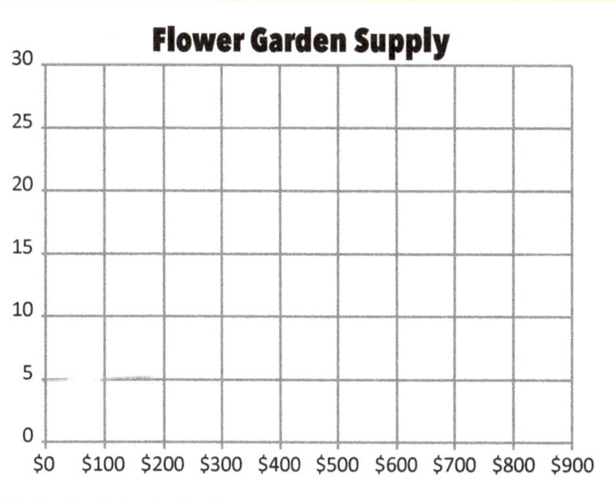

4. Why is Tom willing to plant fewer flower beds at $900 per bed than at $800 per bed? *(3 points)*

____

____

____

____

____

____

Lesson 11B Reading

Now that you understand the concept of supply, let's turn our attention to the concept of demand. **Demand** is the willingness and ability of consumers to utilize goods and services. Demand cannot exist without both prerequisites. You may want to buy a newer car, but your pocketbook prevents you from making this purchase at the present time. You have the desire to acquire an updated vehicle, but not the means to acquire one.

Like suppliers, consumers are very price conscious. *Ceteris paribus*, buyers are willing to consume more goods and services at lower prices than at higher prices. Let's look at a demand chart for Happy Cola in Mark Me Up's village of Liquidity.

Price	Demand
$0.00	400
$0.05	322
$0.10	275
$0.15	213
$0.20	198
$0.25	110
$0.40	69
$0.50	63
$0.75	42
$1.00	27

If he were extremely generous, Mark could give away 400 cans of Happy Cola each week. More than 200 cans could be sold at prices below Mark's manufacturing costs. Demand remains extraordinarily high for such a small community until the price reaches 40 cents per can. A few residents are even willing to pay one dollar for a 12-ounce can of liquid refreshment known as the "fizz that undoes frowns."

Let's graph the demand information from the chart. Like the supply curve, we show the various price levels of the product on the horizontal (X) axis. The vertical (Y) axis shows the quantity demanded. After plotting the 10 points from the demand curve chart, we connect the dots to complete the curve. The demand curve slopes downward from left to right, showing us that buyers are willing to consume less as the price increases.

Many factors influence demand. Perhaps the most obvious is a nation's population—a growing population creates greater demand for goods and services. Abortion, besides being morally reprehensible, negatively impacts our country's economy by killing unborn consumers.[11] Fifty-one million U.S. abortions (and counting) decrease demand for diapers, food, clothing, teachers, bicycles, bedroom furniture, houses, cars, jobs, computers, cell phones, and a host of other consumer goods and services. Aborted babies never get the opportunity to become taxpayers, military personnel, voters, or consumers. Pray for an end to this spiritual and economic tragedy plaguing our nation.

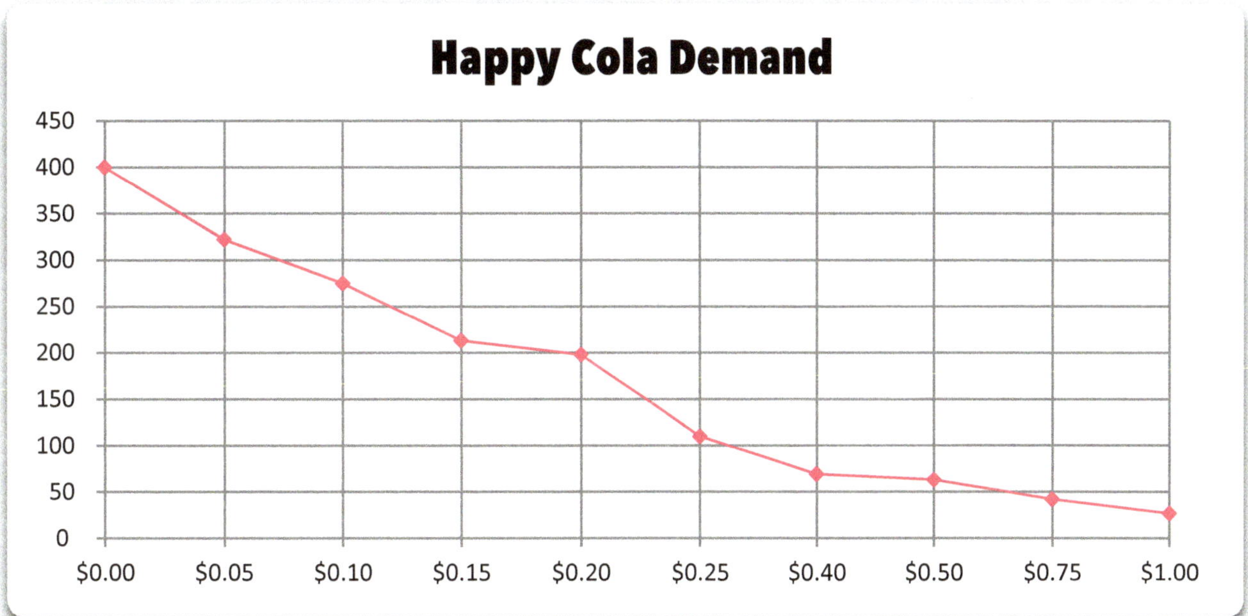

People's tastes also impact demand. The author's father-in-law despises broccoli, so he'll never personally spend a dime on this extremely nutritious vegetable. The author's family loves broccoli. They buy it fresh or frozen, and grow it in their garden. Remember when minivans were in? Then the automobile designers came out with the sport-utility vehicle. Their popularity declined due to skyrocketing fuel costs, so the auto manufacturers came out with a compromise known as the crossover—a trendy new design that will itself eventually fall victim to a shift in consumer desires.

Demand also depends on personal income. The more money a person makes, the more "stuff" he can acquire.

Government policies can inhibit or encourage demand. Lowering taxes gives consumers more money to spend on other items. With the U.S. economy mired in a deep recession, the federal government's Car Allowance Rebate System ("cash for clunkers" program) helped the automobile industry sell over 690,000 vehicles between July 1, 2009, and August 24, 2009.[12] Even with this incentive, U.S. auto sales were down 21.4 percent from 2008.[13] In that same year (2009), the government's cash for appliances program created artificial demand for Energy Star-rated appliances and HVAC equipment (furnaces and air conditioners). Without the tax benefits and rebates, consumers would have purchased fewer appliances during the same time period.

---

[11] For a great study on this topic, see Dennis Howard's article, "Economic Impact of Abortion" at http://www.movementforabetteramerica.org/economicimpact.html.

[12] http://www.dot.gov/affairs/2009/dot13309.htm

[13] http://www.usatoday.com/money/autos/2010-01-05-auto-sales_N.htm

Alternative or substitute products have a cause-effect relationship on demand. Suppose you like cream cheese, grape jelly, or marmalade on your breakfast bagel. Disruptions to the grape jelly supply or skyrocketing jelly prices will not adversely affect your morning repast—you simply switch to a less-expensive alternative topping. However, if you only like cream cheese on your bagel, and the price of cream cheese becomes more than you're willing to pay, you no longer eat bagels with cream cheese for breakfast. Your demand for bagels and cream cheese ceases, to be replaced by an alternative breakfast food (oatmeal).

Fads and crazes, fueled by creative advertising, create short-term demand. Fads are a temporary fashion, notion, manner of conduct, etc., especially one followed enthusiastically by a group.[14] A craze is a popular or widespread fad, fashion, etc.; a mania.[15] Fads and crazes create "flash-in-the-pan" demand that may or may not revive at some point in the future (can you do the hula hoop?).

Review Questions

Directions: *Answer the following questions based on the Lesson 11B reading.*

1. Why would a multimillionaire who despises compact cars not contribute to the demand for small, fuel-efficient vehicles? *(1 point)*

____

____

____

____

____

____

____

2. Why must demand include both a willingness and the ability to consume a good or service? *(1 point)*

____

____

____

____

____

____

____

____

---

[14] fad. (n.d.). *Dictionary.com Unabridged.* Retrieved March 15, 2011, from Dictionary.com website: http://dictionary.reference.com/browse/fad

[15] craze. (n.d.). *Dictionary.com Unabridged.* Retrieved March 15, 2011, from Dictionary.com website: http://dictionary.reference.com/browse/craze

3. Why does a typical demand curve slope downward from left to right? *(1 point)*

____

____

____

____

____

4. Can you think of a situation in which increased demand is not tied to decreasing prices? *(2 points)*

____

____

____

____

____

____

5. List six factors that influence demand. *(3 points)*

____

____

____

____

____

____

____

____

6. Draw a demand curve for flower beds in Tom's neighborhood based on the information in the chart. *(5 points)*

Price per Flower Garden	No. of Flower Gardens Demanded
$0	36
$100	30
$200	26
$300	19
$400	11
$500	7
$600	4
$700	2
$800	1
$900	0

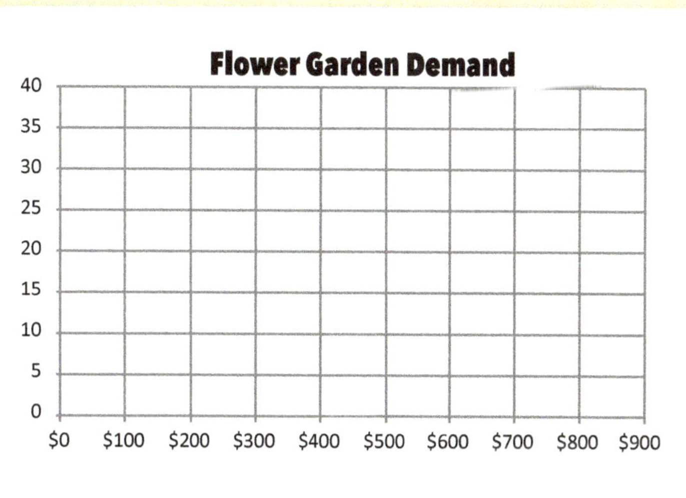

LESSON 12

NAME

DATE

Quiz Study Guide for Lessons 9-11 / Scripture Memorization Verse 2

Directions: *Review the following information from Lessons 9-11 before taking the Lesson 12 Quiz.*

Scripture Memory

- **Psalm 33:12**—Blessed is the nation whose God is the LORD; and the people whom He hath chosen for His own inheritance.

Concepts to Review

- Value exists in the mind, but value changes with time, place, and circumstances.
- Subjective value contains non-measurable variables. Objective value is measurable.
- Man's basic economic problem is limited resources (everyone cannot have everything they want). Limited resources force us to make choices.
- Opportunity cost is the next best alternate choice. Individuals and nations experience opportunity costs.
- The supply side of the market focuses on the willingness and ability to produce goods and services. *Ceteris paribus*, suppliers are willing to supply more at a higher price than at a lower price.
- Demand is the willingness and ability of consumers to utilize goods and services. *Ceteris paribus*, buyers are willing to purchase more at a lower price than at a higher price.
- Many factors influence demand—a nation's population, personal income, consumer tastes, government policies, and alternative products.

Practical Application

- Illustrate value and opportunity cost by selecting a specific home style.
- Demonstrate a personal concept of value by designing a kitchen or recreational room.

The Lesson 12 Quiz is located in the assessments section on page 221.

NAME

DATE

Imprimis Article #2

Dinner Table Discussion/Co-op Class Discussion

Directions: *Read the following article and prepare a list of five discussion questions based on the reading. Have your parents and any siblings old enough to engage in the conversation read the article, then schedule a mealtime to discuss the article as a family, using your discussion questions. You will be graded on your understanding of the article (10 points), list of discussion questions (10 points), and participation in the discussion (30 points). If doing this assignment as part of a co-op class, your supervisor will ask you to write five discussion questions prior to the class discussion. Grading will be the same as if doing the assignment in a family setting.*

Imprimis article—The Great (and Continuing) Economic Debate of the 20th Century

Steve Forbes

The following is adapted from a speech delivered at Hillsdale College on January 29, 2006, during a five-day seminar co-sponsored by the Center for Constructive Alternatives and the Ludwig von Mises Lecture Series on the topic, "Great Economists of the Twentieth Century."

The great economic debate of the twentieth century was between collectivists and free-marketers. In one sense, the free-marketers won: When the Berlin Wall fell in 1989, it was widely acknowledged that Soviet socialism had been a catastrophic, not to say murderous, failure. But in another sense, the debate continues. Democratic capitalism still has not vanquished the idea of collectivism. Far from it.

At the beginning of the last century, free markets seemed to be on the ascendancy everywhere. But two events gave collectivism its lease on life. The first was World War I. In addition to the slaughter—and to breeding the ideologies of communism, state fascism, Nazism, and even the Islamic fascism we are battling today—World War I served as an intoxicating drug to those in the West who believed that a handful of people in government could manage affairs better than the messy way in which free peoples tend to do so. Massive increases in government powers, coupled with massive increases in taxation, gave many the idea that you can achieve massive increases in production by commandeering the financial resources of society.

The second event that served as a boon to collectivism was the Great Depression, which was widely seen as a free market failure. This view was false. Misguided government policies were at fault—the Smoot-Hawley Tariff, for instance, which dried up the flow of capital in and out of the country. If you track the stock market crash of 1929, it parallels the course of this tariff bill through Congress. When Smoot-Hawley arose in the fall of 1929, the markets fell; when it looked like the tariff bill was sidetracked in late 1929, the markets revived (the Dow Jones went up 50 percent from its loss in November); in the spring of 1930 it was signed into law, and the rest is history. There were other factors at work in the Great Depression, of course, such as President Hoover's gigantic tax increases of 1931. But despite the fact that these also involved bad policies, the lesson taken away by many was that economies will implode unless the government manages them. John Maynard Keynes, the intellectual guiding light behind New Deal

economics, believed that an economy was like a machine: If you put doses of money into it or pull money out at the right times, he thought, you can achieve an equilibrium. This idea that government can drive an economy as if it were an automobile has had baleful consequences.

Other leading economists at the time, such as Joseph Schumpeter, recognized that an economy is an aggregate of disparate activities—thus that the idea of achieving equilibrium, while it makes for a neat theory, is nonsense in the real world. A vibrant economy is full of constant *dis*equilibria: New enterprises rise up, old ones decline, etc. Snapshots of such economies mean very little. In the real world, therefore, free markets operate rationally and efficiently in a way that government regulators simply can't. Here in America we came to this realization at the end of the 1970s. Following World War II, we largely bought into the idea that government must play an active role to prevent the economy from going off the cliff. But in the late 1970s, the devastation of inflation and high taxes brought about a reassessment. With the election of Ronald Reagan, the U.S. took a step back from Keynesian economics. Since then, as Western Europe has stagnated—creating, for instance, only a fraction of the private sector jobs that the U.S. has created—our country has undergone an economic revival.

Nonetheless, democratic capitalism often still seems on the defensive. Why?

Is Democratic Capitalism Good?

One of the great vulnerabilities of capitalism is the perception that it is somehow less than moral, if not positively amoral. A common view of business was depicted in the movie *Wall Street*, in which Michael Douglas's character made famous the phrase, "Greed is good." Capitalism is widely seen as promoting selfishness. We tolerate it because it gives us jobs and prosperity, but many look on this as a Faustian bargain. Charity and capitalism are seen as polar opposites. Thus there's a phrase that's often used today—I myself use it from time to time without thinking—which is "giving back." If you've succeeded in business, it's counted a good thing if you "give back" to the community. And charity is, of course, a good thing. The problem with this phrase is its implication that by succeeding, we have taken something that wasn't ours. The same idea is summed up in the cynical saying, "Behind every great fortune lies a great crime." This way of thinking about democratic capitalism is wrong.

In fact, philanthropy and capitalism are two sides of the same coin. To succeed in business in a free-market economy, one must meet the needs and wants of others. Even someone who makes babies cry is not going to succeed unless he or she provides a product or service that people want. This system weaves intricate webs of cooperation that we don't even think about. Take a restaurant: Someone who opens a restaurant assumes that farmers will provide the food and that someone else will process and package it and that someone else will deliver it, having been supplied the fuel to do so by yet someone else, etc. These marvelous webs of cooperation happen every day throughout a free economy. No one is commanding it. It occurs spontaneously in a way that economists like Schumpeter understood.

Free markets also force people to look to the future and take risks. Misers do not found companies like Microsoft. Nor should we look on it as immoral for people to work for the betterment of themselves and their families. We are all born with God-given talents, and it is right to develop them to the fullest. The great virtue of democratic capitalism is that it guarantees that as we develop our talents, we're contributing to the public good. Statistics show that the U.S. is both the most commercial nation and the most philanthropic nation in human history. And this is no paradox. The two go hand-in-hand.

Another vulnerability of democratic capitalism is that although it leads to progress and to an increase in our societal standard of living, progress is usually disruptive. This allows collectivists to play on people's natural fear of change. We saw this with the rise of industrialism in the 19th century. We had paintings and writings depicting a pastoral agricultural past. Then railroads came along to disrupt the canals, and cars came along to disrupt the railroads. Buggy-whip makers and blacksmiths were done for. One can imagine what *60 Minutes* would have been investigating 100 years ago: the poor blacksmiths being put out of work by Henry Ford. Likewise, when TV came along in the late 1940s and early 1950s, most movie theaters in the country went broke. Now the Internet is disrupting newspapers and Craig's List is disrupting classified advertising. Disruptions are inevitable in a free-market system. The political challenge is to allow these disruptions to take place—they are ultimately constructive, after all—rather than reacting in a way that stymies progress.

In recent decades, collectivists have also hijacked the cause of environmentalism to promote their agenda. I'm not talking about the desire to have clean water; we're all in favor of that. Or clean air; one of the great things we've done in the last century is getting lead out of the air. Saving tigers and elephants is also a good thing. I'm talking about those who use the mantra of environmentalism to try to control the economy the way the old-time socialists wanted to, breathing hellfire and damnation on those who don't subscribe to their new, post-Christian religion. The fact is, if our goal is to improve the environment, increasing government regulation and destroying manufacturing is counterproductive. Affluence is the friend, not the enemy, of the environment. As people become better off, they want a higher quality of life, including environmental improvements. Consider the east coast of the U.S. Even though its population has more than doubled—in some areas, it's tripled—and even though there are more developments, mall, and urban sprawl, there are more trees today than there were 80 years ago. Why? Because of technology that allows us to grow more food on less land. Technology is a friend of the environment.

Additional Collectivist Myths

Let me mention three additional myths that are used to promote collectivism. One is the idea that demand is the key to economic growth. Collectivist economists often talk about means to increase "aggregate demand," as if that would ensure that the economy will grow. Following Keynes, they assume that the economy is like a machine. But again, the economy is an aggregate of tens of millions of people, millions of businesses, millions of technologies. We don't know how it interacts on a day-to-day basis. We don't know what's going to work or not work. Who could have conceived of eBay ten to twelve years ago? But today, 400,000 people make their livings on eBay. When Google was launched, there were ten other search engines. Who would have thought another one was needed? Isn't that how you get so-called "bubbles"? But Google found a way to do it better and ended up on top. Innovation is the key. Whether it's railroads, cars, computers, the Internet, or iPods, risk-taking is messy. It is often irrational, and seemingly wasteful. But it's the only way to determine what works best and what doesn't.

Another collectivist myth concerns trade. If I were dictator of the world—even though I believe in the First Amendment—I would ban trade numbers, especially merchandise trade numbers. They just lead to mischief. We are given the impression that a trade surplus is like a profit and a trade deficit is like a loss. But trade is not a transaction between countries. It takes place between parties. For example, *Forbes* magazine buys paper. For all of the 88 years that we've been in existence, we've run a trade deficit with our paper suppliers. If you look just at that trade deficit, you might think we are doing poorly. But if you look at the two parties involved, that turns out to be an illusion. The paper supplier thinks he's going to make money selling his paper. We think we're going to make money by taking the paper and putting print on it, with value added. So it's a mutually profitable transaction, even if it looks like a trade deficit. Or consider a book printed in Taiwan. Looking at the trade number alone, it appears there is a two dollar trade deficit with Taiwan. Yet the book comes back here and retails for $24.95. The value added is in the U.S. The author gets a cut, the publisher gets a cut, booksellers get a cut, distributors get a cut, and remainder stores get a cut. Something similar happened with iPods: A lot of its parts are made overseas, but where is most of the value added? Here in the United States. North America has had a merchandise trade deficit 350 out of the last 400 years, and we have done very well, thank you.

The final myth I'll mention concerns budget deficits. Milton Friedman said several years ago that if he had a choice between a federal budget of $1 trillion that was in the red and a federal budget of $2 trillion that was balanced, he would take the former. Deficits, in and of themselves, are not evil. Deficits must be put in context, because Washington's inability to curb spending is often used as an excuse to raise taxes.

Principles of Prosperity

Now let me turn to five basic principles of economic growth. First and foremost is the rule of law: Without individual equality before the law, entrepreneurs cannot challenge already existing businesses. Alliances between the latter and government regulators who place barriers before entrepreneurs must be guarded against.

The second essential principle is property rights. We take it for granted in this country that if you buy a piece of property, everyone acknowledges that you own it. Most countries don't have that kind of uniform property system. A few years ago, Hernando DeSoto, a great economist from Peru, saw that in countries like his, although there is entrepreneurial activity, there isn't the corresponding prosperity found in the U.S. And he wondered why. In his recent book—*The Mystery of Capital: Why Capitalism Triumphs in the West and Fails Everywhere Else*—one of the key factors he cites is the absence in so many other countries of a legal foundation for property rights. In Brazil's shanty towns, an individual may know that he owns the house in which he lives, and his neighbors may know it, but the fact is not recognized elsewhere.

Mr. DeSoto was asked by the Egyptian government a few years ago to determine who owns the businesses and residences in Egypt. His finding was that 88 percent of the businesses in Egypt are illegal. Why is that? Here in the U.S., it is possible to set up a business legally in a matter of days. In Egypt, it takes a couple of years. It requires going through numerous bureaucracies, doling out numerous bribes, etc. So it makes sense to proceed "informally." On the other hand, running a business outside the law limits its growth. Most "informal" enterprises never grow beyond the level of family enterprises, because if they get too big, they might attract the attention of the tax collector. DeSoto's group also reported that 92 percent of Egyptian housing is illegal. People living in residences may have deeds; but only a few miles away, those deeds are not recognized. In Egypt, as in so many other places, there is no uniform system of establishing and protecting property rights. As a result, four billion people around the world own $9 trillion of assets that amount to dead capital.

What do I mean by "dead capital"? Remember that here in the U.S., the most important source of capital for new ventures is not Wall Street, the local banker or the venture capitalist. It is the mortgage market. People either increase their mortgage or take out a second mortgage in order to start businesses. This is not possible in countries like Egypt. Understanding this was the key to Japan's post-World War II economic boom. General MacArthur reformed a feudalistic property system, in which the peasants had only an informal system of property exchange, into a system with formalized property rights. Immediately, the Japanese economy took off. The importance of property rights is not sufficiently recognized by those of us who take them for granted.

The third principle of economic prosperity is low taxes. Taxes are not just a means of raising revenue for the government. They are also a price. Income taxes are a price paid for working; taxes on profits are the price paid for being successful in business; taxes on capital gains are the price paid for taking risks. In light of this, the importance of low taxes is easy to see: When you lower the price of good things—things like work, success, and risk-taking—you tend to get more of them. Raise the price of these good things and you get less. In 2003, we lowered tax rates in the U.S. and the economy started to grow again. As we've seen time and again, tax cuts do not mean a loss of tax revenue. By increasing incentives, the government comes out ahead. Washington's revenues in the last fiscal year were up 15 percent—$100 billion above expectations. Washington's problem is not revenue, but spending.

The fourth principle I would mention is making it simpler to launch legal businesses. Getting bureaucracy out of the way will inject a new vibrancy into the economy. The fifth and final principle is free trade. Expanding markets and creating greater opportunity for trade benefits us all.

In closing, I will remind you of a point I made earlier. The reason that the great economic debate continues into the 21st century, despite the proven superiority of free markets in terms of delivering prosperity, is because of the misperceptions that keep democratic capitalism from capturing the moral high ground. Dispelling the misperceptions should be our priority as we carry on that debate in the years ahead.

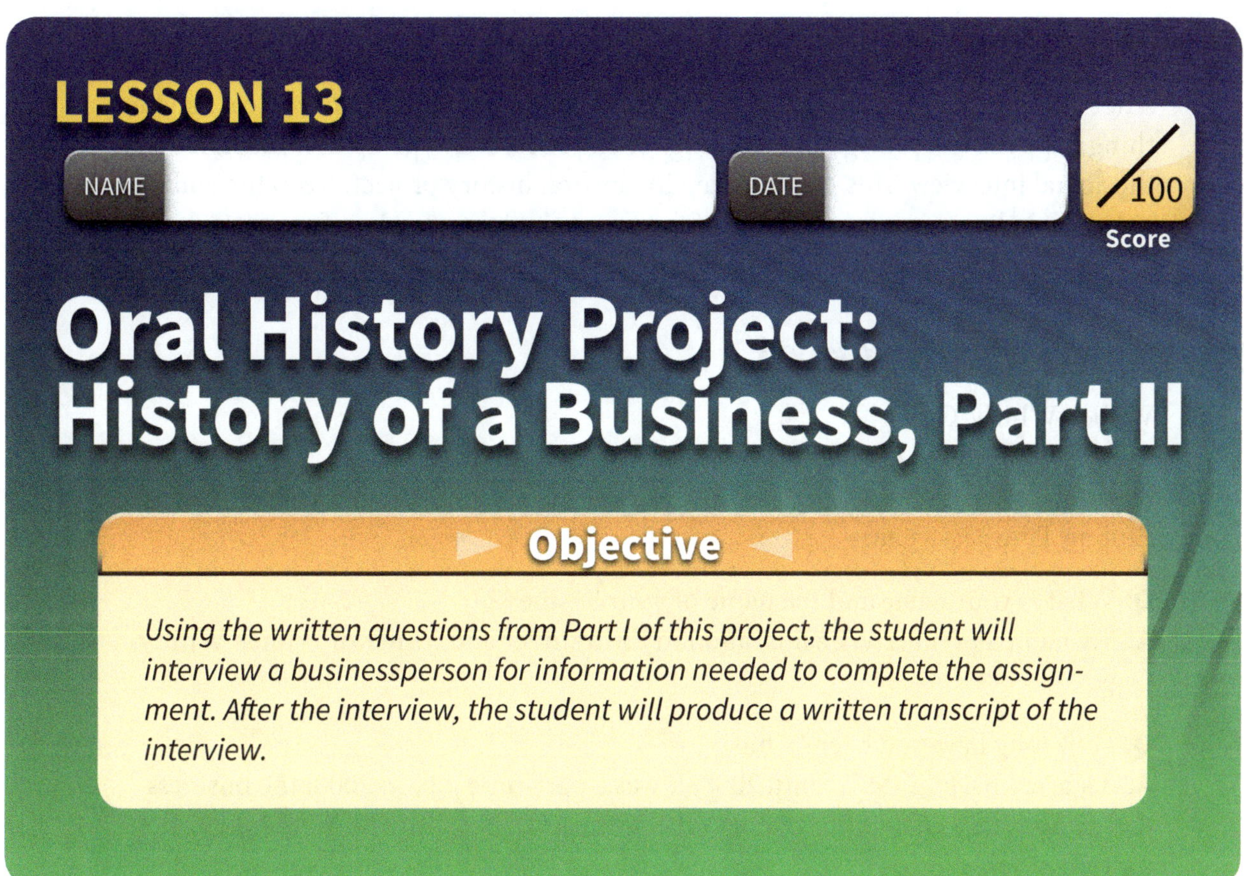

Oral History Project: History of a Business, Part II

Objective

Using the written questions from Part I of this project, the student will interview a businessperson for information needed to complete the assignment. After the interview, the student will produce a written transcript of the interview.

Directions: *During this lesson, you will interview the entrepreneur responsible for starting the business. Use a recording device to obtain an audio or video transcript of the entire interview. After the interview, use the recording to make a written transcript of the interview questions and answers. The transcript will be the "research" needed to write the two- to three-page paper.*

Grading: *See answer key for grading rubric.*

Here are some helpful tips for conducting a successful interview.

- Dress professionally and appropriately.
- Be on time (early) for the interview.
- Bring an extra copy of the interview questions in case the interviewee has misplaced the copy you sent previously.
- Before starting, thank the interviewee for their time and willingness to help you with this project.
- Ask the interviewee if any of the questions need clarification before starting the interview.
- Check the sound level on your recording device before starting the interview to ensure that the questions and answers can be easily heard.
- Express genuine interest in the interviewee's responses with appropriate facial gestures (smiles, nods, etc.). Don't slouch—remember that body language communicates your interest in the person and the information they are providing you for this project.
- After completing the interview, thank the person again for their time and offer them a copy of the final paper after its completion.
- Send the interviewee a thank-you note.

Post-Interview

After the interview, make a backup copy of the audio/video interview in case something happens to the original recording. Then proceed to type up the transcript of the actual interview. This is a vital step in any oral history project. Keep the audio/video recording and a second copy of the transcript in a safe place for posterity. Set the transcript aside until it's time to complete this project in Lesson 26.

Sample Transcript

Willie's Whirly-Gigs
Interview Recorded on 3/13/2011 at the owner's residence
Starting Time: 3:15 p.m.
Ending Time: 3:45 p.m.

1. **Q:** What is your name and the name of your business?
A: My name is Wilber Williams, and I'm the founder and owner of Willie's Whirly-Gigs.

2. **Q:** How long have you been in business?
A: It started back in 1997. Until 2008, it was a part-time job. In 2008, the business had grown large enough to support my family, so it's been my full-time job for the past three years.

3. **Q:** You are a skilled woodworker. Tell us how you got started in this craft.
A: My interest in woodworking began back in junior high school. Mr. Knot nurtured my interest in the woodworking machinery and encouraged me by giving me more challenging projects than my peers. His motto was "it's the little things that matter." I believe Mr. Knot's constant repetition of this phrase drilled into me the importance of quality work and attention to detail. With Mr. Knot's help, I was actually doing high school projects in junior high. I took shop all four years of high school. My senior project was a grandfather clock for my parents' 25th wedding anniversary. I had a part-time job in construction during my junior and senior years of high school, serving as an apprentice to a finish carpenter. He taught me a great deal about joinery, Victorian embellishments, and trim work.

4. **Q:** Why did you start Willie's Whirly-Gigs?
A: I wanted to combine my love of woodworking with a business that would let me be my own boss, set my own hours, and initially supplement my income from my regular job as an office manager. Working in the shop with my hands was a nice change of pace from my full-time desk job. Woodworking helps me relax after a stressful day at the office. It was a business I could do part time until it grew large enough for me to quit my other job and pursue the woodworking full time.

5. **Q:** How did you acquire the capital needed to start Willie's Whirly-Gigs?
A: Before starting the business, I already owned a table saw, miter saw, planer, router, drill press, and band saw. To start the business, I took out a $10,000 home equity loan from my bank. This enabled me to expand my workshop space by building a small addition to the back of my two-car garage, giving me room for all my tools

without having to move the vehicles out of the garage. With my Christmas bonus, I purchased a freestanding storage shed for lumber storage. My wife surprised me with a gift card that enabled me to acquire a joiner and a lathe. The capital needed to start the business came from a home equity loan, a bonus from work, and a nice birthday present from my lovely wife.

6. **Q:** What kinds of products does Willie's Whirly-Gigs specialize in?
   A: We build just about anything—lawn ornamentation, furniture, birdhouses, kitchen cabinets, and even doghouses. If it's made of wood, we can build it. Our specialty is one-of-a-kind items—reproductions of antique furniture styles, unusual decorative profiles for upscale homes, or customer-designed pieces. Just last week I finished a unique coffee table for the wife of the bank president. She created the sketch and I transformed her vision into reality. So although I do cookie-cutter work—dozens of the same whirly-gigs and two or three different birdhouse designs, I love the challenge of custom work, especially if it challenges me in new skill areas. Oh, yes, I've even built a Victorian playhouse for one of the neighborhood children.

7. **Q:** What are some of your favorite projects from past years?
   A: I think my all-time favorite was building some items for a local historic village. I had to research wooden items from the 18th century and replicate them for this historical site, which operates as a living-history museum. I built wood barrels, wood buckets, trenchers (wooden plates), and two working farm wagons for the village. I also built a large apple cider press for a local orchard. Several years ago I carved a totem pole for a customer fascinated with Native American artwork. Shortly after I started the business, a local contractor asked me to build custom doors for a multimillion-dollar mansion. The customer wanted a different wood trim package in each room. Every interior door had two different wood veneers, like maple on the room side of the door and oak on the hallway side. No two doors (interior or exterior) in the entire house were alike.

8. **Q:** What challenges have you had to overcome in your business?
   A: I have to be careful that I don't become a workaholic. I love my woodshop, but I have to keep my priorities straight. My wife reminds me when my work becomes more important than the things that really matter. Another challenge is completing large projects on time. I don't want to hire additional employees, so building a bunch of kitchen cabinets in a three-week window can be stressful. The amount of paperwork seems to increase every year—more forms to file and compliance with new regulations. I'd much rather be making stuff in the shop than filling out tax forms. Fortunately, my wife enjoys the office side of my work, and she takes care of most of it, leaving me more time to do what I really love. With several vendors selling my products at trade shows, I have to produce enough stock so they don't run out of an item during the show. With two shows in the same week, it's difficult to provide both vendors with enough product to guarantee they don't sell out before the show ends. Getting quality raw materials is another difficulty. My clients deserve the very best, and I can't give it to them if the lumber is of poor quality.

9. **Q:** What makes Willie's Whirly-Gigs unique or different from other woodworking shops?
A: I'm the only employee, so work is done to my exacting standards. I don't tolerate inferior work. I'm willing to tackle any woodworking project, even projects in which the customers specify all hand-tool construction (no power tools). Limiting the number of orders I take gives me plenty of time to do a quality job without making customers wait an extraordinary amount of time before receiving the finished product.

10. **Q:** How has your business changed in the last two years?
A: I haven't built a doghouse since Dan's Deluxe Doghouses expanded its operations into this region of the country. Several vendors now sell my whirly-gigs and birdhouses at various home and garden shows east of the Mississippi River. I spend 40 percent of my time in the shop building items for them to sell at the shows. Since we now sell our whirly-gigs on the Internet, my wife processes those orders in addition to her full-time job as a nurse.

11. **Q:** What are your plans for the future?
A: I need to get my wife some help in filling our Internet orders. Sometimes she works the night shift, then comes home and packs orders before going to bed. I'd do it if I didn't need all my time in the workshop manufacturing product. We're thinking about hiring our youngest daughter to come in a couple of hours three days per week to handle the shipping. We don't really need the income from Internet sales, but it does give our product name recognition in locations where our vendors sell at shows, so it helps them out, so I guess we'll keep selling on the Internet for the time being. I'd like to semi-retire in about 10 years, and go back to working part time (about 20 hours per week), leaving me more time for travel and the grandkids. At that point we'll probably stop selling on the Internet and cut back on the number of vendors selling our product. I have a buddy who wants to start a sleigh-ride business using the old-time, horse-drawn sleighs, so I'm currently researching how to build three of them for his business. Before I give up this business entirely, I'd love to build a Victorian house as my retirement home. It will have all the ornamentation bells and whistles for that style.

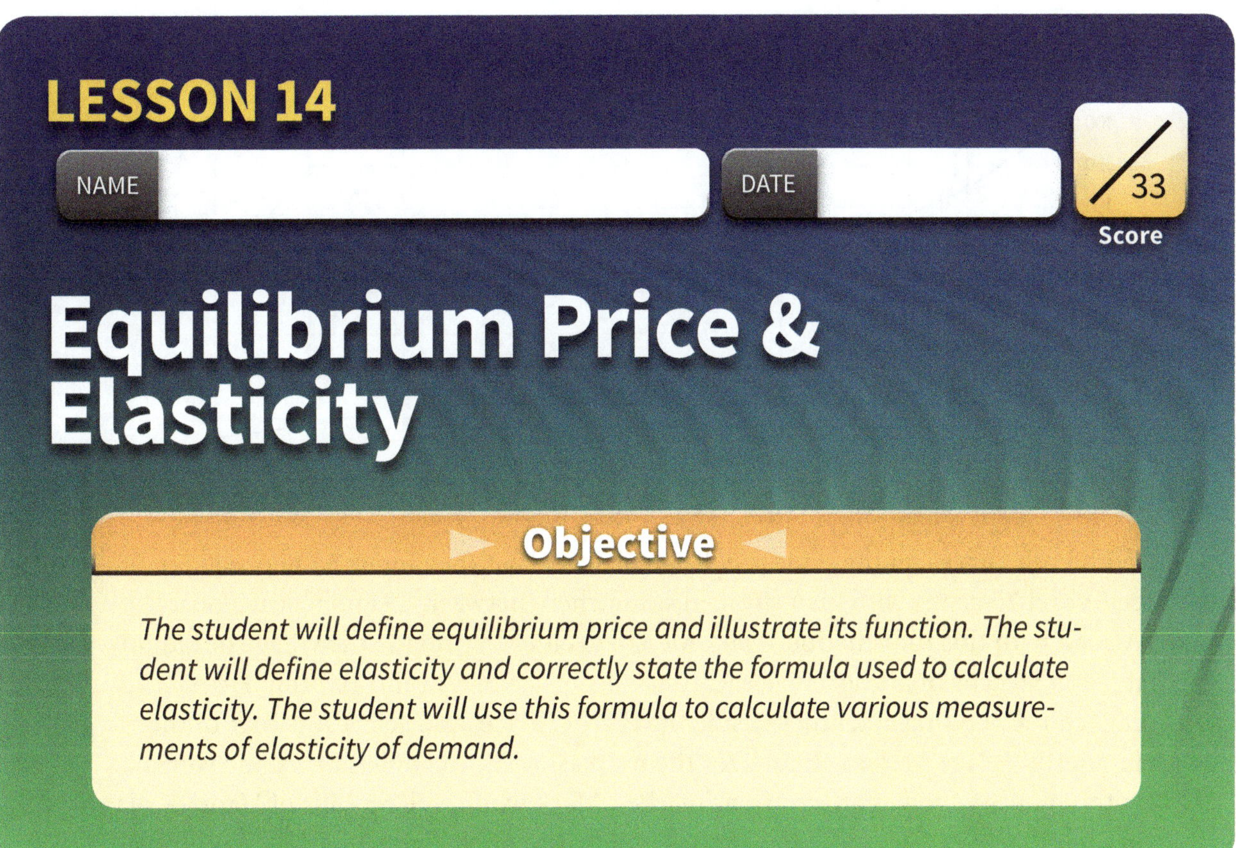

LESSON 14

NAME DATE

/33 Score

Equilibrium Price & Elasticity

Objective

The student will define equilibrium price and illustrate its function. The student will define elasticity and correctly state the formula used to calculate elasticity. The student will use this formula to calculate various measurements of elasticity of demand.

Lesson 14A Reading

The author's wife bought him a suit for his 48th birthday. She insisted that his 15-year-old suit was no longer in style, so after work one day they drove to a nearby shopping plaza. The author had never been to this department store previously. Every display rack contained sale notices advertising 40 to 70 percent off the regular price. As he left the store with his new suit (a real bargain), he wondered if anyone ever paid the "regular" price for clothing items at this store. Were the regular prices greatly inflated so the store could keep everything perpetually "on sale" and still make a profit? How do stores set prices in a free-market economy?

The price at which exchanges take place is the intersection of the supply and demand curves for that good or service. We call this intersection the **equilibrium price**. In a free-market economy, this is the point and price at which supply balances demand. This point is also known as the **market-clearing price.**

Let's revisit our Happy Cola illustration from Lesson 11, but this time we'll overlay the supply and demand curves.

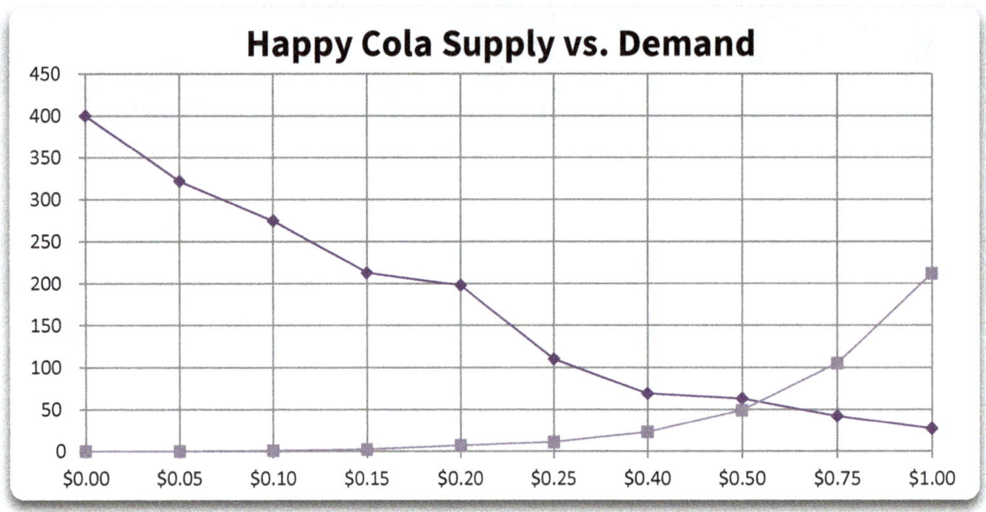

With both curves on the same graph, we observe that they intersect between 50 cents and 75 cents, with quantity sold somewhere between 49 and 63 cans of cola. Armed with this information, Mark Me Up decides to provide the village of Liquidity with 55 cans of his beverage each week at a price of 60 cents per can. He puts 15 cans in the vending machine outside the Petrol Palace, and sells the owner of the Liquidity Village Market 40 cans for the market's walk-in cooler. In a static world without outside forces affecting the market, Mark would sell 55 cans of Happy Cola in Liquidity every week. However, the equilibrium point fluctuates due to multiple factors at work in the market. Let's look at a positive and negative illustration of the forces affecting the sale of Happy Cola.

Seven months ago, a tour bus driver stopped to refuel his bus at the Petrol Palace. Tedd's Old-Town Tours bypassed Liquidity for 10 years until the Petrol Palace installed a tank and pump for diesel fuel. During the fueling stop, an adventurous tour group member purchased a can of Happy Cola and enthusiastically promoted it to his fellow travelers. The 43 passengers on the bus bought the remaining cans from the vending machine and demanded more. The gas station attendant referred them to the village market, and the thirsty tourists bought out the market's remaining stock. Now Tedd's Old-Town Tours makes a weekly stop to refuel the bus and refresh its passengers with Happy Cola. The tour bus business boosted Happy Cola sales in Liquidity by 73 percent. Mark now sells 75 cans of Happy Cola at 65 cents per can each week.

Sales of Happy Cola remained at this elevated level until last month's guest lecture series at the Liquidity Town Hall. Health-Nut Harry presented a paper entitled "Soda Pop: The Unhealthy Beverage." Harry's lecture caused considerable consternation among Liquidity's soda-drinking citizens. Many village residents signed a pledge to stop drinking soda pop. After Harry's speech, sales of Happy Cola plummeted. Average weekly demand decreased from 75 cans to 20 cans, even though Mark lowered the cost to 40 cents per can.

In the previous illustrations, tourists and a health-conscious lecturer contributed to a change in demand for Happy Cola. Many other factors, such as a competitor's sale price on cola or extremely hot weather conditions, could decrease or increase Liquidity's demand for Happy Cola. With a multitude of market-changing forces constantly at work affecting the demand side of the market, suppliers like Mark Me Up must respond to the changing dynamics of the market or see their sales suffer.

The supply side of the market also causes changes in equilibrium price. When supply exceeds demand, sellers must lower prices to move their surplus inventory. Demand that exceeds supply results in shortages. The equilibrium price increases, forcing some customers out of the market temporarily or permanently.

Review Questions

Directions: *Answer the following questions based on the Lesson 14A reading.*

1. In a free market, what sets the equilibrium price? *(1 point)*

____

____

2. For the following scenarios, predict an increase or decrease in the equilibrium price and give a reason for your answer. *(1 point each)*

   Ticket prices for a championship baseball team **Decrease** **Increase**

   ____

   Celebrity endorsement of a certain brand of tennis shoes **Decrease** **Increase**

   ____

   Last year's fashions in a department store **Decrease** **Increase**

   ____

3. Draw the demand and supply curves for Tom's flower gardens (see Lesson 11) on a single graph. Circle the point at which the curves intersect. At what price and quantity will amount supplied equal quantity demanded? *(10 points)*

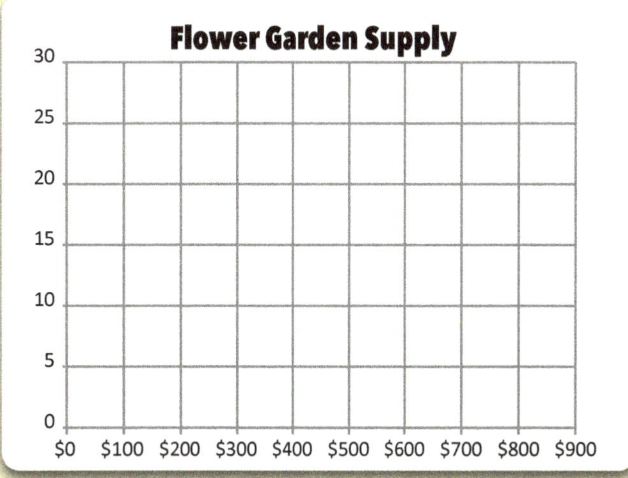

4. What will happen to prices if supply exceeds demand? *(1 point)*

____

____

Lesson 14B Reading

In this section of our lesson, we'll be discussing the economic concept of **elasticity**—how people respond to changes in price. Both suppliers and consumers respond to changing price levels. To calculate elasticity, we need to know the quantity supplied or demanded at the previous price and the quantity supplied or demanded at the new price. We can then use the following formula to calculate the elasticity of the good or service.

% Δ Quantity / % Δ Price

In this equation, the delta symbol (Δ) stands for change. Stated in words, the formula reads "the percentage of change in quantity divided by the percentage of change in price." You calculate elasticity using the *percentage* of change, not the numeric quantity or dollar amount of change from the former to the latter. Suppose, by way of example, that your local appliance store has a sale on a washer-dryer set which normally retails for $500. The following chart shows the before and after sales results.

Price	No. of Washer-Dryer Sets Sold
$500	4
$400	8

Before the 20-percent-off sale, the sales associates sold only four washer-dryer sets. The week-long sale convinced four additional customers to purchase a washer and dryer. The 20-percent-off sale ($100 divided by $500 equals .20, or 20 percent) resulted in a 100 percent increase in sales (four additional pairs sold divided by the previous four sold equals 1.00, or 100 percent). Plugging these numbers into the formula gives you an elasticity measurement of 5 (100 divided by 20 equals 5).

What if the 20-percent-off sale results in only one additional sale?

Price	No. of Washer-Dryer Sets Sold
$500	4
$400	5

In this case, the denominator (the percentage of change in price) remains the same (20). The numerator (percentage of change in quantity) is now 25 (1 additional pair sold divided by the original 4 sold gives you .25, or 25 percent). The new elasticity number is 1.25.

Now suppose that the store had a 50-percent-off sale with only one more washer-dryer set sold.

Price	No. of Washer-Dryer Sets Sold
$500	4
$250	5

In this scenario, the numerator (percentage of change in quantity) remains at 25 while the denominator changes to 50. The elasticity measurement is .5—a disappointing result based on the size of the sale.

An elasticity measurement greater than 1 (>1) illustrates **elastic** supply or demand. The price change had a significant effect on supply or demand. An elasticity number less than 1 (<1) signifies **inelastic** supply or demand. The price change did not result in a significant increase in supply or demand. Necessity items and low-cost purchases tend to have inelastic demand. Luxury items, products with many substitutes, and large purchases tend toward elastic demand.

Review Questions

Directions: *Answer the following questions based on the Lesson 14B reading.*

1. Write and explain the formula used to calculate elasticity. *(2 points)*

____

____

____

____

____

2. If the price of airline tickets doubles just before summer vacation season, would demand for airline tickets be elastic or inelastic? Why? *(3 points)*

____

____

____

____

____

____

____

____

____

3. If gasoline goes from $3.05/gallon to $3.37/gallon in one week (a 9 percent increase), do you think demand for gasoline would be elastic or inelastic? Why? *(2 points)*

___

___

___

___

4. Calculate the elasticity of demand for the following price changes. Round your answer to two decimal places. *(9 points)*

Price	Quantity	Elasticity
$237	2	********
$209	4	
$195	8	
$189	12	
$143	18	
$125	30	
$116	33	
$109	40	
$99	50	
$78	43	

5. If the price of bread goes up five cents, would suppliers bake millions more loaves in response? Why or why not? *(2 points)*

___

___

___

___

___

___

___

___

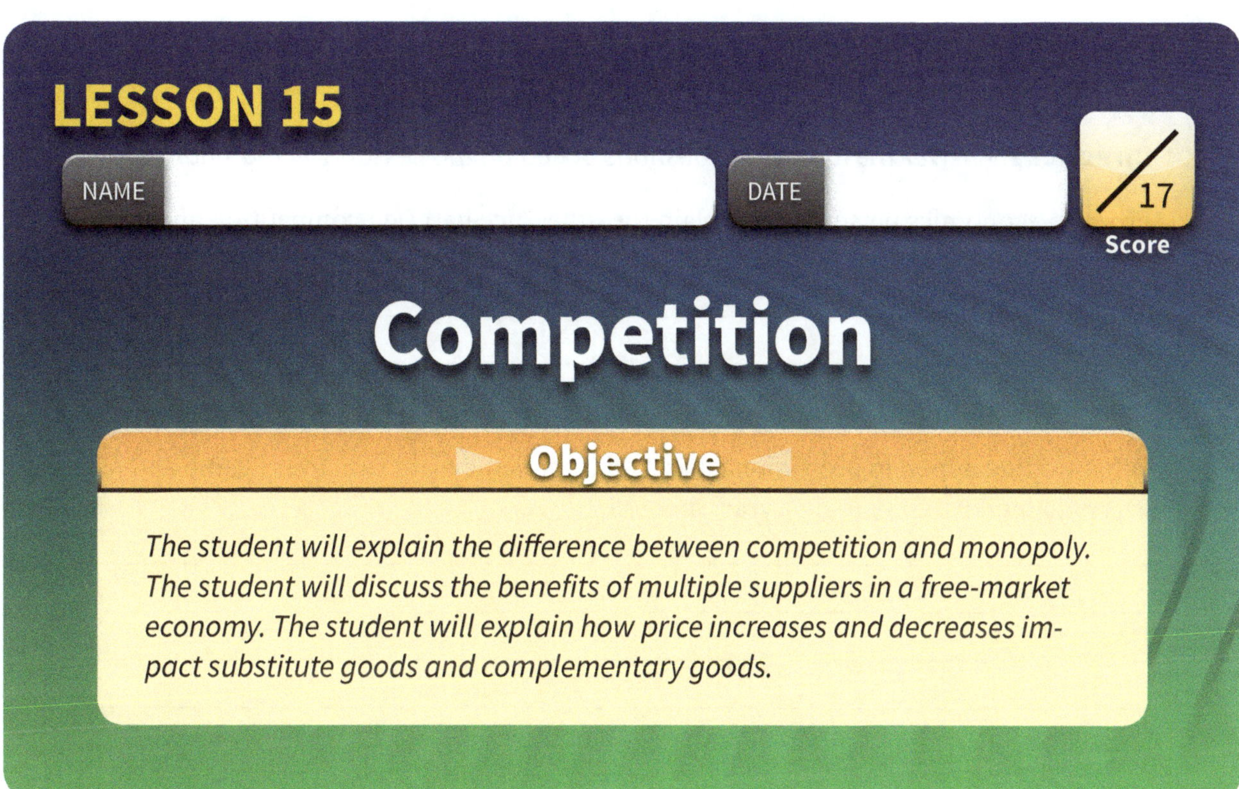

LESSON 15

NAME DATE /17 Score

Competition

Objective

The student will explain the difference between competition and monopoly. The student will discuss the benefits of multiple suppliers in a free-market economy. The student will explain how price increases and decreases impact substitute goods and complementary goods.

Lesson 15A Reading

Americans love sports. We thrive on competition, both as participants and spectators. In the economic realm, **competition** (multiple suppliers competing for customers) is a good thing for the economy, while **monopoly** (one supplier controlling the entire market) is a bad thing for customers. Consumers win when multiple businesses compete. Having multiple producers results in more variety, better quality, and lower prices.

Review Questions

Directions: *Answer the following questions based on the Lesson 15A reading.*

1. From an economics perspective, explain the difference between competition and monopoly. *(2 points)*

   ____

   ____

   ____

2. What would happen to professional baseball if the same team won every game and every championship year after year? *(2 points)*

   ____

   ____

   ____

   ____

3. What would happen to concession prices at professional sporting events if multiple vendors could supply fans with food and beverages? *(2 points)*

   ____

   ____

   ____

Lesson 15B Reading

Walk into a large grocery store's snack aisle and count the number of suppliers of potato chips. You'll probably find three or more major snack food producers and at least one generic brand on the shelves. Each supplier has its own method of making chips that leads to that brand's unique flavor and texture. Our capitalist economy and the American penchant for snacking while watching television or a movie enables multiple suppliers to profitably produce potato chips. For purposes of understanding the concepts of substitute goods and complementary goods, let's refer to the name-brand potato chip suppliers as brands A, B, and C, with the generic brands labeled X, Y, and Z.

Brand A dominates the potato chip market in Anytown, Ohio. They sell more of every potato chip variety in this region than the other two major suppliers and the three generic suppliers combined. Some economists might categorize Brand A chips as a competitive monopoly based on their large market share in Anytown. How does Brand A maintain its dominance of the Anytown potato chip market? Unique advertising commercials ("snack the right way with Brand A") and effective marketing strategies coupled with their "melt in your mouth" flavor keep consumers coming back for more.

Unfortunately, a transportation strike in its third week prevents Brand A from resupplying the Anytown markets and all their stores east of the Mississippi River. With store stocks of Brand A chips dwindling rapidly and no end to the strike in sight, consumers will have to make some tough choices. Will they rush to the stores with Brand A chips and snatch up the remaining inventory, hoping their hoarded bags of chips will outlast the transportation strike? Should they pay to have their relatives in Arizona buy and ship them a dozen bags of Brand A chips? Can they bring themselves to eat the less-delectable Brands B, C, X, Y, and Z chips? Will they riot in the streets demanding an end to the strike that is preventing them from consuming Brand A chips? Let's hope not! While management at Brand A fumes over the ongoing strike, and the Anytown consumers impatiently await the return of their favorite snack food, market analysts at Brands B, C, X, Y, and Z are hard at work on a strategy to topple Brand A's dominance of the potato chip market in Anytown. Brand B's sales experts think a "buy one, get one free" sale on their chips might entice some of Brand A's loyal customers into the Brand B fold. Brand C strategizes that a higher preprinted retail price on their chips with constant sales prices might convince some potato chip connoisseurs that Brand C is the gourmet line of snack food. Brands D, Y, and Z think now's the time for updated packaging that might attract Brand A customers. Brand X decides to tinker with their manufacturing process until their chips taste similar to Brand A. Their generic packaging will trumpet "compare to Brand A."

What will go down in Anytown's history as the "potato chip famine of 2011" doesn't mean there were no potato chips at all in Anytown. With five other suppliers producing potato chips and additional snack food options readily available, there were plenty of substitute products to fill the Brand A shortage. Notice in our hypothetical illustration that Brand A's five competitors took advantage of the situation to improve their market share of Anytown's potato chip sales. Brand A's competition used various methods such as lower prices, marketing gimmicks, and a "new improved taste" strategy to increase sales. Brand A's return to the Anytown supermarket shelves will enable the other brands to gauge the effectiveness of their decisions.

Observe one of the major benefits of multiple suppliers in the market. When an outside force (transportation strike) disrupted the Brand A supply chain, five other suppliers were there to meet consumer wants and needs. The impact of price increases or shortages is lessened when multiple suppliers can provide substitute goods. In our hypothetical illustration, the goods (potato chips) are **perfect substitutes**—they are exactly alike (potato chips) and the demand for and consumption of this snack food remains constant. Anytown's residents would not consume significantly fewer potato chips during Brand A's absence—they would eat similar amounts of chips supplied by Brand A's competitors. **Imperfect substitutes** could also help to meet the snack needs of Anytown's residents. Electronic zombies who get the "munchies" could chow down on popcorn, pretzels, or similar snack food items. Imperfect substitutes provide a close enough alternative to the unavailable or higher-priced item. If the price of soda pop increases beyond what buyers are willing to spend, thirsty consumers could select a lower-priced imperfect substitute like lemonade or iced tea to quench their thirst. Both perfect substitutes and imperfect substitutes respond to the parent product in similar ways. A price *increase* for Product C will result in increased demand for Product D (its substitute). A price *decrease* for Product C will cause a drop in demand for Product D.

Complementary goods (goods that go together and rely upon each other) react just the opposite of substitute goods. If the price of Product C *increases*, demand for Product D *decreases*. For example, if the price of hot dogs and hamburgers skyrockets, leading to significantly less consumption, demand for ketchup will likely decrease. If the price of Product C *decreases*, demand for Product B *increases*. If the price of burgers and hot dogs decreases, demand for ketchup increases. Anytown's potato chip crisis could affect sales of chip dip or salsa. **Perfect complementary goods** must be consumed together. Your inkjet printer needs inkjet cartridges to operate. As the price of inkjet printers drops, consumers will purchase more of them, creating additional demand for replacement ink cartridges and/or refill inks. The printer also needs paper, but regular printer paper sales may or may not mutually correspond to the increased printer sales. If 95 percent of consumers bought the inkjet printers to print out photos from their digital cameras, then photo paper sales would more accurately mirror the increased demand for inkjet printers than would the sale of regular printer paper.

Review Questions

Directions: *Answer the following questions based on the Lesson 15B reading.*

1. What are the benefits of having multiple suppliers of same or similar items? *(2 points)*

____

____

____

____

2. Explain the difference between perfect substitutes and imperfect substitutes. Give an example of each. *(2 points)*

Tasty complementary goods!

3. Why would a price decrease for a product lead to decreased sales for its perfect and imperfect substitutes? Give an example of this phenomenon in action. *(3 points)*

4. List an example of a perfect complementary good. *(2 points)*

5. Why do perfect complementary goods respond the way they do to price increases or decreases? *(2 points)*

NAME

DATE

Practical Application Activity: *Competition*

Directions: *Take this form with you to a local store selling similar items from multiple suppliers. Complete the information comparing pricing, packaging, and rating of the products. Rating should be your evaluation of the product based on attractiveness of the packaging, advertising, or personal consumption of the product. Rate the product using the numbers 1-5, with 1 being undesirable and 5 being highly desirable. In the rating evaluation column, list one reason to support your rating number in the rating column. You may not need to use all of the lines provided. After completing the chart, circle the brand or product you prefer. Then discuss with your home school supervisor the following two questions.*

1. What factors contributed to your selection?
2. Would more or less competition for this product be beneficial? Why or why not?

Brand/Product Description	Package Size/Wt.	Price	Rating (1-5)	Rating Evaluation

Grading: *See answer key for grading rubric.*

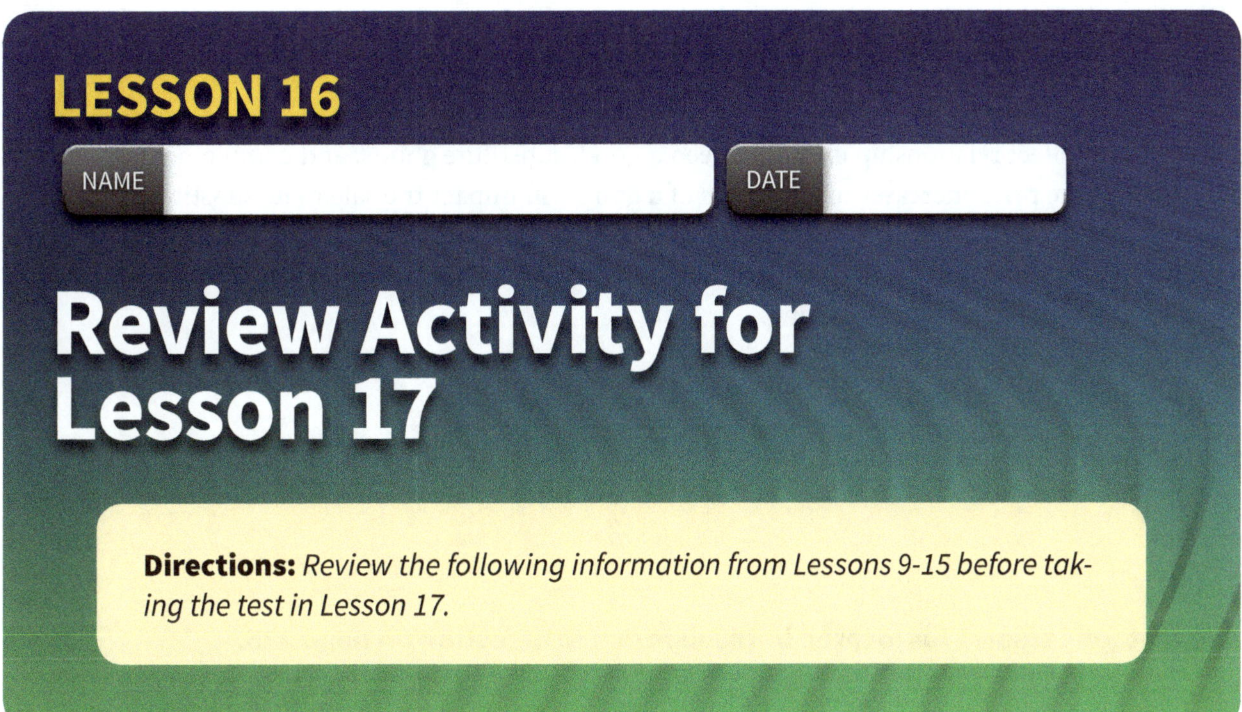

Review Activity for Lesson 17

Directions: *Review the following information from Lessons 9-15 before taking the test in Lesson 17.*

Scripture Memory

- **Psalm 33:12**—Blessed is the nation whose God is the LORD; and the people whom He hath chosen for His own inheritance.

Concepts to Review

- Value exists in the mind, but value changes with time, place, and circumstances.
- Subjective value contains non-measurable variables. Objective value is measurable.
- Man's basic economic problem is limited resources (everyone cannot have everything they want). Limited resources force us to make choices.
- Opportunity cost is the next best alternate choice. Individuals and nations experience opportunity costs.
- The supply side of the market focuses on the willingness and ability to produce goods and services. *Ceteris paribus*, suppliers are willing to supply more at a higher price than at a lower price.
- Demand is the willingness and ability of consumers to utilize goods and services. *Ceteris paribus*, buyers are willing to purchase more at a lower price than at a higher price.
- Many factors influence demand—a nation's population, personal income, consumer tastes, government policies, and alternative products.
- Equilibrium price (the price at which sales take place) is the intersection of the supply and demand curves for that good or service. Various factors cause equilibrium price to fluctuate.
- Elasticity measures people's response to changes in price. Understand and utilize the formula that is used to calculate elasticity measurements.

- Economic competition benefits consumers by lowering the cost of items and improving the quality of the products. Monopoly hurts consumers because without competition, prices increase and product quality might suffer.
- A cause-effect relationship exists between a good, substitute goods, and complementary goods. The price increases or decreases of a good will impact the sale of its substitute goods and complementary goods. Perfect substitute goods are exactly the same as the product they are replacing. Imperfect substitutes are similar enough to act as a stand-in for the product they are replacing.

Practical Application

- Using what you've learned in this unit, evaluate the cost of a glass of lemonade at a lemonade stand.

The test for Lesson 17 is located in the assessments section on page 225.

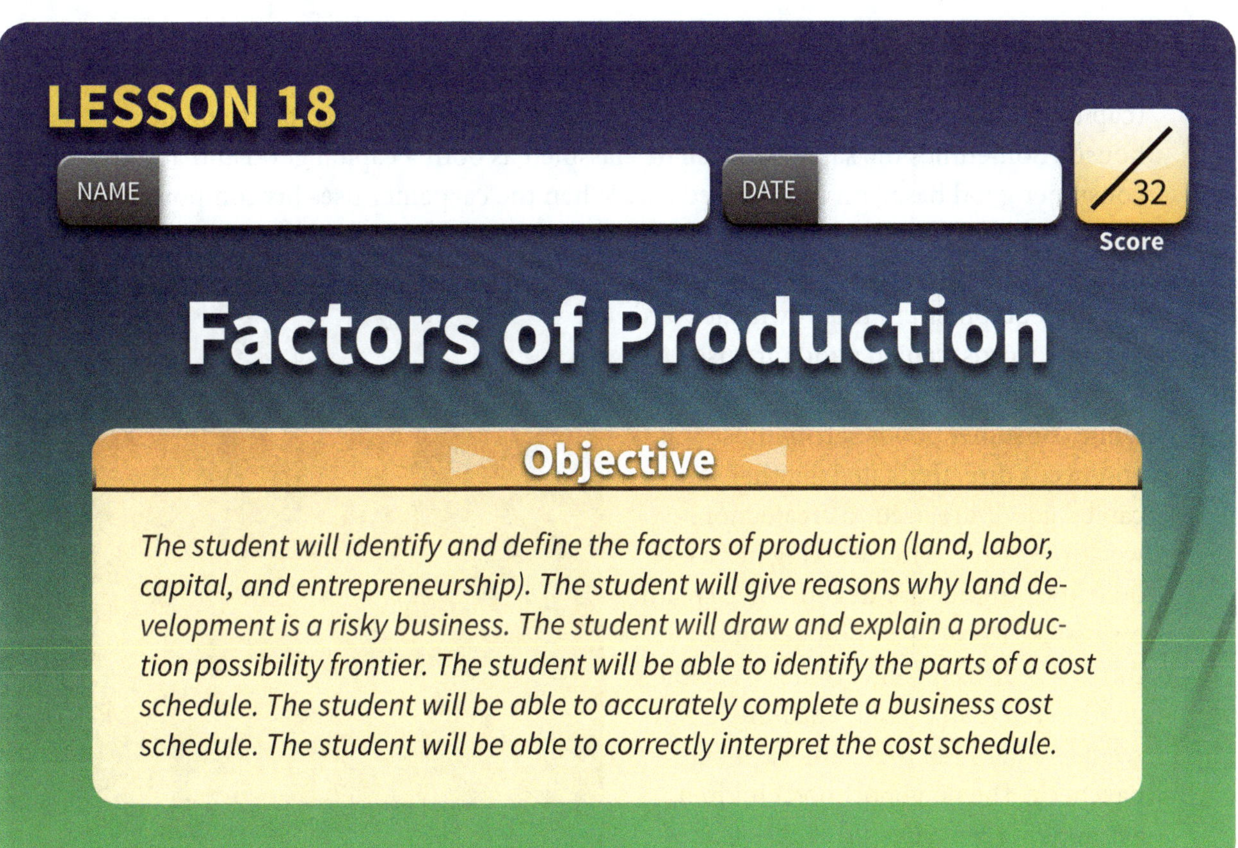

Lesson 18A Reading

Because man was made in the image of God, man can, like his Creator, make things using the resources God has given him. In the productive process, man utilizes the four factors of production to design and create useful items. These four factors of production are **land**, **labor**, **capital** and **entrepreneurship**.

Land is defined as the earth in its natural state exclusive of man-made objects—in other words, land without the application of human effort. The early pioneers blazing trails through the trackless wilderness were altering the natural state of the land, making it more useful (and thus more valuable economically) to those who followed. The virgin forests contained valuable timber and other natural resources such as iron ore, coal, and petroleum that the settlers would soon discover and exploit. The soil would produce crops once the land was cleared for farming by human effort. The economist must make a distinction between land in its natural state and land with man-made improvements in order to evaluate the impact of the other factors of production.

Labor is mankind's physical and mental human effort. Labor is the most important factor of production. It's also the one factor that every individual can completely control. Unless you're a slave, you can do what you want with your labor. Notice that labor includes mental effort. An accountant may not expend as many calories as a migrant farm worker picking tomatoes or an Olympic weight lifter working out in a gym, but he is still laboring as he uses his knowledge to do his job.

Capital refers to the machines, tools, and buildings used to create wealth (man-made goods that have value). An automobile manufacturer uses robotic welders (capital) to make cars. A carpenter uses a compound miter saw (capital) to build houses. Sometimes the same item can be classified as both a capital good and a consumer good based on its intended use. When the carpenter uses his compound miter saw to build his kids a swing set, his saw is considered a consumer good—it's being used to satisfy his children's desire for play equipment in their own backyard. In other words, capital goods are used to satisfy human wants and needs indirectly, while consumer goods satisfy those wants and needs directly. Stated another way, capital goods are used to create more wealth. A mail carrier walking her route on a hot summer day devours "ice cream on a stick" to cool off and quench her thirst. The frozen confection is a capital good to the mail carrier, enabling her to complete her mail route and earn her paycheck. The neighborhood children eating the same type of treat use it as a consumer good—increasing the enjoyment of a leisurely day at play.

Entrepreneurship, which could be classified as labor, is often categorized as a fourth factor of production. This factor of production encompasses a risk-taking mindset and the ability to project what consumers will want once the product or service finally hits the market. A person could have a great idea for a new product but lack the "drive" and willingness to launch this new enterprise. With no guarantee that the idea will succeed, the entrepreneur gambles that others will desire his creation. Profits are the rewards given to a successful entrepreneur.

Every good or service available on the market mixes various inputs of land, labor, capital, and entrepreneurship to produce that good or service. A newly discovered vein of coal lying just 20 feet below the surface in a remote region of Pennsylvania may not be worth mining at the moment due to the cost of extracting it from the ground. As the price of coal rises, however, a mining company may purchase the property, believing that it can profitably mine the previously untapped coal seam. The process will involve bringing in heavy equipment to build temporary roads and strip off the thin layer of soil, extracting the coal and hauling it away, regrading the land once the coal plays out, and restoring the region's vegetation before leaving the area. The coal-mining company has a major outlay of cash before its efforts begin to show a profit. The labor and capital inputs needed to get the coal might be more costly than anticipated, meaning the company could lose money on this venture. Management must weigh the rewards versus the risks and determine if the potential gains outweigh the potential losses.

Land development is an extremely risky business that can fluctuate wildly depending on the overall state of the economy. Investors who seek to profit from residential or commercial construction could find themselves with unsellable land or unrentable property for a prolonged period during an economic recession or depression. For example, a land developer buys a 10-acre tract of timberland to subdivide into 40 one-quarter-acre building lots. After the deal closes, the developer must prepare the lots for his potential clients. He hires a logging company to clear the land so homes can be built on what was once forested land. He needs to survey and subdivide the tract of land into individual building lots. He must build paved streets and bring the utilities (water, sewer, gas, electric) to each lot. Let's assume that all these expenses (the initial purchase price of the land and the improvements) total one million dollars. The developer must sell each lot for $25,000 just to break even—more if he wants to realize a profit. If people are not buying and building homes in the developer's region, then it might be years until the last lot is finally sold. If the developer borrowed money to buy the land, then he might not be able to make the payments on the loan, with the attendant financial consequences that would involve.

Sometimes a once-profitable site may become unprofitable because of future development. Think of all the small-town businesses bypassed by the building of the interstate highway system, or the shopping centers put out of business by a new mall. Communities cannot always protect the status quo from future progress, even if the "progress" is bad for the local economy.

Review Questions

Directions: *Answer the following questions based on the Lesson 18A reading.*

1. List and define the four factors of production. *(4 points)*

____
____
____
____
____
____
____
____

2. Why would a developer who bought 100 acres of farmland for $1,000 per acre charge $25,000 for a one-quarter-acre building lot on that same piece of property? Is the developer making an excessive profit? Why or why not? *(5 points)*

____
____
____
____

Lesson 18B Reading

Economists and entrepreneurs use a **production possibility frontier** to evaluate the dual usage of a factor of production. One use is shown on the X-axis, and the other use is shown on the Y-axis. In Figure 18:1, you see Susan's production possibility frontier for working at the grocery store and the ice cream stand. The X-axis shows the hours worked at the grocery store, and the Y-axis reveals the hours worked at the ice cream stand. The line on the graph is the **line of maximum production.** Anything to the left of the line can be achieved without increasing the number of hours worked. Notice that Susan currently works 40 hours per week between the two jobs. She could work 0.5 hours at the ice cream stand and 39.5 hours at the grocery store. She could work 10 hours at the ice cream stand and 30 hours at the grocery store. Anything to the right of the line is unobtainable unless Susan decides to work more hours per week. If Susan gets paid the same for both jobs, *ceteris paribus*, it doesn't really matter where she works as long as she gets her 40 hours. However, if she gets tips for working at the ice cream stand, Susan probably wants to get as many hours as possible selling ice cream because it means more income.

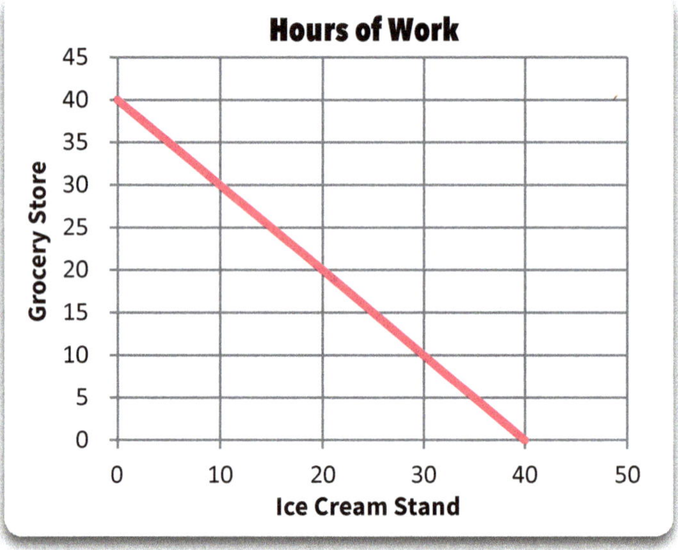

Figure 18:1 Susan's Production Possibility Frontier

Suppose a farmer might want to know how much income he could generate from his property if he grew soybeans and/or used the land to raise grass-fed beef. Using a production possibility frontier, he could illustrate all possible combinations for the two uses of the land to achieve maximum profit. Let's imagine that this farmer has 500 acres suitable for cultivation or raising beef cattle. Soybean income last year was $380/acre, while grass-fed beef income averaged $490/acre. If the farmer planted all soybeans on the 500 acres, he would bring in $190,000. If he raised grass-fed beef on the entire plot of ground, he would gross $245,000. However, he doesn't have enough customers to buy all the meat if he only raised beef cattle. So this intelligent farmer draws a production possibility frontier to show all possible combinations of the two agricultural products he can produce. Last year he planted 100 acres of soybeans and used 400 acres to graze cattle, giving him a gross income of $234,000.

Many factors will influence the farmer's decision about land usage for this coming year. Has the price of soybeans gone up or down? If soybean prices went up significantly, he might put more land into soybeans. If the almanac predicts a drought during the growing season, the soybean yield (bushels per acre) might decline along with his income. If he could attract more grass-fed beef customers, more land could be used for grazing cattle. The production possibility frontier is a useful analytical tool for comparing two alternative uses of a factor of production.

Review Questions

Directions: *Answer the following questions based on the Lesson 18B reading.*

1. Why would an economist use a production possibility frontier? *(1 point)*

2. Draw a production possibility frontier given the following information. You currently have two part-time jobs, working at each 20 hours per week. Job #1 (landscaping) pays you $8/hour. Job #2 (pizza delivery) pays you $10/hour. *(10 points)*

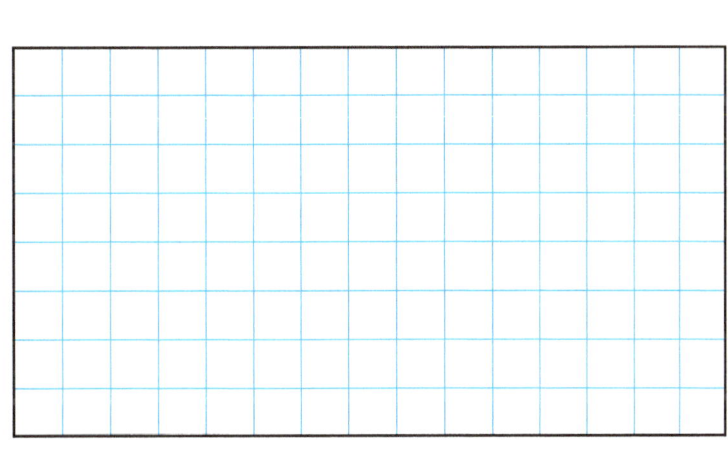

Lesson 18C Reading

Manufacturing goods or providing services involves a mixture of the four factors of production. The entrepreneur inputs land, labor, and capital to produce a good or provide a service. In order to maximize profits, the entrepreneur must determine the optimum level of production. Perhaps the company needs more land to expand its manufacturing capability. Maybe the company needs to hire more workers at its existing facilities to increase output. New machinery at its current plant could make the employees more productive. The entrepreneur can examine the factors of production both in relationship to each other and in isolation. For example, will the manufacturing process be **labor-intensive** or **capital-intensive**? An excavating company could dig

ditches using men with shovels or a single backhoe operator. The former method would be labor-intensive (digging by hand), while the latter method would be capital-intensive (a machine is doing most of the work). In this situation, the entrepreneur can easily determine which method to use. The high cost of labor in the United States and the speed of excavating with a backhoe compared to hand digging makes investing in an excavating machine an easy decision.

Not all interrelationships between the factors of production are so readily apparent to the entrepreneur. A company the author worked for used to subcontract out the powder coat painting of parts used by the company. The facility at which the author worked made the parts and shipped them out for painting before returning them to the author's factory for assembly. Many of these parts received scratches and dings during transport from the painting facility to the manufacturing plant. An extra employee had to work the assembly line to do touch-up painting on the finished product. Dozens of the assembled product surrounded the packing workstation waiting for the touch-up paint to dry before final packaging. The painting subcontractor blamed the trucking company for the blemishes, while the trucking company blamed the painting contractor employees who loaded the trucks. With no one willing to accept responsibility for the damaged parts or fix the problem, the author's employer finally decided to install an expensive automated paint line at the manufacturing plant. Quality control improved significantly once the parts never left the plant—proof of the old adage "if you want something done right, you have to do it yourself." In this case, the company made an expensive capital outlay (the automated paint line) rather than continue to use the cheaper but inferior painting subcontractor. In the short run, the company's profitability declined due to the expense of the paint line. In the long run, profitability and the overall quality of the product increased.

To examine a factor of production in isolation to determine optimum output, the entrepreneur can use a **cost schedule**. The cost schedule enables management to statistically quantify output at various levels of input. Figure 18:2 shows a typical cost schedule. Column 1 shows the factor of production under consideration. Column 2 lists the quantity produced at each level of input. Column 3 contains the total fixed cost for the company, which does not change with each variable input. Such costs might be taxes on the facilities or rent for the building. Column 4 shows the total variable cost with each additional input. These costs might include salary and benefits for additional employees, additional wages paid to the current workforce for working longer hours, higher electric bills due to longer working hours or additional machinery, and additional raw materials to make the finished product. Column 5 (total cost) can be found by adding columns 3 and 4. Column 6 (average fixed cost) is found by dividing column 3 (total fixed cost) by column 2 (quantity). Column 7 (average variable cost) is found by dividing column 4 (total variable cost) by column 2 (quantity). Column 8 (average cost) is the sum of columns 6 (average fixed cost) and column 7 (average variable cost). Column 9 (marginal cost) is the cost of going to the next level of production. To calculate marginal cost, take the *increase* in total variable cost (column 4) and divide it by the *increase* in quantity (column 2). Note that you must calculate the *numerical increase* between two levels of total variable cost and two levels of quantity to determine marginal cost. This column helps the entrepreneur determine if it's worthwhile to go to the next level of production. You will need to know these formulas for the Lesson 18 practical application activity and the assessments for this unit.

Input	Q	TFC	TVC	TC	AFC	AVC	AC	MC
1	30	1,000	470	1,470	33.33	15.67	49.00	*****[16]
2	36	1,000	560	1,560	27.78	15.56	43.34	15
3	47	1,000	740	1,740	21.28	15.74	37.02	8.89
4	51	1,000	830	1,830	19.61	16.27	35.88	22.50
5	53	1,000	1,500	2,500	18.87	28.30	47.17	335

Figure 18:2 A Typical Cost Schedule

Review Questions

Directions: *Answer the following questions based on the Lesson 18C reading.*

1. Why would an entrepreneur use a cost schedule? *(2 points)*

___

___

___

2. List and define the nine columns of a cost schedule. *(5 points)*

___

___

___

___

___

___

___

___

___

3. Give the formula for calculating TC, AFC, AVC, AC, and MC. *(5 points)*

___

___

___

___

___

[16] You cannot calculate marginal utility for Level 1 input because you need two levels to make a comparison.

NAME

DATE

Practical Application Activity:
Cost Schedule

Dan Anyman went into business for himself five years ago. Dan's Deluxe Doghouses produces custom-built pooch palaces complete with air-conditioning, automated food and water dispensers, sound and video systems, and of course, very cushy doggie beds. Depending on upgrades and accessories, each doghouse retails for $10,000 to $18,000.

Working by himself, Dan can build 22 deluxe doghouses in a year, but he cannot keep up with current demand for his quality creations. Some customers wait almost two years from the time they order until delivery of their finished doghouse. Dan needs help to meet customer demand more quickly, so he created a cost schedule to determine his ideal level of production.

Directions: *Complete the following cost schedule for Dan's Deluxe Doghouses. You may use a calculator to complete this part of the assignment. (10 points—1/5 point per answer)*

Input*	Q	TFC	TVC**	TC	AFC	AVC	AC	MC
1	22	200,000	35,000					
2	36	200,000	70,000					
3	45	200,000	105,000					
4	58	200,000	140,000					
5	67	200,000	175,000					
6	79	200,000	210,000					
7	81	200,000	245,000					
8	80	200,000	280,000					
9	78	200,000	315,000					
10	71	200,000	350,000					

*No. of employees **includes salary, benefits, and additional expenses such as tools and electrical usage for each new employee

Directions: *Answer the following questions based on the cost schedule.*

1. Why wouldn't production double when Dan hired another employee? *(3 points)*

____
____
____
____
____

2. Why did total product start to decrease when eight employees worked for Dan's Deluxe Doghouses? *(2 points)*

____
____
____
____

3. How many employees should Dan have working at Dan's Deluxe Doghouses? Why? *(3 points)*

____
____
____
____
____

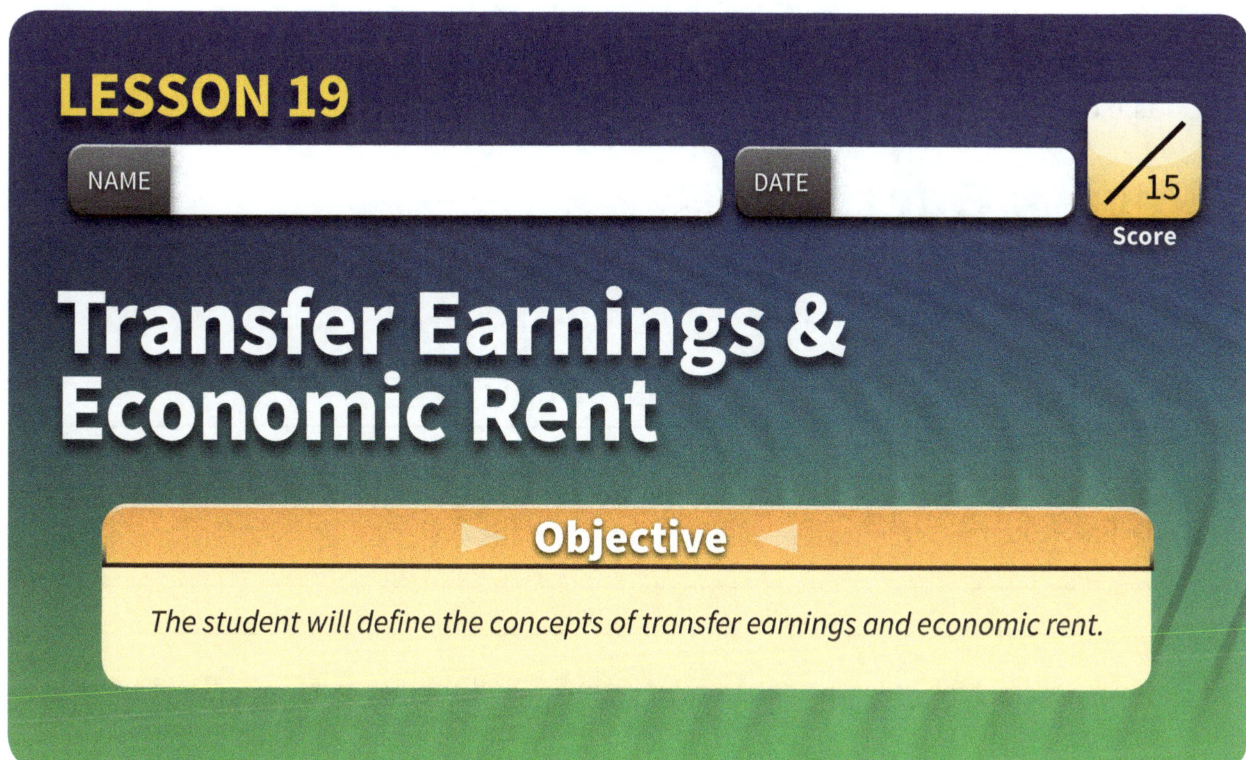

Lesson 19A Reading

Transfer earnings are what a factor of production must earn in order to keep it in its present use. If a farmer receives a satisfactory income from his land, he will continue to utilize the land for farming. If raising crops fails to meet his living expenses, however, he will seek an alternative, more lucrative use of a portion or all of his land. **Economic rent** is income earned above transfer earnings. Suppose our previously mentioned farmer needs an average of $750 per acre to make a living. If he averages $1,000 per acre, we note that he received $750 per acre of transfer earnings and $250 per acre of economic rent. Both concepts include objective (monetary) and subjective (non-monetary) elements.

Why are these two concepts important? They force us to consider the most efficient use of the various factors of production. *Ceteris paribus*, the opportunity cost of alternative uses of factors of production leads us to put the factors of production into their most profitable use.

There are times when transfer earnings trump economic rent. When the author got married in 1989, he and his wife rented a duplex from the widowed landlady who occupied the other unit. They lived in that apartment for 13 years until she passed away. In that entire time, she raised the rent only one time—after their second child was born and they needed to use an additional upstairs bedroom. Of course, the author mowed the grass, shoveled snow from the driveway and sidewalks, and did repairs about the house to help his landlady out financially. This was a win-win situation for both the author and the landlady—it enabled him to teach in a Christian school, his wife to finish college, and the landlady to have someone to look after her in her declining years (she had no children and her husband had previously passed away). She was more than willing to give up a significant amount of economic rent from the apartment rental to get a reliable long-term tenant who helped her maintain the property.

Review Questions

Directions: *Answer the following questions based on the Lesson 19A reading.*

1. Define transfer earning. *(1 point)*

2. Define economic rent. *(1 point)*

3. If your current job only pays you transfer earnings, and another employer offers you a similar job at a higher salary, what factors might influence you to keep your current job? *(3 points)*

4. Could farming ever become so unprofitable compared to other uses of land that all land would be utilized for something other than farming? Explain and defend your answer using what you've already learned in this course. *(5 points)*

5. If you own commercial real estate, should you always rent to the highest bidder? Under what circumstances might you rent to someone other than the highest bidder? *(5 points)*

NAME ______________________ DATE ____________

Practical Application Activity: *Transfer Earnings and Economic Rent*

(1 point each unless otherwise indicated)

1. Do you currently have a job? **Yes** ________ **No** ________
   If yes, where do you work? ______________________________
   If no, where would you like to work? ______________________________

2. If you answered "yes" to question #1, how much do you make per hour?
   $________/hour

3. If you answered "no" to question #1, what would be your starting wage at the place where you would like to work? **$________/hour**

4. Would you be willing to work at this job if you had to take a pay cut of

25 cents/hour?	**Yes** ________	**No** ________
50 cents/hour?	**Yes** ________	**No** ________
$1.00/hour?	**Yes** ________	**No** ________
>$1.00/hour?	**Yes** ________	**No** ________

5. What do you like about your job? ______________________________
   ____

6. What do you dislike about your job? ______________________________
   ____

7. If another company in a similar business offered you more money, would you switch jobs? **Yes** ________ **No** ________

8. If you answered "yes" to question #7, how much more would you have to make per hour to induce you to switch? **$________**

9. If you answered "no" to question #7, what factors might influence you to pass up the other company's pay increase and stay with your current job?
   ____
   ____
   ____
   ____

NAME DATE

Transfer Earnings Case Study: *The Smiths*

Mr. Smith (age 51) works for a large corporation in the city where he grew up (Columbus, Ohio). He lives with his wife and two teenage children (a sophomore boy and a junior girl) in a beautiful suburb just a short 15-minute drive from his place of work. They own their $475,000 home (no mortgage). They own two vehicles (two older cars for the teenagers to drive) and lease two new vehicles for the parents to drive. Mr. Smith's parents live four blocks away, but for health reasons, his wife's parents moved to southern Arizona after retirement. They currently use one of Mr. Smith's two weeks of vacation to fly out and visit his wife's parents. His daughter plays volleyball and basketball for her public school teams, but she's not a starter, and sometimes never gets to play against their better opponents. His son participates in an excellent program for students with learning disabilities (he's dyslexic). Mrs. Smith is a stay-at-home mom, but she's very involved in the school's PTA, a quilting club, and church activities. The entire family attends church, but Mr. Smith's work schedule (10-hour days—six days a week) prevents him from holding any church offices. He does, however, sing in the church choir, along with his teenage children. Mr. Smith makes $300,000 per year. His benefits include full medical coverage and two weeks' paid vacation. He currently has $50,000 set aside for his children's college education and $25,000 in a retirement fund.

Just last week, Mr. Smith's boss asked him to consider a temporary assignment in northern Mexico. He would oversee his company's start-up of a new plant in Mexico for three years. Mr. Smith would work 40 hours per week, live in company housing on the plant site, set his own hours, and have a company car to use for personal transportation and company business. His salary would increase to $500,000, and he would get four weeks of paid vacation. His benefits package would still include the full medical coverage. If he takes the job, however, his current position would not be waiting for him when he returns. He could take a $150,000-per-year job in the Louisville, Kentucky, plant (working a 40-hour week) or a $275,000-per-year job (working a 50-hour week) in the Portland, Oregon, plant. Both positions offer three weeks of paid vacation. The compensation package at the Louisville plant would include 1,000 shares of company stock (currently valued at $75/share), while the Portland plant would give him 5,000 shares of stock. Should Mr. Smith take the job?

Directions: *The following chart lists several considerations showing positive and negative aspects of taking the job in Mexico. For each consideration, put a plus or minus sign in the fourth column along with a reason why you believe that factor is advantageous or disadvantageous.* *(13 points)*

Job Considerations	Positive	Negative	+ or – and reason
Salary	$200,000/year increase for three years; Mr. & Mrs. Smith would put the increase toward their children's college education and the retirement fund	$25,000 to $150,000 decrease in salary after three years	
Work Hours	Work 20 less hours/week for three years (and set own hours), and 10 to 20 less hours/week after three years	Need to continue working 60-hour weeks	
Vacation Time	Two-week increase for three years and one-week increase for his remaining employment	Current job only gives him two weeks	
Housing	Free housing for three years	Rent or sell the home in Columbus?	
Stock Compensation	Not currently available; would be available after three years	What would the stock's value be in three years?	
Vehicles	Free use of a car for three years	Would the Smiths be able to have four cars in Mexico? Can the Smiths get out of the lease agreement on two cars?	

His parents	Could use extra vacation time to visit them periodically	Away from them permanently unless Mr. Smith finds other work after three years	
Her parents	Only two hours away from them for three years	Still far away after three years, with Mr. Smith making less money	
Daughter's school	Don't know	Miss her senior year with her friends in Columbus	
Son's school	Don't know	Taken out of the dyslexic program	
Church	Don't know their church options	Mom would lose her church family	
Distance from his parents	Current Job: 4 blocks	Louisville 206 miles Portland 2,422 miles	
Distance from her parents	Current Job: 1,910 miles	Louisville 1,753 miles Portland 1,451 miles	

Subjective Considerations: List five subjective or unknown factors which will influence Mr. Smith's decision. *(5 points)*

____

____

____

____

____

____

LESSON 20

NAME ______ DATE ______

Score

Productivity

Objective

The student will define productivity and explain its importance to economics. The student will explain how the division of labor, specialization, and technology impact productivity. The student will discuss how absolute and comparative advantage should be used to make decisions concerning productivity. The student will explain the difference between labor productivity and multifactor productivity.

Lesson 20A Reading

Can you write faster than you can type? If your answer is no, then the computer makes you more productive as a writer. You should produce your high school research paper using the computer rather than handwrite it using pen and paper. In today's lesson, we'll be discussing various aspects of **productivity** and why this concept is so important to a free-market economy.

From a microeconomics standpoint, productivity focuses on an individual worker's efficiency—how much output per unit of labor input. Increased productivity helps businesses remain competitive in today's global business environment. Remember Dan's Deluxe Doghouses from Lesson 18? Dan needed to increase production so that his potential customers didn't have to wait almost two years for a custom-built pooch palace. Since he was already working as efficiently as humanly possible by himself, hiring more carpenters enabled Dan to build his doghouses faster to keep pace with current demand. The broader macroeconomics view of productivity looks at how a nation can

effectively use its human and physical resources to bring about economic growth. Without increased productivity, a growing population will experience a decline in its standard of living due to already limited resources having to meet the needs of more people. For example, if a nation's population doubles, but its food production does not increase accordingly, that nation will experience food shortages or be forced to import food from other countries. In a global economy, productivity helps a nation's business firms remain competitive with foreign firms by lowering manufacturing costs. Productivity growth at the macroeconomic level is a win-win situation. Employees receive higher wages, businesses earn higher profits, corporate shareholders get larger dividends, consumers pay lower prices, and governments receive greater tax revenue. In the next reading section, we'll look at three ways to increase productivity: division of labor, use of technology, and specialization.

Review Questions

Directions: *Answer the following questions based on the Lesson 20A reading.*

1. If you can type faster than you can write in longhand, why would you choose to write your sweetheart a love letter rather than type it on the computer? *(2 points)*

___

___

___

2. Explain the difference between microeconomic productivity and macroeconomic productivity. *(2 points)*

___

___

___

3. Why must productivity continue to increase? *(2 points)*

___

___

___

4. How does productivity interact with supply and demand to benefit consumers? *(3 points)*

___

___

___

___

5. List three benefits a nation receives from increased productivity. *(3 points)*

___

___

___

Lesson 20B Reading

One of the most obvious ways to increase productivity is through a technique known as the **division of labor**. Instead of one employee making a product from start to finish, multiple employees perform specific steps in the manufacturing process. Using assembly-line techniques, these employees produce a much greater number of the finished product than if they each tried to build the entire product on their own. Years ago, the author worked on an assembly line in a manufacturing plant. Not counting the individuals who kept the line supplied with the necessary parts, the five-person assembly-line team could crank out 300 items in an eight-hour shift. The author's job, the next-to-last station on the line, involved attaching two braces using four screws and wiping the then-finished product with a cleaning solution. Although extremely boring work, it didn't take him very long to master the rhythm of the conveyor belt. He was a pro at "bracin' and cleanin' " after just a few minutes on the line. With the division of labor, the five employees on that assembly line didn't have to be skilled craftsmen capable of building the entire product on their own—they just had to be experts at a portion of the entire assembly process.

Productivity Techniques
- *Division of Labor*
- *Technology*
- *Specialization*

Technology is another method of increasing productivity. Imagine the author's speed on the assembly line if he had to use a hand-powered screwdriver rather than an air-driven one to attach the two braces. While a blessing to productivity in many areas, and creating new employment opportunities as it develops, technology is a two-edged sword, responsible for "technological unemployment" in certain situations. For instance, a contractor the author worked for won a bid from a medium-sized business to install concrete foundations for $500,000 machines capable of performing multiple milling operations. This fantastic piece of technology displaced several skilled machine operators while creating jobs in other areas. The author's company got temporary work pouring the concrete foundation and core-boring precise holes to anchor the machine into the pad. The machine required a trained operator to program it, load bar stock into the machine for milling, and check the quality of the parts periodically. Highly trained technicians had to service the machine —a job that might require the company to hire additional maintenance personnel or utilize technicians from the machine's manufacturer. If the machine's speed and versatility allow the factory to create new product lines, more employees would be needed to produce, package, and promote the new products (tooling for the new products, retail sales outlets, etc.). In the short run, several machine operators at the plant experienced technological unemployment

due to a machine that doesn't take home a paycheck and need benefits (health care, paid vacations, paid sick days, etc.). Those employees displaced by the new machines could look for work elsewhere with their existing skills set, which might require geographic relocation, or train for work in an entirely different field, necessitating a personal expenditure of time and money. In the long run, the company's productivity and profitability increased, thanks to an amazing piece of technology.

Another way to increase productivity is through **specialization**. Division of labor is a type of specialization in that it breaks down the production process into smaller components. Another aspect of specialization is to focus on something using readily available resources. For instance, you wouldn't try to grow citrus fruit in the Arctic because the climate is not favorable to this type of farming. You would have to utilize a great deal of costly technology (greenhouses, imported soil, heating apparatus and growth-stimulating lighting during the long Arctic winters). On the other hand, you might be able to start a packaged ice business using the icebergs that break off the glaciers—a plentiful Arctic resource. Nations with the right type of soil and climate could specialize in growing coffee, tea, or bananas. Still another example of specialization would be to focus on just one aspect of providing a good or service. Your local bike repair shop doesn't try to manufacture tires and all the various repair parts, but buys the needed tires and parts from others who specialize in tire manufacturing and machining parts to concentrate on what it does best—servicing this two-wheeled means of transportation. For most of us, it's to our advantage to hone our skills in a limited area and pay other specialists to more efficiently do tasks we could do, but choose not to do. Let's assume, for instance, that you're a salaried teacher making $50,000 a year. The concrete driveway at your home needs to be replaced. You have the knowledge and ability to pour a new driveway, but specialization argues that you should focus on teaching and hire a concrete contractor to redo your driveway. You solicit three estimates for the project, and receive bids of $10,000, $12,000, and $15,000 from the concrete contractors. Those bids seem high to you, so you consider doing the job yourself. You'll need to rent a jackhammer to break up the old concrete, a bull float for the day of the pour, and a floor saw to cut the control joints. You'll have to pay someone to dispose of the old concrete. You must purchase reinforcing wire, stone, expansion joint material, and lumber to make the forms for the driveway. You'll need to provide a steak dinner for several buddies to help you on the day of the pour, and you'll have to pay for ready-mix concrete delivered to the job site. You're responsible for contacting the city building department for the necessary permits. Even with all these expenses, your research reveals you can do the job yourself for $8,000—$2,000 less than the cheapest estimate from a concrete contractor. Should you do the job yourself, or hire the specialist? Before answering that question, you need to consider the economic concepts of **absolute advantage** and **comparative advantage**.

Not a profitable Arctic crop!

Review Questions

Directions: *Answer the following questions based on the Lesson 20B reading.*

1. List three factors affecting productivity. *(3 points)*

2. Is technological unemployment necessarily a bad thing? Explain your answer. *(3 points)*

3. How could an interlibrary loan system (utilizing an online card catalog and the Internet) create employment? *(2 points)*

4. Why do general contractors hire subcontractors (electricians, plumbers, roofers, etc.) to help them build houses? *(2 points)*

5. What if you cannot find gainful employment in your area of expertise? Is this an argument against specialization? *(3 points)*

6. If you were an employer, who would you rather hire—Pablo Picasso or Leonardo da Vinci? Why? Does your reasoning reflect an argument against specialization? *(5 points)*

Lesson 20C Reading

Absolute advantage is "a business situation in which a provider of goods or services is more profitable or efficient than all of its competitors, by having a smaller total input per unit of output."[17] **Comparative advantage** is "the ability of an individual or group to carry out an economic activity, such as production, at a lower cost and more efficiently than another entity."[18] In the concrete driveway illustration, the $10,000 bidder has an absolute advantage over the other two contractors, assuming that all three contractors could provide a finished driveway of comparable quality. Do you, as a do-it-yourselfer, have a comparative advantage over the concrete contractors? You can do the job cheaper, just not as efficiently as they can. Conventional wisdom says you should let the contractor do the work and focus on teaching, but the $2,000 difference is a lot of money, especially if you have to take out a home equity loan to pay for the new driveway. As Ben Franklin used to say, "A penny saved is a penny earned." You have the time to do the job yourself during summer break, and you cannot make $2,000 in the time it would take you to redo the driveway, so you should proceed with the project on your own. You can still take advantage of specialization, even when you do the job yourself. You rent the technology needed to do the job, pay someone else to haul away the debris from the old driveway, and pay to have the stone and ready-mix concrete delivered to the job site.

Business managers concerned about productivity will pay close attention to the absolute advantage and comparative advantage of their employees to effectively utilize their skills. The author's assembly-line job mentioned previously came through a temporary employment agency. Part of the application process with the agency was a dexterity test to assess his ability to perform tasks using the fine motor skills of his hands. Although not as qualified in this area as many of the other applicants, he did well enough to get the assembly-line job. A retail establishment would be foolish to put its best salesperson in an office doing paperwork all day instead of on the showroom floor making sales. A multinational corporation wouldn't send its French-speaking leadership to negotiate business deals in Spanish-speaking countries—they would assemble a team fluent in Spanish. An automotive repair shop in the area of the country the author grew up in had a blind mechanic. This blind mechanic could do brake jobs on vehicles—an amazing feat for someone without the ability to see what he was doing. Although he didn't have an absolute advantage over all the other mechanics at the shop, particularly in diagnosing problems that required visual inspection of the vehicle, he did have a comparative advantage in certain areas such as brake repairs. Absolute and comparative advantage information determines effective and efficient use of human resources.

[17] absolute advantage. (n.d.). *Dictionary.com's 21st Century Lexicon*. Retrieved April 12, 2011, from Dictionary.com website: http://dictionary.reference.com/browse/absolute advantage

[18] comparative advantage. (n.d.). *Dictionary.com's 21st Century Lexicon*. Retrieved April 12, 2011, from Dictionary.com website: http://dictionary.reference.com/browse/comparative advantage

Review Questions

Directions: *Answer the following questions based on the Lesson 20C reading.*

1. Explain the difference between absolute advantage and comparative advantage. *(2 points)*

2. Who has an absolute advantage in doing the dishes at your house? Do you have a comparative dishwashing advantage? Why or why not? *(2 points)*

3. Even though you might have a comparative advantage in replacing your concrete driveway, what arguments might be made against your doing so? *(2 points)*

Lesson 20D Reading

Technology doesn't always result in higher productivity. While a cell phone could help a salesman make and maintain contacts with clients while on the road, the plethora of apps available on his phone might make him less productive. He could be playing games or watching sports instead of using the phone as a tool to make more sales. Do computers make us more productive, or must there be a corresponding increase in other capital to take full advantage of the computer's productivity possibilities? One computer could control the three dozen separate milling operations on the previously mentioned $500,000 machine. Today's powerful computers could be underutilized—a business might need to invest in additional technology to take full advantage of the computer's productivity. Then the business owner must decide if the additional investment is worth the expense. If the business *could make* more products but *could not sell* the increased output, then it should not spend the money for the additional capital.

The pace of technological advancement creates a phenomenon that could be called "planned obsolescence." Within a year, items with faster processing speeds, better apps, and sharper images will hit the market. Consumers bent on having the "latest and greatest" will ditch their "antiquated" technology for the newest models. In the early months of 2011, the author saw an advertisement from a major electronics retailer promoting their "buy back" program. Being a somewhat cynical person, he had to know more about this marketing strategy that would help consumers remain "cutting edge." The company's website announced that those enrolled in the program could receive up to 50 percent back if they traded in the original item in good condition with all its accessories within six months. Of course, consumers had to purchase the "buy back" program for an additional cost when acquiring the original item. The trade-in value had to be redeemed as instant store credit or be placed on a store gift card. Considering the limitations of the program, individuals most likely would recover more of the original purchase price selling the used item in another venue rather than utilizing the retailer's "buy back" program. That's because the retailer cannot give them top dollar for the obsolescent item and still make a profit reselling the used item.

Does "planned obsolescence" hinder productivity? Consider the number of computer-operating systems the industry leader in computer software has unveiled in the last decade. If the old operating system works fine, and the new operating system has a learning curve for the company's computer operators with no real productivity increase in the future, then the new operating system hurts the company's productivity and profitability in the short run with no perceivable benefits in the long run. Businesses must decide if switching to the upgraded operating system is absolutely essential for their business—a moot point once the company's software upgrades cannot run on the older operating system or technical support is no longer available for the older software and operating systems.

Review Questions

Directions: *Answer the following questions based on the Lesson 20D reading.*

1. Can a computer make a church secretary, who is skilled on the electric typewriter, more productive? How? *(3 points)*

____

____

____

____

____

2. Give two examples of decreased productivity due to technology. *(2 points)*

____

____

____

____

3. Do the productivity benefits of technology outweigh the real or potential drawbacks? Explain your answer. *(5 points)*

____

____

____

____

Lesson 20E Reading

Can increased productivity alone keep a country with a high standard of living competitive with a developing nation whose citizens live in poverty? The author doesn't think so—not in the long run. With automation and the simplification of the manufacturing process, less-expensive labor in developing countries means greater profits for businesses that don't require highly skilled labor. In the HBO documentary entitled *Schmatta: Rags to Riches to Rags*, Marc Levin and Daphne Pinkerson chronicle the growth and decline of the U.S. garment industry. In 1965, 95 percent of American clothing was manufactured in the United States. As of 2009, only 5 percent was manufactured domestically. According to Stanley Garfunkel of Kent State University, contributing factors to the decline of the Cleveland, Ohio, garment industry were higher-than-average wages, unionization, technology, foreign competition, and an inability to respond quickly to changing market conditions.[19] Real estate greed, according to Kevin Strouse, contributed to the decline of the New York City garment industry. Building owners drove out garment manufacturers in favor of high-tech or advertising firms that could afford to pay higher rents for the space.[20] American seamstresses, no matter how productive, couldn't profitably compete with less-expensive labor in other parts of the world or with corporate greed.

There are two different ways to measure productivity—**labor productivity** and **multifactor productivity**. *Labor productivity* compares the value of the output to the input of labor (number of employees or hours worked). The five-person assembly-line team mentioned in the Lesson 20B reading could make 300 products in an eight-hour shift. To calculate the team's efficiency, note that the group produced 60 products per person or 7.5 products per person per hour worked. Based on these numbers, the team considered themselves to be highly productive. The *multifactor*

[19] http://ech.cwru.edu/ech-cgi/article.pl?id=GI, an article entitled "Garment Industry" from *The Encyclopedia of Cleveland History*

[20] http://www.gothamgazette.com/iotw/garments/, "The Fraying of the Garment Industry" September 18, 2000

method of calculating productivity, however, provides a more accurate picture of the team's manufacturing efficiency, as explained in the next paragraph.

At stage two of the manufacturing process, the entire assembly-line team had to take the first hour of the workday to help the employee at the second workstation assemble the mechanisms that were attached at the third workstation. Without the entire team's help, employee #2 could not keep up with the rest of the assembly line. Twelve man-hours (five hours by the entire team and seven additional hours by the person at workstation #2) per shift were required to construct the mechanisms. Were the other four employees on the assembly line skilled at producing the mechanisms? If not, finding another way to get the devices completed should improve the assembly team's productivity. Would two people producing the mechanisms at workstation #2 enable the team to manufacture finished product for the entire shift? Would pre-assembling the mechanisms elsewhere in the plant and using only four employees on the assembly line be a more productive way of making the items? These questions must be considered if management desires to find optimum labor productivity.

Measuring productivity based solely on labor does not take into account other factors that affect worker's performance. What if medieval monks had computers and modern-day printing presses to make copies of the Holy Scriptures? The Bible would have reached the masses several centuries before Gutenberg and movable-type printing. To understand the impact of technology, capital, working conditions, etc., we need to utilize multifactor productivity.

Multifactor productivity takes into account the impact of capital or other factors over which workers have little or no control.

Multifactor productivity compares output to the input of labor and capital. This method takes into account the impact of capital or other factors over which workers have little or no control. In a hot, humid climate, for instance, workers in air-conditioned buildings will be more productive than workers doing the same type of work in oppressively hot rooms. The air-driven screwdriver made the author more productive on the assembly line compared to a hand-operated screwdriver. Multifactor productivity gives business owners a more valid assessment of their employees' productivity.

Review Questions

Directions: *Answer the following questions based on the Lesson 20E reading.*

1. Besides lower labor costs, what factors might attract American businesses overseas? *(3 points)*

2. Explain the difference between labor productivity and multifactor productivity. *(2 points)*

3. Why is using hours worked rather than number of employees a more accurate measurement of labor productivity? *(3 points)*

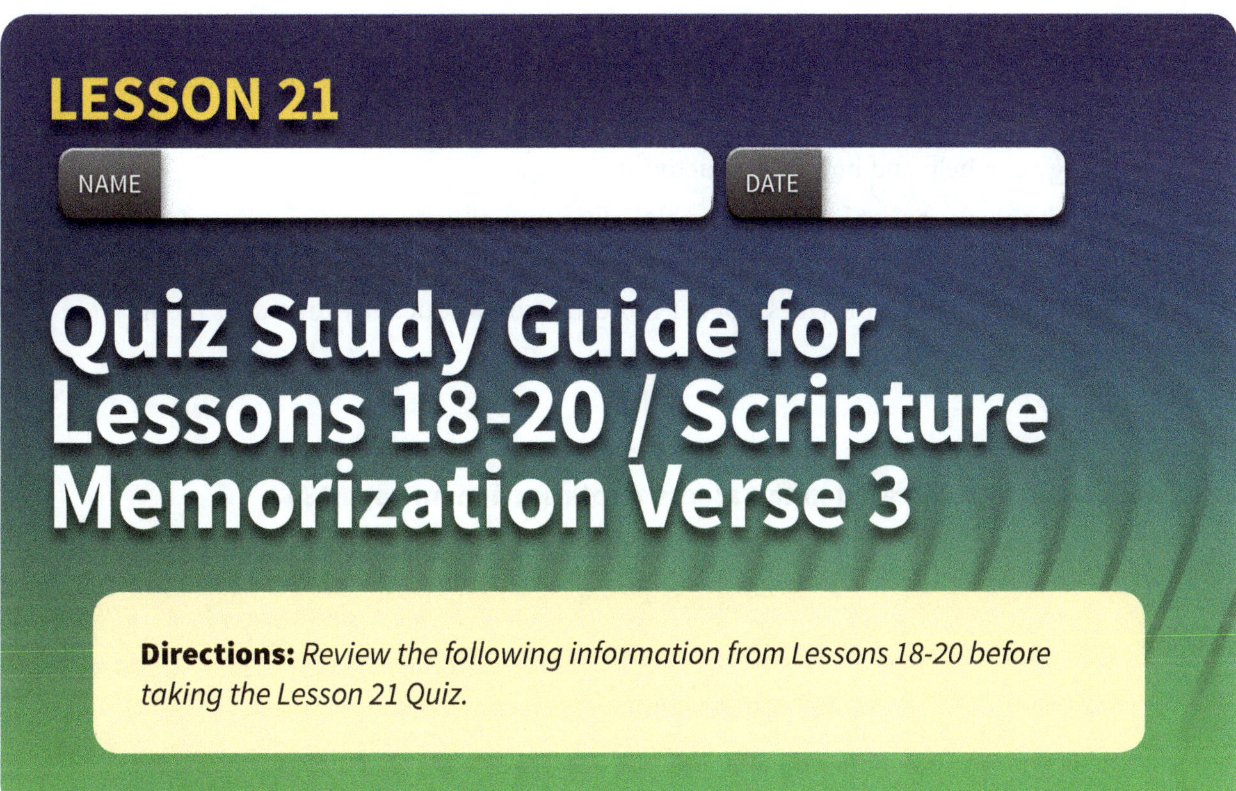

Quiz Study Guide for Lessons 18-20 / Scripture Memorization Verse 3

Directions: *Review the following information from Lessons 18-20 before taking the Lesson 21 Quiz.*

Scripture Memory

- **Matthew 6:33**—But seek ye first the kingdom of God, and His righteousness; and all these things shall be added unto you.

Concepts to Review

- Land, labor, capital, and entrepreneurship are the basic factors of production.
- Land is the earth in its natural state. Labor includes both physical and mental human effort. Capital refers to the machines, tools, and buildings that help us produce wealth. An entrepreneur plays two roles in a free-market economy: he takes a risk in starting a business and he must try to predict consumer wants and needs.
- Producing goods and services involves varying mixes of the factors of production.
- Its intended use determines if a good is a capital good or a consumer good.
- Production possibility frontiers show all possible combinations of two uses of a factor of production.
- Labor-intensive production relies on man's physical effort, while capital-intensive production takes advantage of technology.
- Cost schedules help entrepreneurs determine the optimum level of production for their business.
- Transfer earnings and economic rent help us efficiently utilize the factors of production.
- Increased productivity helps a nation maintain its standard of living and compete in a global economic environment.

- Productivity can improve using division of labor, technology, and specialization.
- Absolute and comparative advantage helps individuals, business firms, and nations increase their productivity.
- Technology can help and hinder productivity.
- Productivity alone cannot keep a nation globally competitive.
- Because it takes into account the impact of capital and environmental conditions, multifactor productivity provides a better indication of productivity than does labor productivity.

The Lesson 21 Quiz is located in the assessments section on page 231.

NAME DATE

Imprimis Article #3

Dinner Table Discussion/Co-op Class Discussion

Directions: *Read the following article and prepare a list of five discussion questions based on the reading. Have your parents and any siblings old enough to engage in the conversation read the article, then schedule a mealtime to discuss the article as a family, using your discussion questions. You will be graded on your understanding of the article (10 points), list of discussion questions (10 points), and participation in the discussion (30 points). If doing this assignment as part of a co-op class, your supervisor will ask you to write five discussion questions prior to the class discussion. Grading will be the same as if doing the assignment in a family setting.*

Imprimis article—The Entrepreneur As American Hero

Walter E. Williams

The following remarks were delivered on February 6, 2005, on the Hillsdale College campus, during a seminar on "Entrepreneurship and the Spirit of America," co-sponsored by the Center for Constructive Alternatives and the Ludwig von Mises Lecture Series.

Let's start off talking about the entrepreneur with a brief discussion of the sources of income. Some of the rhetoric one hears gives the impression that income is somehow distributed—that there's a dealer of dollars. Thus, one might think that the reason some Americans have more income than others is that the dollar dealer is a racist, a sexist or a multi-nationalist who deals out dollars unfairly. Alternatively, some suggest that the reason that some Americans are richer than others is because they got to the pile of money first and took an unfair share. In either case, justice requires that government take the ill-gotten gains of the few and restore them to their rightful owners—in other words, redistribute income. While no one actually describes the sources of income this way, the logic of their arguments for redistribution implies such a vision.

In truth, in a free society, income is earned through pleasing and serving one's fellow man. I mow your lawn, repair your roof or teach your kids economics. In turn you give me dollars. We can think of dollars as certificates of performance. With these certificates of performance in hand, I go to my grocer and ask him to give me a pound of steak and a six-pack of beer that my fellow man produced. In effect the grocer says, "You're making a claim on something your fellow man produced. You're asking him to serve you—but did you serve him?" I say, "Yes I did." The grocer responds, "Prove it!" That's when I show him my certificates of performance—namely, the money my fellow man paid me to mow his lawn.

Contrast the morality of having to serve one's fellow man as a condition of being served by him with the alternative. Government can say to me, "Williams, you don't have to serve your fellow man in order to have a claim on what he produces. As long as you're loyal to us, we will take what your fellow man produces and give it to you."

Obviously, some people are more effective at serving and pleasing their fellow man than others. They earn a greater number of certificates of performance (i.e., higher income) and hence have greater claims on what their fellow man produces. Take Luciano Pavarotti. Why is his income much higher than mine? It's because of discriminating people like you. You will plunk down $75 to hear him sing an aria from *La Boheme*; but how much would you be willing to pay to hear me do the same? Those who would call Pavarotti's income unfair and would have government take part of it to give to others are essentially saying, "We disagree with the decisions of millions upon millions of people acting voluntarily that resulted in Pavarotti's higher income. We are going to use the coercive powers of government to cancel out the full effect of those decisions through income redistribution." I might add that income redistribution is simply a legal version of what a thief does—namely, take the rightful property of one person for the benefit of another. The primary distinction between his behavior and that of Congress is legality.

For the most part, in a free society, people who are wealthy have become so through effectively serving their fellow man. Cyrus McCormick and his reaping machine, Thomas Watson Sr., the founder of IBM, and Lloyd Conover, who created the antibiotic tetracycline in the employ of Pfizer Company are just a few of the exceptional contributors. And while these people and their companies became extremely wealthy, society benefitted far more than they did in terms of the value of healthier lives and the millions and possibly billions of lives saved.

Capitalism Raises All Boats

Propaganda and stubborn ignorance has it that the advances of capitalism benefit only the rich. The evidence, as I've already pointed out, refutes that. Let's look at more: The rich have always been able to afford entertainment, but it was the development and marketing of radio and television that made entertainment accessible to the common man. The rich have never had the drudgery of washing and ironing clothing, beating out carpets or waxing floors. It was the development and mass production of washing machines, wash and wear clothing, vacuum cleaners and no-wax floors that spared the common man of this drudgery. At one time, only the rich could afford automobiles, telephones and computers. Now all but a tiny percentage of Americans enjoy these goods.

Today, as it has always been, the direct impetus for technological innovation and progress has been the entrepreneurial search for profits and the competitive economy. As Stephen Moore and Julian L. Simon point out in their 1999 article, "The Greatest Century That Ever Was," over the course of the 20th century life expectancy rose from 47 to 77 years of age; deaths from infectious disease fell from 700 to 50 per 100,000 of the population; agricultural workers fell from 35 to 2.5 percent of the workforce; auto ownership rose from one to 91 percent of the population; and patents granted rose from 25,000 to 150,000 a year. Controlling for inflation, household assets rose from $6 trillion to $41 trillion between 1945 and 1998.

Let's consider another factor that is nearly completely ignored. The output and wealth generated through free enterprise contributes to a more civilized society. For most of mankind's existence, he has had to spend most of his time simply eking out a living. In pre-industrial society and in many places in the world still today, the most optimistic scenario for the ordinary citizen was to be able to eke out enough to meet his physical needs for another day. But with the rise of capitalism and the concomitant rise in human productivity that yielded seemingly ceaseless economic progress, it was no longer necessary for mankind to spend his entire day simply providing for minimum physical needs. People were able to satisfy their physical needs with less and less time.

This made it possible for them to have the time and resources to develop spiritually and culturally.

In other words, the rise of capitalism enabled the gradual extension of civilization to greater and greater numbers of people. More of them have time available to read, become educated in the liberal arts and gain more knowledge about the world around them. Great wealth permits them to attend the arts, afford recreation, contemplate more fulfilling and interesting life activities and enjoy other culturally enriching activities that were formerly within the purview of only the rich. How was all this achieved? In a market system, enterprise profits are performance-related; they come about through a process of finding out what human wants are not being met and finding ways to meet them.

. . . the rise of capitalism enabled the gradual extension of civilization to greater and greater numbers of people.

In reference to the motivations of the entrepreneur, Adam Smith says this: "By directing that industry in such a manner as its produce may be of the greatest value, he intends only his own gain, and he is in this, as in many other cases, led by an invisible hand to promote an end which was no part of his intention." That might very well describe an entrepreneur like Thomas Watson Sr., founder of IBM. Such previously unimaginable progress as we have seen in recent decades is the direct result of having methods of handling large amounts of data accurately and rapidly. From the 1930s onward, IBM was at the forefront in the development of the machinery to do this. The huge benefits we enjoy as a result of IBM's pioneering work was no part of the intention of Thomas Watson or his successors. They were in it for profits.

In Defense of Profit

Profit has almost become a dirty word, so let me spend a few minutes talking about the magnitude of profits and the role that they play in a free market economy. Regarding their magnitude, only roughly six cents of each dollar companies take in represent after-tax profits. By far, wages are the largest part of that dollar, representing about 60 cents. As percentages of 2002 national income, after-tax profits represented about five percent and wages about 71 percent.

I'll discuss first what might be called normal profit and later turn to the more emotional topic of "windfall profits"—what some have labeled "obscene profits." Normal profit is the opportunity cost of using entrepreneurial abilities in the production of a good. It's what the entrepreneur could have earned in his next best alternative—say, another business venture. Just as wages, rent and interest must be paid in order to employ the services of labor, land and capital, normal profits must be paid to employ entrepreneurial services—the decisions, innovations and risks that drive economic progress.

Whether an entrepreneur makes a profit depends essentially on two things. The first is whether he is producing a good that consumers value and are willing to pay for; the second is whether he's using the scarce resources of society in the most efficient manner to produce the good.

Let's look at an example of the role of profits in providing incentives to produce what the consumer wants. Remember when Coca Cola introduced the "new" Coke in 1985? Pepsi Cola president Roger Enrico called it "the Edsel of the '80s," representing one of that decade's greatest marketing debacles. Who made the Coca Cola Company bring back the old Coke? Was it Congress, the courts, the president or other government officials acting in the interests of soda-drinking Americans? No, it was the specter of negative profits (i.e., losses) that convinced Coca Cola to bring back the old Coke. Thus, one role of profits is to discover what consumers want and to correct producers who make mistakes.

Profits also force producers to employ resources wisely. If producers waste inputs, their production costs will be higher. In order to cover their costs, they must charge prices higher than what consumers are willing to pay. After a while the company will incur unsustainable losses and go out of business. As a result, the company's resources will become available to someone else who'll put them to wiser use. This process is short-circuited if government offers bailouts in the forms of guaranteed loans, subsidies or restrictions such as tariffs and import quotas on competitive products from abroad. Government "help" enables failing companies to continue squandering resources. In this context it is important to remember that a business going bankrupt doesn't mean that its productive resources will vanish into thin air. It means someone else will own them.

So-called windfall profits are profits above and beyond those needed to keep an entrepreneur producing a good or service. But they serve a vital social function. They serve as a signal that there are unmet human wants. One of the best examples of the role of windfall profits are those that arise in the wake of a disaster and are often condemned as price gouging. In the wake of a disaster, such as a hurricane, there is an immediate change in scarcity conditions that's reflected in higher prices for goods and services. Assume, for example, that a family of four sees their home damaged or destroyed. At before-disaster prices, they might decide to rent two adjoining hotel rooms. However, when they arrive at the hotel and see that room prices have doubled, they might easily decide to tough it out in a single room. Doing so makes a room available for someone else whose home was damaged and who needs a place to spend the night. Thus, higher prices give people an incentive to economize on scare resources.

In the wake of Florida's Hurricane Andrew, windfall profits played a vital though unappreciated role. Plywood destined to be shipped to the Midwest, West, and Northeast suddenly was rerouted to South Florida. Lumber mills increased production. Truckers and other workers worked overtime in order to increase the availability of plywood and other construction materials to Floridians. Rising plywood prices meant something else as well. All that plywood heading south meant plywood prices rose in other locations, discouraging "lower valued" uses of plywood such as home improvement projects. After all, rebuilding and repairing destroyed homes is a "higher valued" use of plywood.

What caused these market participants to do what was in the social interest, namely, sacrifice or postpone alternative uses for plywood? The answer reveals perhaps the most wonderful feature of this process. Rising prices and opportunities for higher profits encouraged people to do voluntarily what was in the social interest: help their fellow man recover from disaster.

Williams' Law

At this juncture let me say a few words about the modern push for corporate social responsibility. Do corporations have a social responsibility? Yes, and Nobel Laureate Professor Milton Friedman put it best in 1970 when he said that in a free society "there is one and only one social responsibility of business—to use its resources and engage in activities designed to increase its profits so long as it stays within the rules of the game, which is to say, engages in open and free competition without deception or fraud.

It is only people, not businesses, who have responsibilities. A CEO is an employee, an employee of shareholders and customers. The failure of the corporate executive community to recognize this, and its willingness to engage in activities unrelated to the pursuit of profits, means national wealth will be lower, product prices will be higher and the return on investment lower.

If we care about people's wants, rather than beating up on profit-making enterprises, we should pay more attention to government-owned non-profit organizations. A good example are government schools. Many squander resources and produce a shoddy product while administrators, teachers and staff earn higher pay and perks, and customers (taxpayers) are increasingly burdened. Unlike other producers, educationists don't face the rigors of the profit discipline, and hence they're not as accountable. Ditto the Postal Service. It often provides shoddy and surly services, but its managers and workers receive increasingly higher wages while customers pay higher and higher prices. Again, wishes of customers can be safely ignored because there's no bottom line discipline of profits.

Here's Williams' law: Whenever the profit incentive is missing, the probability that people's wants can be safely ignored is the greatest. If a poll were taken asking people which services they are most satisfied with and which they are most dissatisfied with, for-profit organizations (supermarkets, computer companies and video stores) would dominate the first list while non-profit organizations (schools, offices of motor vehicle registration) would dominate the latter. In a free economy, the pursuit of profits and serving people are one and the same. No one argues that the free enterprise system is perfect, but it's the closest we'll come here on Earth.

LESSON 22

NAME

DATE

/72 Score

Circular Flow of Goods & Services: Households, Businesses, & Government

Objective

The student will explain how households, businesses, and government function as both producers and consumers in their economic interactions with each other. The student will identify problems associated with government involvement in the circular flow of goods and services.

Lesson 22A Reading

In every society, there are three economic entities—**households**, **businesses**, and **government**. Each entity interacts with the other two entities as both a producer and consumer. To simplify this complex interaction, let's start by examining the relationship between a single household and a single business.

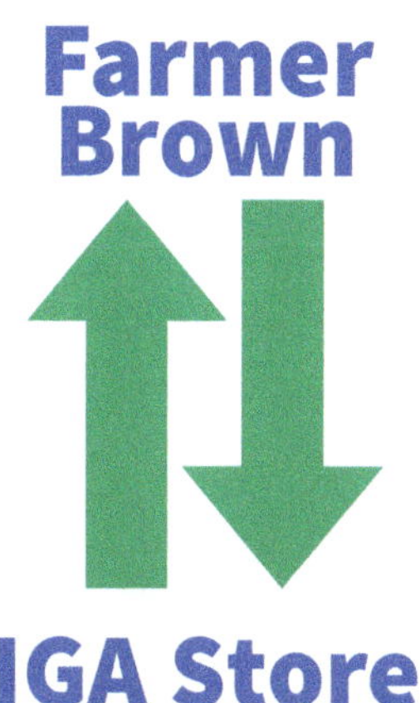

Farmer Brown owns two hundred acres of prime farmland in the midwestern United States. He grows a variety of produce for his hometown IGA grocery store. As a way of saying thanks for their business, Farmer Brown does his other grocery shopping at IGA. The graphic illustrates this interaction between Farmer Brown's household and the IGA store. Farmer Brown produces food for the IGA, and consumes certain of their grocery items that he cannot or doesn't find profitable to grow on his own land. The IGA store manager acts as a consumer when she purchases Farmer Brown's produce, then acts as a supplier by stocking additional grocery items that Farmer Brown's family wants or needs. This symbiotic relationship has benefits for both parties involved in the transactions. Farmer Brown receives income for his produce—a portion of which he returns to the IGA by purchasing some of their other grocery items. The store pays out money to stock its produce aisle with fresh, locally grown vegetables, but gets some of its outlay back when Mrs. Brown does her weekly shopping. Just last week, the IGA hired daughter Susie Brown as a cashier. Now the Brown family supplies both produce and labor for the grocery store. When the IGA decided to dispose of its day-old donuts by feeding them to Farmer Brown's pigs, the store created another supply link between itself and the Brown family.

Review Questions

Directions: *Answer the following questions based on the Lesson 22A reading.*

1. List the three economic entities found in every society. *(3 points)*

2. Draw a diagram detailing the producer-consumer relationship between Farmer Brown's household and the IGA store. *(5 points)*

Lesson 22B Reading

Now watch what happens when we add the third economic entity (government) into the relationship. Farmer Brown receives agricultural subsidies from the U.S. government, enabling him to compete against cheap vegetables grown and trucked in from Mexico. Other government agencies such as the Food and Drug Administration and the U.S. Department of Agriculture oversee the items for sale at the IGA to protect shoppers from harmful products. The Browns must pay sales tax on certain items they purchase from the grocery store, while both the store and the Browns pay property taxes. The store withholds taxes from Susie's paycheck, and Farmer Brown pays income and self-employment taxes on the profits from his farm. Mrs. Brown works for the local Bureau of Motor Vehicles, and their oldest son Matt serves his country as an officer in the U.S. Navy. Local health officials periodically inspect Farmer Brown's liquid manure pit and manure disposal practices to ensure that his farming techniques do not pose a health hazard to the local community. Farmer Brown uses information he learned from adult education classes at the local vocational-technical school to keep his farm equipment in good working order. The local agricultural extension office provides free soil testing and advice on controlling topsoil erosion from his somewhat hilly farmland. The local government uses some of its tax dollars to repair the roads and plow the snow between Farmer Brown's place and the IGA store. As you can see, the relationship becomes much more complex by adding local, state, and national government into the mix. While some government services benefit Farmer Brown and the IGA store (street repair, agricultural subsidies, job opportunities, etc.), government regulation drives up the cost of doing business, while taxes siphon off additional funds from Farmer Brown and the grocery store. Let's examine the benefits and drawbacks of government involvement in the circular flow of goods and services by looking at a historical example.

The U.S. Department of Agriculture oversees meat processing in the United States. Before the Meat Inspection Act of 1906, unscrupulous entrepreneurs sold adulterated meat products to American consumers. Some of the alleged ingredients in ham salad, for instance, included ground up rope, sawdust, and rats. Upton Sinclair's book *The Jungle* exposed these unsanitary conditions in the Chicago meat plants. On-site inspections of these plants by commissioners appointed by President Theodore Roosevelt led to federal regulation of meat processing. The Meat Inspection Act and its companion Pure Food and Drug Act created a federal bureaucracy to regulate the business practices of those industries that produced the nation's food—a necessary step to improving its quality and fitness for consumption. The American public could confidently buy groceries knowing that the products for sale wouldn't be harmful to their health, but this peace of mind came at a price. Greater government regulation and an expanded bureaucracy meant more tax dollars from taxpayers. Because the meat packers wouldn't police themselves, the federal government had to step in to make them do the right thing. New rules and regulations had to be written, enforced, and expanded as new situations developed.

Officials at the Food and Drug Administration have the final say on what is okay for consumption and what is potentially or actually harmful. These officials could be bribed to overlook illegal activity by those they are supposed to be regulating. They could also be misled by misinformation presented to them by "experts" seeking approval for new products. Multiple layers of government bureaucracy create more paperwork and additional costs for businesses; these costs must be passed on to consumers via higher prices for the firm's products. Do the benefits outweigh the drawbacks? In this situation, probably yes. The news media from time to time reports nationwide or regional recalls of contaminated or potentially contaminated food—in many cases the food has harmful *e coli* bacteria. In this situation, it's

important to have a regulatory agency monitoring the food supply for dangerous food products. Another advantage of federal oversight of the nation's food is proper labeling of the ingredients on the packaging. This enables shoppers to avoid purchasing certain items that have ingredients approved by the FDA but that their families don't want to consume because of the long-term health risks. It also helps those with certain food allergies to avoid consuming products that may trigger their allergies. So while the regulations are a burden to business and costly to consumers and taxpayers, they improve our quality of life. It's sad, however, that we have to have the octopus arms of the government so entwined in the circular flow of goods and services. Man's sin nature, resulting in greed and corruption, makes it necessary for government to step in and police what should be an economic system capable of functioning without government interference.

Review Questions

Directions: *Answer the following questions based on the Lesson 22B reading.*

1. Complete the diagram detailing the relationship between Farmer Brown, the IGA store, and the various levels of government mentioned in the reading section. *(10 points)*

2. Why did the U.S. government have to intervene in the meatpacking industry? *(2 points)*

____

____

3. What is an "unfunded mandate?" Did the Meat Inspection Act and the Pure Food and Drug Act fit into this category? Explain your answer. *(5 points)*

____

____

____

____

____

4. Why is government regulation necessary? *(2 points)*

____

____

____

Lesson 22C Reading

If government's involvement in the circular flow of goods and services stopped with necessary regulation of the interactions between consumers and businesses, then government would still be within its biblical role as mentioned by the Apostle Paul in Romans, Chapter 13. Regulation to prevent wrongdoing falls within the scope of punishing evildoers. However, like households and businesses, government acts as both an economic consumer and an economic producer in our society. Where does government get the ability to be a producer? Government can use its legislative or administrative power to create an advantageous business climate. For example, the Free Trade Agreement Tariff Tool[21] created by the Office of the U.S. Trade Representative, the Commerce Department's International Trade Administration, and the Small Business Administration, helps U.S. small businesses expedite the process of exporting goods to other nations with which we have trade agreements. The online information provided at this website can help U.S. businesses increase their exports.

Government can also use its legislative or administrative power to demonstrate favoritism toward certain businesses. Protective tariffs throughout our nation's history have promoted American manufacturing at the expense of those engaged in importing foreign-made goods. On May 17, 2011, the U.S. Senate blocked a bill that would have eliminated $2 billion a year in tax breaks for the five largest U.S. oil companies—even after those five companies posted a $36 billion profit in the first quarter of 2011.[22] With such large profits on the heels of rising gas prices, most Americans probably agree that the said oil companies don't need such tax breaks.

In order to be a producer in the circular flow of goods and services, government must collect taxes from households and businesses. The French political economist Frederic Bastiat (1801-1850) referred to taxation as legalized plunder. Taxes siphon away income from individual consumers and businesses for purposes over which they (households and businesses) have little or no control. The government spends much of this money on things other than its biblical mandates or the protection of life, liberty, and property. Perhaps the following example will help you think through the ramifications of this legalized plunder for American taxpayers.

In a *PlaceEconomics* article entitled "Save America's Treasures Update," Donovan Rypkema notes that the $220 million spent by the federal government between 1999 and 2009 on the Save America's Treasures Program generated $330 million from other sources and created 16,012 jobs (a job being defined as a full-time equivalent for one year).[23] Mr. Rypkema laments that President Obama wants to cut this program, which cost taxpayers $13,780 per job created while the Stimulus Package that President Obama signed in 2009 cost taxpayers $248,000 per job created. I know that $220 million spread out over a decade doesn't sound like much in an era when Congress tosses around hundreds of billions of dollars every year. I'm also a history teacher who likes visiting historical sites with my family and students. From a biblical or constitutional perspective, however, I don't believe that historic preserva-

[21] www.export.gov/FTA/FTATariffTool

[22] http://news.yahoo.com/s/ap/20110517/ap_on_bi_ge/us_oil_tax_breaks

[23] http://www.placeeconomics.com/archives/476

tion is a responsibility of the federal government. In my opinion, monies for historic preservation should come from memberships and private sources. Perhaps historic preservation wouldn't cost so much if the federal government wasn't throwing money at it. In addition to criticizing the expenditure of taxpayer dollars on historic preservation, citizens opposed to excessive government involvement in the economy might also disagree with President' Obama's stimulus package, the bailout of failing financial firms, government assistance to General Motors, federal funding for Planned Parenthood, and a host of other government programs.

Federal, state, and local governments have become major players in the American economy. At the national level, the U.S. government negatively impacts the American economy due to its inability to live within its means. Deficit spending has been the norm for the past two generations. Putting more economic power back in the hands of consumers and businesses would go a long ways toward fixing our economic woes.

Review Questions

Directions: *Answer the following questions based on the Lesson 22C reading.*

1. According to Romans 13 in the Bible, what are government's two biblical responsibilities? *(2 points)*

____

____

____

2. List two ways government uses its power to aid business. *(2 points)*

____

____

____

3. How does government acquire the resources to be a producer in the circular flow of goods and services? *(2 points)*

____

____

____

4. Why is deficit spending a "smoke screen" enabling government to be a producer? *(4 points)*

____

____

____

____

5. The Teacher Next Door Program, established by the Department of Housing and Urban Development, enables certified teachers and administrators working with K-12 students to obtain a foreclosed, single-family home at a 50 percent discount. The U.S. government "pays" the remaining mortgage amount after the teacher meets the three-year residency requirement. Should the federal government continue this program that aids such a limited segment of society? Why or why not? *(5 points)*

____

____

____

____

____

6. Below are 10 statements listing economic categories that receive financial assistance or are fully funded by the government. In the first column, put an X next to those categories that fall under the government's biblical or constitutional authority. In the second column, put a Y if you believe this to be a legitimate government expenditure. Put an N if you believe the government should not be spending money on this program. After completing column 2, discuss and defend the reasons for your responses with your school supervisor. Your supervisor will grade you based on the validity of your defense. *(10-30 possible points)*

Government Expenditure	Column 1	Column 2 Y or N	Points Awarded 1-Weak 2-Adequate 3-Excellent
Space exploration			
Art projects			
Scientific research			
Military defense			
ATF (Bureau of Alcohol, Tobacco, and Firearms			
Medical research			
Education			
Welfare			
Family planning			
TSA (Transportation Security Administration)			

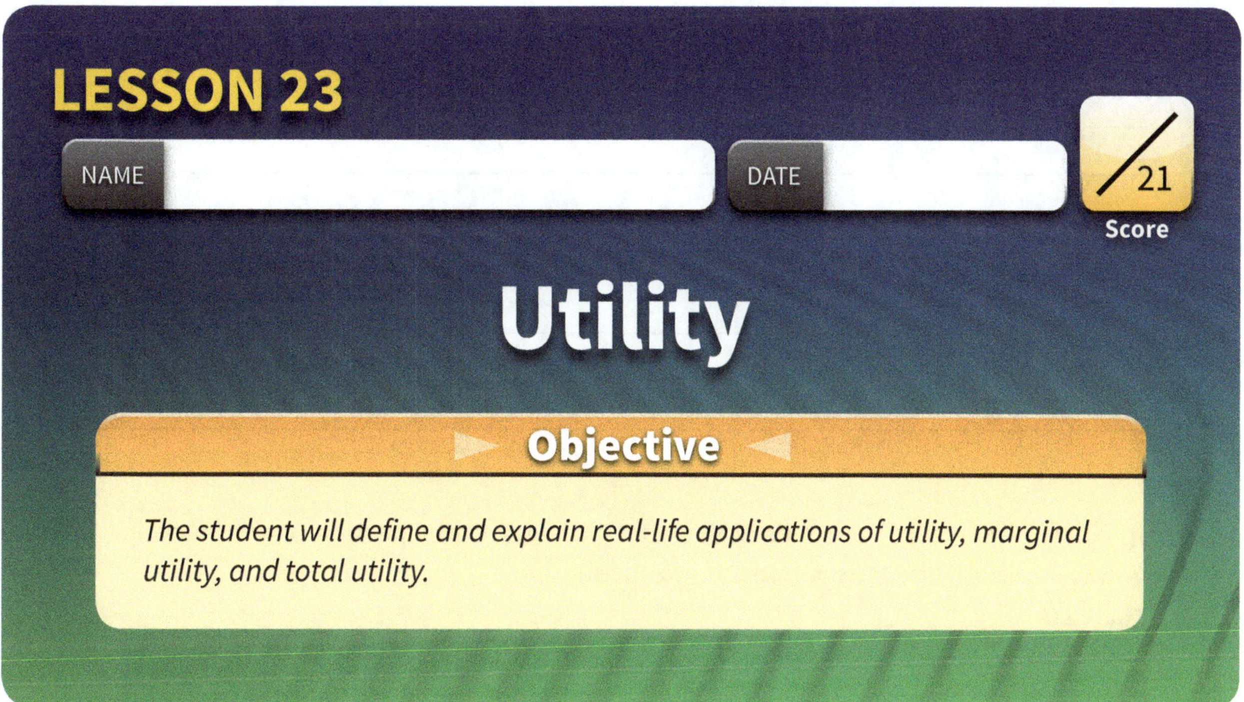

Lesson 23A Reading

Would a blind man need a pair of binoculars? Of course not! This economic good designed to give the user a close-up view of faraway objects has no value to a person who cannot see. If you gave a blind man a pair of binoculars, he might sell them or give them away to someone who could make use of them. By doing so, he would receive money in exchange for this unusable gift or experience the joy of knowing someone else is using them. This illustration helps us understand the concept of **utility**, or the usefulness of a good or service to an individual. Simply stated, utility is "the satisfaction derived from consuming a good or service." Let's demonstrate this concept by indulging in one of your favorite snack foods. For this experiment, you will need to consume similar-sized, multiple servings of the same item and record objective data about your satisfaction after each serving. Before you start, make sure your experiment time does not conflict with family meal plans. After obtaining permission from a parent, get out your snack, any necessary items to serve it (if you're having ice cream, you'll need an ice cream scoop, bowl, spoon, etc.), and a pen or pencil to complete this lesson. Then answer the following questions and follow the directions to complete the remainder of this lesson.

Review Questions

Directions: *Answer the following questions based on the Lesson 23A reading.*

1. Define "utility." *(1 point)*

____

____

____

2. What snack item did you select for the utility experiment? *(1 point)*

____

____

____

3. Identify the serving portion (one scoop, one slice, one bowl, 5 oz., etc.). *(1 point)*

____

____

____

____

4. In Chart 23A, record your satisfaction after consuming one portion of the snack. You can express this satisfaction as a whole number. *(1 point)*

Chart 23A

Snack Item	Portion No.	Utility (Satisfaction)
	1	

Lesson 23B Reading

How was your snack? Pretty tasty, you say? That's good, because you're about to consume more of it. In this portion of the experiment, we'll be learning about the law of **marginal utility**. Marginal utility is the satisfaction derived from consuming an additional unit of a good or service. To a hungry football player, the first piece of pizza provides the most satisfaction. However, since his stomach isn't full after the first slice, he has a second, third, fourth, fifth, sixth, seventh—wait a minute, he just ate the whole pizza! The second slice through the eighth slice gave him additional satisfaction. By quantifying this additional (marginal) satisfaction, we can acquire a set of numbers known as **total utility**. Total utility is the sum of all satisfaction derived from consuming a good or service. It's important to remember that each person's utility may be different. The author experiences a larger level of utility from consuming water rather than coffee. Since he doesn't like coffee, his total utility for a cup of coffee would be less (zero) than for someone who likes coffee. Calculating total utility is easy. With each additional input, simply add the new input's marginal utility to the previous total utility measurement. During this part of the experiment, you'll be consuming additional portions of your snack and recording the marginal utility and total utility for each additional portion. Your marginal utility numbers should decrease with each additional portion consumed.

Review Questions

Directions: *Answer the following questions based on the Lesson 23B reading.*

1. Explain the difference between marginal utility and total utility. *(2 points)*

2. Complete Chart 23B based on your snack food consumption. Use the information from Chart 23A (question #4 in Review 23A) to complete the first row of Chart 23B. Use whole numbers to express marginal utility and total utility. Cease consumption once you're totally satisfied at the moment and before making yourself sick. You may not need all the rows provided on the chart. *(5 points)*

Chart 23B

Snack Item	Portion No.	Marginal Utility	Total Utility
	1	******	
"	2		
"	3		
"	4		
"	5		
"	6		
"	7		
"	8		
"	9		
"	10		
"	11		
"	12		
"	13		
"	14		
"	15		
"	16		
"	17		
"	18		
"	19		
"	20		

Lesson 23C Reading

At what portion did you stop consumption? Look at the marginal utility column in Chart 23B. With each additional portion consumed, you experienced less additional satisfaction. This decrease in marginal utility is known as the law of **diminishing marginal utility**. You still like the snack, but each additional portion didn't satisfy you as much as the previous portion(s), until you temporarily cease consumption (*ceteris paribus*, you'll enjoy this snack again in the future). As marginal utility decreases, total utility increases, albeit more slowly with each additional input. Let's revisit our football player pigging out on pizza. Chart 23C shows us a utility schedule for his pizza consumption.

Chart 23C

Pizza Slice	Marginal Utility	Total Utility
#1	******	35
#2	29	64
#3	24	88
#4	16	104
#5	12	116
#6	7	123
#7	4	127
#8	1	128
#9	-15	113

After eating a whole pizza to celebrate winning the state championship, the football player tried to finish the quarterback's leftover piece. Too much of a good thing made him ill, as illustrated by the negative marginal utility number for the ninth slice of pizza. The low marginal utility numbers for slices seven through nine should have warned our football player it was time to stop consuming pizza.

Review Questions

Directions: *Answer the following questions based on the Lesson 23C reading.*

1. How can an all-you-can-eat buffet restaurant use the law of diminishing marginal utility to their advantage? *(2 points)*

2. Why would suppliers be interested in the concept of marginal utility? *(3 points)*

____

____

____

____

____

____

____

____

Lesson 23D Reading

Diminishing marginal utility helps explain why people make certain choices. A sports fan may spend hundreds of dollars at the beginning of a season attending the home games of his favorite professional baseball team. As the season progresses and the losses outnumber wins, he attends fewer and fewer games, finally refusing to go at all for the remainder of the season. Knowing his team wasn't going to be in the playoffs, he experiences less satisfaction every time he attends a game. Opportunity cost kicks in, and he finds another venue for his entertainment dollars.

Does every use of a good or service result in diminishing marginal utility? What about a college education? If every day spent in class is an additional input of the service, could you not experience *increasing* marginal utility as you gain knowledge and move one step closer to achieving your diploma and embarking upon your chosen career? Would a violin virtuoso experience diminishing marginal utility every time she performs with the orchestra? Not under normal circumstances (three concerts a month), because she loves to play the violin. Maybe if she had to play nonstop for forty-eight hours without sleep—in that situation, fatigue would cause diminishing marginal utility long before her playing time was up.

One can argue that diminishing marginal utility applies only in the short run (a brief, consecutive time period). This decline in satisfaction has less impact in the long run. You still like your snack. Having recently consumed a large quantity of this item, you probably aren't craving it at this moment. In a couple of days, however, you'll have another heaping helping of the same food item. Your long-term demand for the snack still exists. A brief respite from consumption will cause your cravings to return.

During a high school choir tour, the author and several of his friends spent the night in the home of a wonderful elderly couple. Their home contained dozens of decorative glass dishes filled with a certain round candy-coated chocolate. They encouraged the visitors to help themselves to as many of the mini-confections as they wanted, and showed them grocery bags full of 2-pound packages of the candy, lest they hesitate to imbibe for fear their host might run out. The choir members had a great time indulging from dishes at the bottom of the stairwell, at the top of the stairs, in the bedrooms, on the kitchen counter, atop the television, on the coffee table, in the bathroom, on the kitchen table, and several other locations. While the author and his friends could enjoy this candy lover's dream for only one day, imagine the couple living there constantly. Each candy-filled dish provided them with the opportunity to gratify their love of chocolate. No matter where they were in the house when the desire for chocolate arose, only seconds of time separated them from satisfying their sweet tooth. Candy dishes throughout the house provided constant visual stimulation of their subjective valuation for the candy.

Advertising has the same effect on consumers as the candy dishes in the elderly couple's home. It keeps your long-term demand for various products and services alive. That's why full-color grocery store ads are so effective. They tempt you to purchase food items that you maybe haven't had in a while, especially if those items are "on-sale." If you ate at a certain restaurant yesterday, seeing an advertisement for the restaurant today probably won't prompt you to eat there again so soon. However, if it's been a while since your last meal at that restaurant, the advertisement could prompt an internal rearrangement of your present priorities, and you'll find yourself eating at that restaurant in the very near future—perhaps the same day you saw the advertisement. A car commercial could create diminishing marginal utility for your current clunker, causing you to visit your local car dealerships for a newer vehicle. Why do pizza places advertise during sporting events? Harry and his football buddies see the commercial and they all chip in for an extra-large, two-topping pizza delivered right to the front door. Advertising counteracts the effects of diminishing marginal utility, restoring subjective value lost during previous consumption of the good or service.

Review Questions

Directions: *Answer the following questions based on the Lesson 23D reading.*

1. Why can't diminishing marginal utility sustain itself over a long period of time? *(3 points)*

2. How could diminishing marginal utility cause you to change careers? *(2 points)*

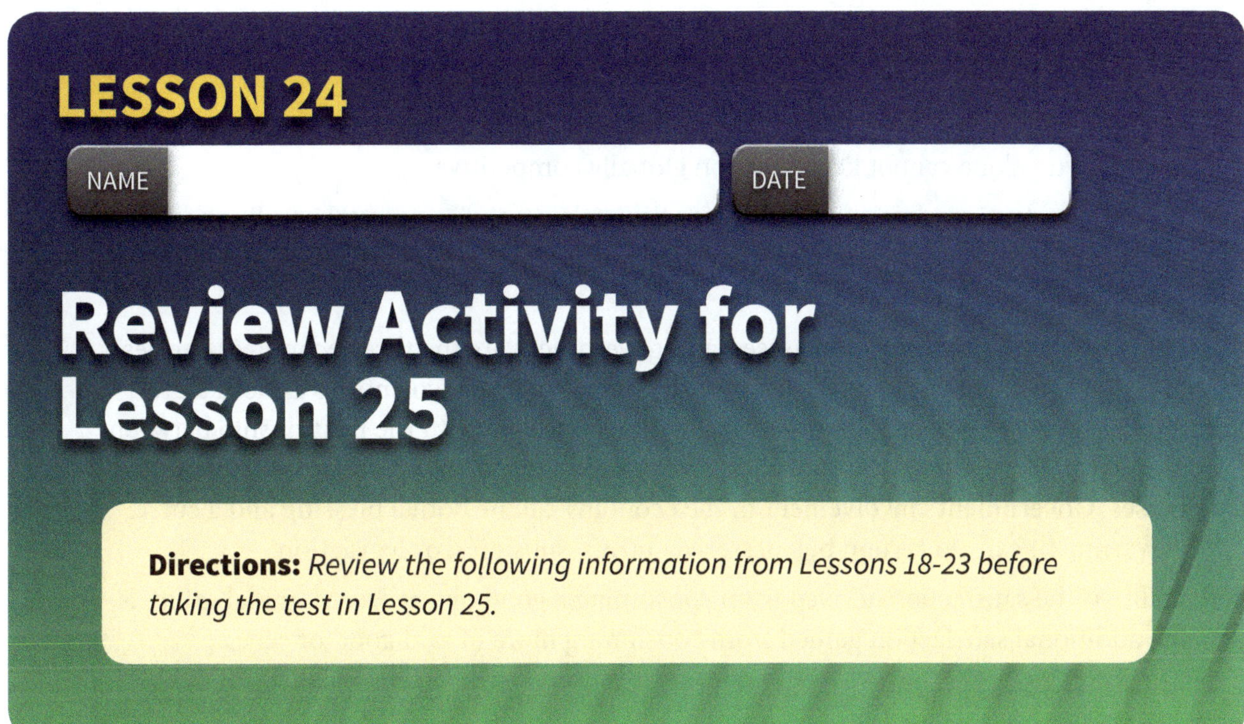

Review Activity for Lesson 25

Directions: *Review the following information from Lessons 18-23 before taking the test in Lesson 25.*

Scripture Memory

- **Matthew 6:33—**But seek ye first the kingdom of God, and His righteousness; and all these things shall be added unto you.

Concepts to Review

- Land, labor, capital, and entrepreneurship are the basic factors of production.
- Land is the earth in its natural state. Labor includes both physical and mental human effort. Capital refers to the machines, tools, and buildings that help us produce wealth. An entrepreneur plays two roles in a free-market economy: he takes a risk in starting a business and he must try to predict consumer wants and needs.
- Goods and services involve varying mixes of the factors of production.
- Its intended use determines if a good is a capital good or a consumer good.
- Production possibility frontiers show all possible combinations of two uses of a factor of production.
- Labor-intensive production relies on man's physical effort, while capital-intensive production takes advantage of technology.
- Cost schedules help entrepreneurs determine the optimum level of production for their business.
- Transfer earnings and economic rent help us efficiently utilize the factors of production.
- Increased productivity helps a nation maintain its standard of living and compete in a global economic environment.
- Productivity can improve using division of labor, technology, and specialization.

- Absolute and comparative advantage helps individuals, business firms, and nations increase their productivity.
- Technology can help and hinder productivity.
- Productivity alone cannot keep a nation globally competitive.
- Because it takes into account the impact of capital and environmental conditions, multifactor productivity provides a better indication of productivity than does labor productivity.
- Households (individuals), businesses, and government are the three economic entities found in every society. Each entity interacts with the other two entities as both a producer and a consumer. Government regulations interfere with the relationship between households and businesses, and taxes siphon away revenue from households and businesses. Government's involvement in the economy can be both a blessing and a curse. Government can aid certain businesses via tariffs, subsidies, or legislation.
- Utility is the satisfaction derived from consuming a good or service. Marginal utility is the additional satisfaction gained from consuming more of said good or service.
- Advertising aims to get consumers to utilize goods and services. Effective advertising motivates consumers to move from mere utility to marginal utility.
- Diminishing marginal utility is a short-run consequence. Time negates diminishing marginal utility.

Practical Application

- Develop a production possibility frontier for a 20′ x 30′ section of your backyard.

The test for Lesson 25 is located in the assessments section on page 235.

NAME DATE

Lesson 26 Oral History Project: *History of a Business, Part III*

Grading: *See answer key for grading rubric.*

Objective: *Using the previously completed written transcript, the student will write a two- to three- page paper on the history of a business.*

In this final phase of the history of a business project, use the completed transcript to write a two- to three-page narrative on the business. The transcript has all the information you need to complete the project. Since the thoughts and ideas for the paper are already in the transcript, you can take this opportunity to improve your writing skills. Focus on using action verbs, varying your sentence structure, minimizing passive voice, and incorporating a healthy dose of adjectives and adverbs. Read the sample paper on the following pages before commencing with this assignment.

History of Willie's Whirly-Gigs

Wilber Williams, founder and owner of Willie's Whirly-Gigs, started his business as a part-time venture in 1997. An office worker for a multinational corporation, Wilber wanted to free himself from the slavery of the computer screen to pursue his passion full time. A woodworking business would enable him to set his own hours and be his own boss. Working with his hands to create beautiful objects was a nice change of pace and a great stress reliever from the pressures of the corporate world. His dream became a reality in 2008. He quit his office job and now supports his family with Willie's Whirly-Gigs.

Wilber's interest in woodworking began in junior high school. The shop teacher, Mr. Knot, noticed Willie's natural talent and nurtured his interest in the woodworking machinery. He challenged young Willie by giving him high school projects in seventh grade. Mr. Knot's interest in Wilber's talent motivated Willie to take shop courses throughout his high school career. He also worked as a finish carpenter's apprentice during his junior and senior years. Mr. Knot gave Willie quite the challenging senior project, knowing he was up to the task because of his extraordinary skill level. He built a grandfather clock for his parent's 25th wedding anniversary. Looking back at his high school experiences, Wilber credits the finish carpenter with teaching him a great deal about joinery, Victorian-style embellishments, and trim work. Quality work and attention to detail, hallmarks of Willie's Whirly-Gigs, can be traced to Mr. Knot's mantra that "it's the little things that matter."

Since he already owned a number of tools needed for his business, Wilber didn't need a great deal of capital to start his business. A $10,000 home equity loan enabled him to build a workshop addition on the back of his two-car garage. His Christmas bonus for 1997 went toward the purchase of a freestanding shed for lumber storage. With the workshop completed, Wilber still needed a joiner and a lathe before the grand opening. Wilber purchased these tools with the gift card that his wife gave him for his birthday.

In the early years of the business, Wilber produced mainly lawn ornamentation items and birdhouses—hence the name Willie's Whirly-Gigs, but he eventually expanded into other areas of production. He built doghouses until Dan's Deluxe Doghouses lured potential customers away with their fancy pooch palaces. Over the past decade, Wilber built furniture, kitchen cabinets, and many unique items such as reproductions of antique furniture or unusual decorative profiles used as trim in upscale homes. One of Willie's recent customers designed a coffee table. She brought him a sketch and Willie transformed her vision into reality. He still mass-produces whirly-gigs and birdhouses, but more and more of his business is custom work. Wilber welcomes the challenge of custom work, as it enables him to develop new woodworking skills.

Willie's all-time favorite project so far was the replication of wooden items for a local historic village. This challenge required him to research items from the 18th century and make faithful reproductions that are used on a daily basis at the historical site's living history museum. Wood barrels, wood buckets, and wood plates known as trenchers enable visitors to the museum to experience life in the 1700s. Crops from the village farm make their way to the barns and storage bins in two wagons Wilber built. Some of his other favorite projects reveal Willie's diverse woodworking talent. He built a large apple cider press for a local orchard. Several years ago Willie carved a totem pole for a customer fascinated with Native American artwork. Shortly after he started the business, a local contractor asked him to build custom doors for a multimillion-dollar mansion. Every interior door had two different wood veneers, and no two doors in the entire house were alike. He's currently researching the process of building horse-drawn wooden sleighs for a friend's new business venture.

Like any business, Willie's Whirly-Gigs faces daily challenges. Willie loves woodworking so much that it sometimes takes precedence over more important matters. His wife steps in and reminds him when he needs to rearrange his priorities. Getting large projects finished on time is another challenge. Willie vividly remembers trying to complete a bunch of kitchen cabinets in three weeks. He struggles to keep up with the paperwork, such as complying with new regulations. Sometimes he cannot get top-quality lumber. With several vendors selling his products at trade shows east of the Mississippi River, Willie must work some long days to supply them with inventory. His wife, who has a full-time job as a nurse, has to pack and ship Internet orders. Willie hopes to soon hire a relative part time to help fill these Internet orders.

Willie attributes his business success to the superior quality of his products and his willingness to take on any type of project. He doesn't cut corners or allow inferior products to leave his shop. He limits the number of orders for custom items so that he can do a quality job in a reasonable amount of time. As the sole employee, he doesn't have to worry about shoddy workmanship from others with less-demanding standards.

In about another decade, Willie plans to semi-retire to spend more time with his wife and grandkids. He wants to work no more than 20 hours per week. Before he puts away his woodworking equipment for good, Willie dreams about building a Victorian-style retirement home.

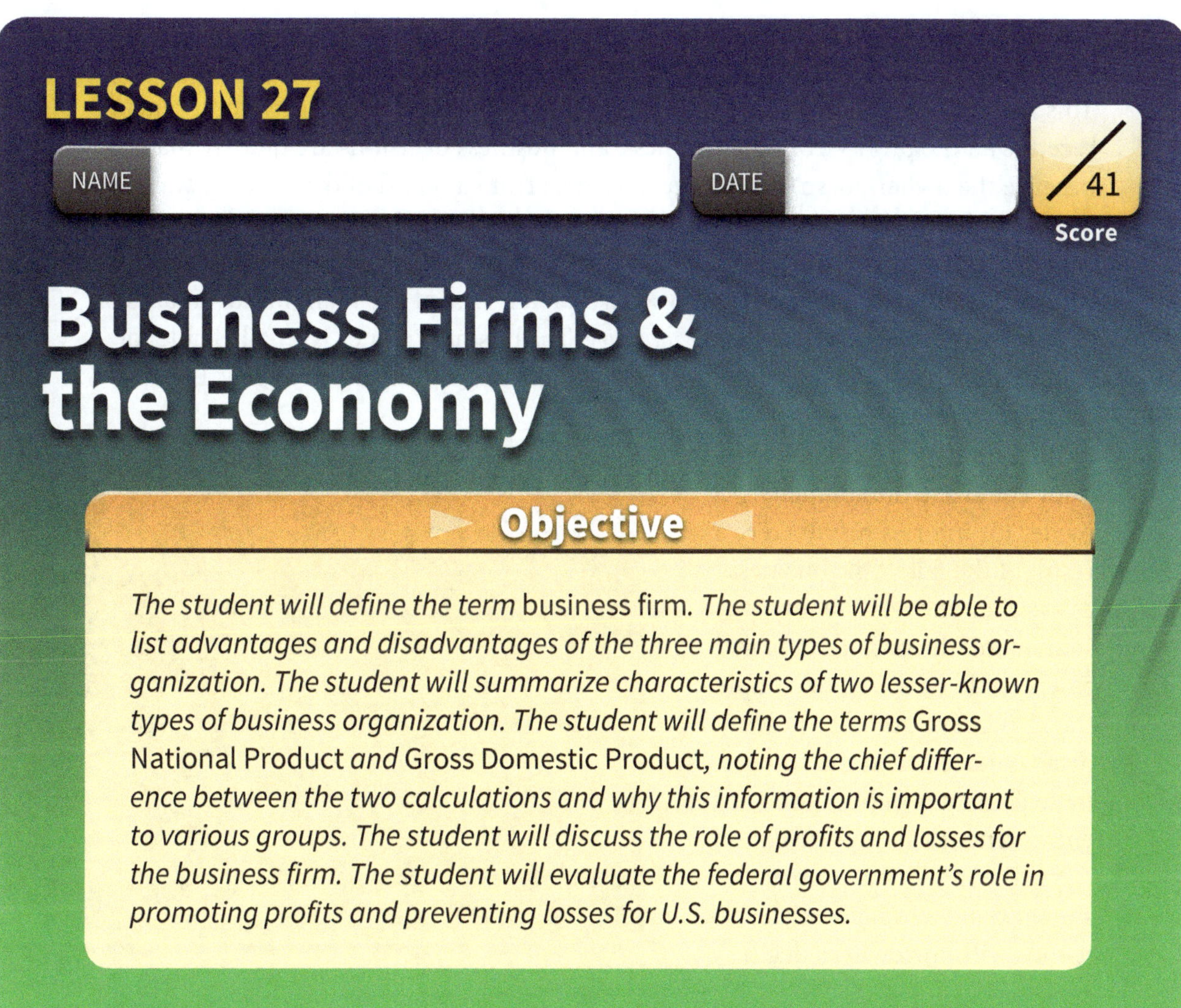

Business Firms & the Economy

Objective

The student will define the term business firm. *The student will be able to list advantages and disadvantages of the three main types of business organization. The student will summarize characteristics of two lesser-known types of business organization. The student will define the terms* Gross National Product *and* Gross Domestic Product, *noting the chief difference between the two calculations and why this information is important to various groups. The student will discuss the role of profits and losses for the business firm. The student will evaluate the federal government's role in promoting profits and preventing losses for U.S. businesses.*

Lesson 27A Reading

In the lessons on supply and demand, and on equilibrium price, we used the fictitious Happy Cola Company to illustrate these concepts. This microeconomic focus on a single business helped us understand how prices are established in a market economy. In this lesson, we'll look at business firms from a macroeconomic viewpoint—as players in our national and world economies. Let's begin by defining the term *business firm*.

According to Tom Rose, author of *Economics: Principles and Policy from a Christian Perspective*, a **business firm** is "any organization or entity that arranges the various factors of production to provide a good or service."[24] Business firms range from the child with the lemonade stand to the multinational corporation with thousands of employees. Large or small, business firms exist to meet consumer wants and needs. There are three main types of business organization: **individual proprietorships**, **partnerships**, and **corporations**.

[24] Rose, Tom. *Economics: Principles and Policy from a Christian Perspective*. American Enterprise Publications, 1996

The **individual** or **sole proprietorship** is the easiest and simplest method of starting a business. As its name implies, a single person owns an individual proprietorship. This has both advantages and disadvantages for the entrepreneur. The entrepreneur receives all the profits from the business, and business decisions are quickly made because the owner doesn't have to get approval from a board of directors or wait for a vote by shareholders at an annual meeting. On the other hand, the amount of capital available to expand the business depends on the business profits or the entrepreneur's collateral available to secure a loan. One of the main disadvantages of the sole proprietorship is *unlimited liability*. The business owner is legally liable for all actions of the company and any incidents related to company property. For instance, a customer who slips and falls on a wet retail establishment floor could sue the company owner for injuries sustained as a result of the fall. If the business assets cannot cover the injury settlement, the owner's personal assets could be seized to complete the settlement. Another potential disadvantage is that the company's management is only as good as the entrepreneur's ability and experience. The individual proprietorship also has a limited existence—it ends with the owner's death.

The **partnership** offers several advantages over the individual proprietorship. With two or more owners, a partnership has access to greater capital resources. With more collateral, the partnership can borrow larger sums of money to start or expand the business. Multiple owners potentially give the partnership better management skills and diversity compared to the individual proprietorship. A legal partnership, for instance, could have lawyers specializing in several specific aspects of the law, thus attracting a larger number of clients. On the other hand, partnerships have some disadvantages. If one member of the partnership dies or decides to leave, the partnership no longer exists as a business firm. Perhaps a more pressing reason not to enter into a partnership is that the partners are legally liable for each other's actions. If a doctor involved in a partnership makes a mistake during surgery, the patient could sue all the doctors in the partnership for medical malpractice.

The corporation offers advantages over both the individual proprietorship and the partnership. A **corporation** is a state-chartered business entity with legal rights as an entity separate from its owners.[25] Stated another way, a corporation is a separate legal entity that is owned by stockholders.[26] The important concept in these two definitions is that the corporation is a separate legal entity. It is similar to creating another person, except that this new person or entity is made up of other people.

---

[25] http://www.investorwords.com/1140/corporation.html

[26] http://www.morebusiness.com/getting_started/incorporating/d934832501.brc

This new "person" (the corporation) can get a loan, pay people, own property, have a separate bank account, and do many other things that individual people do. The corporation is like an individual proprietorship without many of the disadvantages of a sole proprietorship. For example, the individual proprietorship has limited means to finance its business venture—its access to capital being restricted by the owner's resources acting as collateral for a business loan. A corporation can issue shares of stock to investors, making them part owners of the corporation in exchange for monies to grow the business. Individual proprietorships also have unlimited liability—the business owner's personal assets are fair game if the company gets sued. Incorporation protects the company owners from personal liability for the company's actions (the corporate shield). British Petroleum (BP) investors could not be held personally liable for the *Deepwater Horizon* accidental oil spill in the Gulf of Mexico from April to July, 2010. The government or plaintiffs desiring to sue BP for damages resulting from the oil spill could not go after the personal assets of shareholders of BP stock. Shareholders could lose their investment dollars if BP stock plunged or the company declared bankruptcy as a result of the accident, but their homes, vehicles, bank savings accounts, etc., could not be confiscated to compensate those bringing the lawsuit. The corporation also has an unlimited time span of existence—not subject to dissolution at its founder's death. Large corporations can also afford to pay exorbitant salaries and benefits to professional managers for their company.

One disadvantage the corporation has in relationship to the two other major forms of business organization is taxation. General corporations and close corporations must pay business taxes, and their shareholders pay taxes on dividends (earnings) they receive from the corporation. "S" corporations avoid this double taxation by allowing all income (or losses) to be reported on the shareholder's personal income tax return. However, there are important IRS guidelines and restrictions for S corporations. Other corporate disadvantages include a slower decision-making process, as major decisions about the company might need to wait until the next board of directors' meeting or the annual shareholders' meeting, and there are more government rules and regulations to follow.

There are several other recognized types of business organizations in the United States. Too detailed for purposes of our survey course, let's briefly mention just two of these other forms of organization. A **cooperative (co-op)** is a business organization owned and controlled equally by the people who use its services or by the people who work there. Those involved in the cooperative have a vested interest in its success. Cooperatives often benefit from bulk purchasing, passing the savings on to their members. Agricultural, utility, and credit unions are some of the more popular types of cooperatives in the United States. The **Limited Liability Company** (**LLC**) is similar to an S corporation but without all of the Internal Revenue Service rules and regulations. Like the S corporation, an LLC can avoid double taxation by reporting all its income or losses on its shareholders' personal income tax returns. You can be the sole owner of a corporation (an S-corp, LLC, or other form of corporation) and have the advantages of a sole proprietorship while still limiting your liability.

Review Questions

Directions: *Answer the following questions based on the Lesson 27A reading.*

1. What is a business firm? *(1 point)*

2. Why do business firms exist? *(1 point)*

3. Which type of business is the easiest and simplest to start? *(1 point)*

4. What are some disadvantages inherent in the sole proprietorship? *(2 points)*

5. What would be a major disadvantage for a medical partnership? *(2 points)*

6. How does a corporation avoid unlimited liability? *(2 points)*

7. What disadvantage does a general corporation have compared to a sole proprietorship? How does an S corporation avoid this disadvantage? *(3 points)*

8. What is a cooperative? *(1 point)*

____

____

____

____

9. Which form of business organization (S corporation or Limited Liability Company) has fewer Internal Revenue Service regulations? *(1 point)*

____

____

____

Lesson 27B Reading

Business firms play an important role in the macroeconomic concepts of **Gross National Product** (GNP) and **Gross Domestic Product** (GDP). Both concepts measure the total value of goods and services produced for final sale during a year. GNP includes U.S. firms operating outside the geographic boundaries of the United States, while GDP excludes U.S. firms manufacturing in foreign countries but does include foreign firms manufacturing in the United States. GDP is the more commonly used measure of a nation's output. GNP is becoming less and less relevant due to the international nature of many large firms. For example, Toyota was long considered a Japanese company, but they employ tens of thousands of people in the United States and sell cars worldwide. GNP would not count Toyota, but GDP would count those economic activities that occurred within U.S. borders.

The U.S. Commerce Department's Bureau of Economic Analysis reports GDP in both current dollars and constant dollars. The constant dollars amount, adjusted for inflation, allows for valid comparisons between time periods. The information is published quarterly for the previous quarter and released in three stages. The initial estimate is followed by a revised preliminary report. Revisions to the preliminary report result in a final report released about two months after the initial report.

GDP growth is one measure of a nation's economic health. When GDP is used in conjunction with unemployment and inflation information, GDP analysts can evaluate fluctuations in the business cycle, noting periods of business expansion or decline. Governments use this information to pursue policies that they believe will encourage continuing economic growth. Investors use this information to alter their investment strategy and their portfolios. Consumers use this information to make purchasing and borrowing decisions.

Review Questions

Directions: *Answer the following questions based on the Lesson 27B reading.*

1. Explain the difference between Gross National Product and Gross Domestic Product. *(2 points)*

____

____

____

____

2. Why is the GDP measurement in constant dollars more accurate than the GDP measurement using current dollars? *(2 points)*

____

____

____

3. Besides GDP figures, what other measurements help economists evaluate the nation's economic health? *(2 points)*

____

____

____

Lesson 27C Reading

With the exception of nonprofit organizations, individual proprietorships, partnerships, and corporations are in business for one reason—to make money (**profit**). Even business decisions that appear counterproductive to the maximizing-profit motive, such as donations to a charitable organization, may enable the business to receive a tax deduction or create goodwill with the public, resulting in future sales. Profits in a market economy signal that the entrepreneur or business firm is meeting consumer wants and needs. Profits are the rewards for providing a good or service that people want or need.

There are several methods of measuring profits. The simplest and easiest to understand is profit as a **percentage of sales**. The formula for this method is gross sales minus operating costs. Last year, Linda's Luscious Lemonade had $80,000 in gross sales receipts. Linda's operating expenses totaled $71,000, leaving her with $9,000 in profit or 11.25 percent of total sales. Not bad for a 10-year-old with a sidewalk lemonade stand trying to start a college fund.

A second method of calculating profit is **percentage of invested capital**. This method divides the profit by the investment needed to start the business. If Linda used $27,000 of her own money to start the lemonade business, she received a 33.3

percent return based on percentage of invested capital. This is the best method for measuring profits to assure the most efficient allocation of capital resources. If Linda could make more money selling slushies, she should quit the lemonade business and offer her customers slushies instead. Linda's Luscious Slushies has a nice ring to it, don't you think?

A third method of calculating profit is **percentage of ownership equity**. This method takes the profit minus interest payments on borrowed money, then divides it by the amount of money invested. Suppose Linda had to borrow the $27,000 needed to start her lemonade stand. She went to her parents' credit union and borrowed the entire $27,000 at 6 percent interest to be paid back over a 10-year time span. Linda's parents co-signed for her loan using the equity in their home. Her monthly payment (which is part of the business operating expenses) comes to $299.76. In her first year of business, Linda paid $1,299.73 in interest on the loan. Using the formula to calculate profit as a percentage of ownership equity yields the following results.

$$9{,}000 - 1{,}299.73 = 7700.27/27{,}000 = 28.5\%$$

Still not a bad rate of return for a preteen investment! Assuming that business stays the same or continues to grow, Linda should have a nice nest egg put aside for college by the time she graduates from high school.

These methods of measuring profit are *objective* measurements—in other words, they are measurable in terms of dollars and cents. Before we end our discussion of profit, we need to look at the *subjective* side of profit. Subjective profit, like value, exists in the mind, and thus is not measurable in the same way as monetary profit. For instance, why would a person choose to invest in a certificate of deposit (CD) at their local bank rather than in the stock market? The stock market has the potential for significantly greater profits compared to the CD. However, if the stock market declines and then crashes, an investor could lose their initial investment principal and any previous gains earned before the market collapsed. The CD pays much less interest but is guaranteed up to $250,000 by the Federal Deposit Insurance Corporation or the National Credit Union Administration. An investor wary of the stock market might subjectively value the lower rate of return more than the volatility of stocks. The author's landlady for 13 years, who lived through the Great Depression, had this mindset. All of her investments were in government-guaranteed securities. A business owner might help a missionary financially without such help benefiting the business in any way. Such a contribution to the Lord's work is another example of subjective profit at work in the mind of the donor.

As you're probably aware of from personal observation, not every business in the United States turns a profit. Some businesses lose money and eventually go out of business. **Losses** in a free-market economy warn entrepreneurs that they are not meeting consumer wants and needs. Losses signal a need for change—either improve the current business or invest your labor and capital elsewhere. In the town where the author currently lives, there is a quaint little restaurant building on Broad Street (the main thoroughfare through downtown) that cannot keep a business in the building for more than several months or a year at a time. The restaurants attract some customers but not enough to stay in business—they have terrific food (the author has eaten at all of them while they were in business), great service, and reasonable prices, but the number of customers cannot cover building rent, food and labor costs, and miscellaneous expenses. Various entrepreneurs have tried and failed at this location, so it's probably not a lack of business knowledge contributing to the string of failures. As part of the activities for this lesson, you'll be evaluating this business location for potential reasons why the property frequently sits vacant.

Some profits are the result of government intervention in the economy such as through subsidies or advantages extended to certain businesses. The U.S. government in 1816 passed the first of several **protective tariffs** designed to help fledgling U.S. industries in the northern states compete with manufactured goods from Great Britain. Congress revised the tariff in 1824. As part of a political ploy to discredit President John Quincy Adams and get Andrew Jackson elected president in 1828, John C. Calhoun introduced legislation for still higher tariff rates. The plan backfired when northern and western senators passed the bill in spite of high tariffs on imported raw materials needed by northern industries. Nicknamed the Tariff of Abominations by southern states needing to export their cotton to British textile mills, the 1828 tariff created a constitutional crisis when South Carolina proposed nullification of the tariff. The Compromise Tariff of 1833 resolved the immediate crisis but not the tariff controversy. In this situation, the U.S. government promoted the industrial interests of the northern states at the expense of the agrarian interests of the southern states. Throughout our nation's history, the federal government has succumbed to political pressure from special-interest groups to promote or protect their economic success. Farm **subsidies** are another example of this favoritism. The U.S. government pays some farmers not to plant crops in order to prop up agricultural profits. In an article entitled "Agricultural Subsidies," Chris Edwards claims that the U.S. government spends $15 billion to $35 billion annually assisting 800,000 agricultural producers (mostly large-scale enterprises) in the form of direct cash payments, subsidized crop insurance, market support, and other farm-related services.[27] On the other hand, laws preventing *restraint of trade* (contracts or combinations that tend, or are designed, to eliminate or stifle competition, create a monopoly, artificially maintain prices, or otherwise hamper or obstruct the course of trade as it would be carried on if it were left to the control of natural economic forces)[28] are a good thing. Such laws create an even playing field for new businesses to enter the marketplace and compete with existing businesses.

Of greater concern than government policies that protect or promote business profits is government intervention in the economy to prevent business losses. In 1970, the U.S. Congress refused a financial aid package for the struggling Penn

---

[27] http://www.downsizinggovernment.org/agriculture/subsidies June 2009

[28] http://legal-dictionary.thefreedictionary.com/Restraint+of+Trade

Central Railroad. After Penn Central declared bankruptcy, Congress provided the railroad company with over $676 million in loan guarantees. In 1976, the federal government combined six failing railroad companies (including Penn Central) into Consolidated Rail (Conrail). Consolidated Rail finally started turning a profit in 1981, and in 1987, the U.S. government sold the now-profitable company for less than $4 billion. The federal government spent almost $20 billion to bail out the unprofitable railroads. In 1979, the U.S. Congress passed the Chrysler Corporation Loan Guarantee Act—in essence providing a $1.5 billion taxpayer-backed loan to the nation's third-largest automaker. Supporters of the measure argued that the United States couldn't afford to let such a large employer go out of business, even if Chrysler wasn't providing the type of quality cars Americans wanted. This bailout established a precedent for such actions by the federal government—including a $25 billion loan package for General Motors, Ford, and Chrysler as part of the $650 billion spending package in 2008. The website http://www.propublica.org/special/government-bailouts has some interesting information and graphics on how the U.S. government over the past 40-plus years has come to the aid of ailing industries.

Should the U.S. government interfere in the economy to promote profits or prevent losses? Is it true that certain corporations are too big to fail? Adam Smith would roll over in his grave if he could see our capitalist economy in the 21st century. Even before the Great Depression, our national government began to intervene in the economy. Such intervention is needed in situations where a monopolistic corporation puts its employees in unsafe working conditions or provides unsafe merchandise to consumers. Intervention for these or similar reasons falls under the government's Romans 13 mandate to punish evildoers. However, today's government bailouts seem to promote evildoing, as unscrupulous corporate leaders play the system for their benefit. Sure, a few of them will get caught, and some of the guilty will pay hefty fines or go to jail for their crimes, but the risk of punishment doesn't deter the wrongdoing entirely. American taxpayers and investors must repeatedly foot the bill for the greed and corruption of a few. It's no wonder Marxism had such an impact when it appeared on the scene in the mid-19th century. A classless society in which the economic pie is equally divided has a justifiable appeal to the masses suffering for the wrongdoing of others. Seeing evil triumph over good makes the Christian long for the righteous reign of the Prince of Peace.

Review Questions

Directions: *Answer the following questions based on the Lesson 27C reading.*

1. What is the basic assumption about most business firms? *(1 point)*

2. What do profits signal? *(1 point)*

3. List and explain the three methods of measuring profits. *(3 points)* Which method focuses on the efficient investment of capital? *(1 point)*

4. Give an example of a business decision based on subjective profit rather than objective profit. *(3 points)*

5. Losses in a free-market economy send what kind of message to entrepreneurs? *(1 point)*

6. Do you agree or disagree with the federal government's decision to combine the failing Penn Central Railroad with several other struggling railroads to form Conrail? Why or why not? *(5 points)*

7. As part of the North American Free Trade Agreement (NAFTA), the National Park Service regulates amenities available in U.S. national parks. U.S., Canadian, or Mexican businesses wishing to provide these kinds of services in our national parks must obtain a concession from the National Park Service. Making application is no guarantee that the Park Service will grant such a concession or that U.S.-based companies providing these services will be given preference over similar Canadian or Mexican companies. Read the following excerpt from the NAFTA document before answering the following questions.

> "A concession is required to operate hotels, restaurants, gift shops, snack bars, equipment rentals, horseback riding services, guide services, fishing guide services, mountain climbing services, bus transportation and other services in U.S. national parks. The National Park Service regulates all aspects of these services, including building specifications, rates for the services, and hours of operation.
>
> "The National Park Service awards concessions only where they are determined to be 'necessary and appropriate'. In developing its plans for the operation of a national park, the Park Service determines what operations, including concessions, are 'necessary and appropriate'. As a result of this determination, the Park Service may determine that a given concession is not needed."[29]

Is the concession policy in violation of laws preventing restraint of trade? *(4 points)*

____

____

____

____

____

____

____

Does the free-trade agreement give an unfair advantage to Canadian and Mexican companies in the granting of concessions? Would fear of litigation before NAFTA arbitrators influence National Park decision makers to bypass U.S. companies in favor of foreign firms? *(2 points)*

____

____

____

____

[29] North American Free Trade Agreement, Annex V Quantitative Restrictions, Schedule of the United States, Recreation

NAME

DATE

Practical Application Activity:
An Unprofitable Restaurant

Directions: *Using the LESSON 27 AN UNPROFITABLE RESTAURANT map and photos on page 166, answer the following questions.*

1. What problems for this business location can you detect by looking at the map and image on the next page? *(5 points)*

2. How does the building's downtown location hurt dinner sales? *(2 points)*

3. What factors enable the pizza place and the Chinese restaurant across the street to thrive? *(3 points)*

4. The county recently renovated the old train station across the street into a transportation hub and community center with secure parking. Could this downtown upgrade be the salvation of the unprofitable restaurant? *(3 points)*

5. Could the property owner be to blame for the ongoing business failures? Without perfect knowledge of the situation, we can only conjecture, but what might be some owner-related issues that would hurt an entrepreneur wishing to use the building as a restaurant? *(5 points)*

____

____

____

____

____

____

6. Complete the following statement. *(2 points)*

The unprofitable business location cannot make it because ______________ is too low and ______________ are too high.

An Unprofitable Restaurant

LESSON 28

NAME DATE

Score

Government & the Economy: Fiscal/Monetary Policy & the Federal Reserve System

Objective

The student will identify and explain the five parts of the business cycle. The student will list and define the two methods used to regulate the economy. The student will summarize the structure of the Federal Reserve System and explain the tools it uses to regulate the economy. The student will give reasons for government interference in the economy. The student will discuss potential consequences from the fiscal irresponsibility of the United States.

Lesson 28A Reading

In Lesson 6, you studied traditional, command, capitalist, and mixed economies. The United States has a mixed economy tending toward capitalism. However, our free-market-based economy does have a significant amount of government involvement in the economy, some of which is more harmful than helpful. In this lesson, we'll discuss the methods used by government to correct imbalances or alleged injustices in the economy and reasons for government interference in the economy.

Any market-based economy goes through the four stages of expansion and decline shown in Figure 28:1. The trend line shows average economic growth without the steeper ups and downs of real-life periods of expansion and recessions. Economists typically define a **recession** as two consecutive quarters with declining

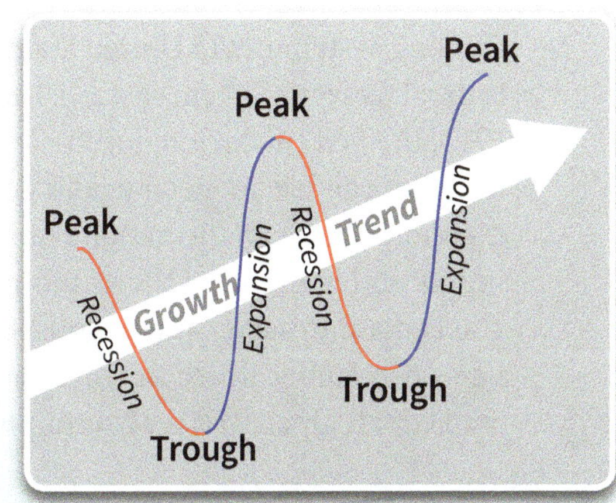

Figure 28:1 The Business Cycle

Gross Domestic Product (GDP). The **peak** marks the end of a period of **expansion**, while the **trough** signals the end of a recession. In other words, the economy tops out at a peak and bottoms out at a trough. Note that expansion and decline can occur both above and below the trend line.

The U.S. government cannot totally eliminate recessions and depressions (a depression being a prolonged period of severe economic decline), but since the Great Depression (1929 to World War II), it has tried to limit their impact and duration. Two methods used to regulate the economy are **fiscal policy** and **monetary policy**.

The term **fiscal policy** refers to government's taxing and spending policies. To stimulate demand in a sluggish economy, government can increase spending, cut taxes, or do some combination of both. This expansionary policy often creates budget deficits due to increased government spending and less tax revenue. Giving consumers more money to spend and businesses more money to invest should encourage production and promote demand for goods and services, but such government policies are risky, as they presume that consumers and businesses will behave a certain way with their increased income. The American Recovery and Reinvestment Act (2009) provided a federal tax credit of $400 per worker or $800 per couple for 2009 and 2010. Would nervous consumers, unsure about their economic futures, decide to save this money rather than spend it? If so, demand would remain stagnant, signaling the policy's failure to achieve the desired goal. The Social Security tax cut for 2011 was supposed to give most Americans $1,000 to $2,000 more in take-home pay. Economists hoped that the tax cut would bring about a better-than-projected growth rate for the struggling American economy. However, higher gas prices forced many consumers to spend that tax-cut money on fuel. Expansionary government policies might also contribute to inflation (a period of rising prices). Such inflation could wipe out any economic gains achieved by the government's fiscal policy. Government could also use fiscal policy to control inflation. Raising taxes would reduce consumers' net spendable income, thus putting the brakes on overall demand in the economy.

A second method used to control the economy is **monetary policy**. Monetary policy is "the regulation of the money supply and interest rates by a central bank, such as the Federal Reserve Board in the United States, in order to control inflation and stabilize currency."[30] Through the central banking system in the United States (the Federal Reserve System) established in 1913, the Fed (nickname for the Federal Reserve) can use monetary policy to expand or contract the nation's money supply and manipulate the economy. The Federal Reserve System consists of a seven-member Board of Governors, the Federal Open Market Committee,

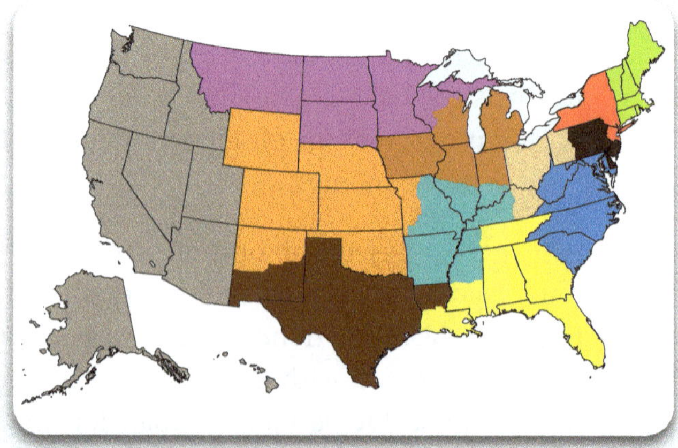

Figure 28:2 Federal Reserve Districts

[30] http://www.investorwords.com/3097/monetary_policy.html#ixzz1O8QCVzkU

and 12 Federal Reserve Banks (one for each of the 12 Federal Reserve districts). Members of the Board of Governors are appointed by the President and confirmed by the U.S. Senate. The Federal Open Market Committee (FOMC) consists of the Board of Governors and five presidents of the Federal Reserve Banks. Figure 28:2 shows the districts of the Federal Reserve Banks.

The Fed has three tools at its disposal affecting monetary policy: **open market operations**, the **discount rate**, and **reserve requirements**. Open market operations involve the purchases and sales of U.S. Treasury and federal agency securities. This is the principal means by which the Fed implements monetary policy.[31] To take money out of circulation, the Fed sells U.S. government securities. To put money back into the economy, the Fed buys back securities from the purchasers.

The discount rate is the interest rate charged to commercial banks and other depository institutions on loans they receive from their regional Federal Reserve Bank's lending facility—the discount window.[32] The Federal Reserve offers three different levels of credit to the financial institutions needing to use this monetary policy tool.

Reserve requirements are the amount of funds that a depository institution must hold in reserve against specified deposit liabilities.[33] Let's take a closer look at this tool of monetary policy—the Federal Reserve requirement or reserve ratio—to see how this tool is used to expand or contract the money supply.

The Federal Reserve requires commercial U.S. banks to have a certain percentage of their deposits available as cash or liquid assets (assets easily converted into cash). The banks must have these funds in their vaults or on deposit with a Federal Reserve Bank in order to cash paychecks or give five-year-old Johnny $10 in cash from his savings account so he can buy his mom a birthday present. This policy creates what is known as a *fractional reserve* banking system. Let's suppose that the Dewey, Cheatum & Howe Bank currently has $100 million on deposit from its customers. If the reserve ratio is 10 percent, the bank must keep $10,000,000 in cash in its vault or on deposit with a Federal Reserve Bank. Dewey, Cheatum & Howe may loan out the remaining $90,000,000 to customers interested in buying an automobile, building a house, or starting a business. If the Federal Reserve wants to expand the money supply, they could drop the reserve ratio to 8 percent. D, C & H Bank would then need to keep $8,000,000 on reserve, giving it $92,000,000 available for loans. Dewey, Cheatum & Howe would drop its loan interest rates to entice consumers to take advantage of the $2,000,000 expanded money supply. If the Federal Reserve wants to contract the money supply, they could raise the reserve ratio to 12 percent. In that case, the bank would need to keep $12,000,000 in cash on hand. Dewey will have to attract more depositors while curtailing all loan activity to meet the higher reserve ratio or call in some of its outstanding loans in order to meet the Federal Reserve requirement. Either way effectively reduces the money supply by eliminating new loans or reducing the number of outstanding loans.

---

[31] http://www.federalreserve.gov/monetarypolicy/openmarket.htm

[32] http://www.federalreserve.gov/monetarypolicy/discountrate.htm

[33] http://www.federalreserve.gov/monetarypolicy/reservereq.htm

The Fed uses the reserve ratio and the other tools in its monetary policy arsenal to regulate the economy via manipulation of the money supply (the total amount of money in circulation in a country at a given time). *Expansionary monetary policy* can stimulate the economy during times of recession or depression. *Contractionary monetary policy* helps to slow down the rate of inflation by reducing the amount of money available in the economy.

Monetary policy should not be confused with **monetizing the debt** (when the government attempts to pay off its debts by printing more money). Politicians not willing to control spending or raise taxes to cover the growing costs of government programs might view monetizing the debt as a less-painful political solution for the problem of government debt. However, monetizing the debt causes hyperinflation (a period of rapidly rising prices as the money supply outstrips the amount of durable goods and services for sale). During the American Revolution, the Continental Congress printed paper money that quickly lost its value, leading to the expression "not worth a continental." Germany experienced hyperinflation shortly after World War I. The Weimar Republic's decision to print more money to meet its obligations led to unbelievable prices for goods and services from July 1922 until November 1923. The commemorative medal on this page contains prices for three common items in Germany on November 1, 1923. One pound of bread cost 3 billion marks. One pound of meat sold for 36 billion marks, and one glass of beer cost the consumer 4 billion marks. German workers received their wages three times per day in order to make purchases before the next round of price increases. Imagine living in Germany during that time period and going out to eat at your favorite restaurant. There are no prices on the menu because the cost of your meal may change from the time you place your order until you finish eating. No wonder Germans used the currency as wallpaper or kindling to light the wood stove. God help us not to make the same mistakes in this country and suffer a similar economic catastrophe.

Review Questions

Directions: *Answer the following questions based on the Lesson 28A reading.*

1. Draw and label a diagram of the business cycle. *(5 points)*

2. Explain the difference between a recession and a depression. *(2 points)*

3. Define "fiscal policy." *(1 point)*

4. Will decreasing taxes always end a recession? Why or why not? *(3 points)*

5. What is the Federal Reserve System? *(1 point)*

6. List and define the three parts of the Federal Reserve System. *(3 points)*

7. What is the principal means by which the Fed regulates the U.S. economy? *(1 point)*

8. What happens to the reserve ratio if the Fed wants to use it to expand the money supply? *(2 points)*

9. Is the U.S. government's burgeoning deficit spending a cause for alarm? *(5 points)*

Lesson 28B Reading

Why do government leaders meddle with the economy? One reason political leaders interfere with a free-market economy is to *maintain economic growth*. As discussed in the previous section, capitalist (free-market) economies are subject to periodic economic declines. Politicians anxious about their approval ratings and re-election chances will try to maintain a satisfactory rate of economic growth or minimize the duration and consequences of a recession or depression.

Another reason for government interference in the economy is to *control inflation*. Excess demand and rising production costs cause inflation. If the demand for goods and services exceeds supply, then prices rise to bump some consumers out of the market at the moment. Remember our beachfront property illustration in Lesson 10? Limited supply coupled with high demand causes a potential shortage of this type of property. Price is the mechanism by which we regulate this scarce commodity. Rising production costs also fuel inflation. If businesses cannot absorb these costs under their current production arrangement, the higher production costs get passed on to consumers in the form of higher prices. With less purchasing power, workers will demand higher wages. The increased paycheck costs must be passed on to consumers as still higher prices. If the process continues, market economies face the prospect of a wage-price spiral that could lead to the previously mentioned situation of hyperinflation. Inflation affects people on fixed incomes by reducing their purchasing power. It also erodes the value of savings accounts, so politicians try to keep inflation in check.

A third reason for government's economic meddling is to *correct economic inequalities*. President Lyndon Johnson's 1965 Executive Order 11246 (E.O. 11246) prohibits federal contractors and subcontractors and federally assisted construction contractors and subcontractors that generally have contracts that exceed $10,000 from discriminating in employment decisions on the basis of race, color, religion, sex, or national origin. It also requires covered contractors to take affirmative action to ensure that equal opportunity is provided in all aspects of their employment.[34] This policy purports to end discriminatory hiring practices for federally funded construction projects.

Some political decisions, however, are counterproductive to a nation's economic well-being. During the 1960s, the United States tried to fight a war in Vietnam and implement social programs without raising taxes. American political leaders and the American public used deficit spending to finance the war effort and fund newly popular entitlement programs like Medicare benefits (Social Security Act of 1965).

---

[34] http://www.dol.gov/compliance/laws/comp-eeo.htm

These deficits, coupled with rising energy prices and high unemployment in the mid-1970s, led to double-digit inflation during President Carter's tenure (1977-1981). In order to understand why some political decisions have harmful economic consequences, we must recognize a fundamental difference between politics and a free-market economy. The political realm operates on the basis of coercion, while a true free-market economy works because of voluntary exchange. This dichotomy in the way the two spheres operate gives lawmakers an unfair advantage, encouraging government leaders to "throw their weight around" to keep the U.S. economic ball rolling. In reality, these coercive policies may do more harm than good. The speculative U.S. housing bubble, which began to burst in 2007 and led to the financial crisis of 2008, was partially caused by government policies encouraging subprime mortgage loans to individuals who were not qualified for such loans. As housing prices began to decline (in many cases, home values dropped below the outstanding loan amount) and homeowners with adjustable-rate mortgages had to refinance at higher interest rates, loan defaults and foreclosures increased dramatically. This led to a U.S. government bailout of major U.S. financial institutions to prevent a worldwide financial markets collapse.

Review Questions

Directions: *Answer the following questions based on the Lesson 28B reading.*

1. List three reasons government leaders meddle with the economy. *(3 points)*

____

____

____

____

2. How does excess demand contribute to inflation? *(2 points)*

____

____

____

3. Why are rising production costs inflationary? *(2 points)*

____

____

____

____

4. How do rising gasoline prices affect everyone, not just motorists? *(2 points)*

____

____

Lesson 28C Reading

Can we as a nation continue to live beyond our means and get away with it? Certainly not! In an April 6, 2011, radio call-in program, the show's host commented on a Congressional Budget Office (the non-partisan watchdog of federal spending) report that unless the United States gets its spending under control, the nation would be bankrupt by the year 2037. In the same talk-show segment, the host mentioned that as of spring 2011, China held 16 percent of the U.S. debt, and that the United States would be unable to pay up should China call in these loans.[35] In an online article, Tom Murse disputes that percentage, claiming that China only holds about 8 percent of the U.S. debt.[36] In a related article, Kimberly Amadeo states that as of mid-July 2012, China holds over $1.1 trillion of our $16 trillion U.S. debt—an analysis closer to Mr. Murse's data. [37] Those are staggering statistics! Our nation's fiscal irresponsibility will result in an economic collapse unless we get our financial house in order. The Tea Party movement, which led to Republican control of the U.S. House of Representatives in the 2010 election, is attempting to cut spending and balance the federal budget, but their efforts are being hampered by the war on terror, colleagues who would rather raise taxes than reduce spending on popular government programs, and special-interest groups who currently benefit from the present arrangement. The problem, as this author perceives it, revolves around the size of the national government and its role in the economy. Until we reduce our national government to its biblical responsibilities or, failing that, to its 1787 constitutional responsibilities, we'll be unable to significantly slash spending. Most Americans receive certain benefits or advantages from the government, and we're perfectly willing for Congress to exercise fiscal restraint as long as it doesn't interfere with our piece of the economic pie being doled out from Washington, D.C.

Our current economic plight should remind us that "some trust in chariots, and some in horses, but we will remember the name of the LORD our God. (Psalm 20:7) David knew that man's devices could fail, but the Holy One of Israel is forever faithful. In Psalm 37:25, David declared, "I have been young, and now am old; yet have I not seen the righteous forsaken, nor his seed begging bread." Like David, Americans in the 21st century need more of God's assurance and less of man's insurance. Where is your trust—in God or in man?

---

35 "Janet Parschel Show," Moody Radio, as heard on WCRF, Cleveland, OH 103.3 FM

36 http://usgovinfo.about.com/od/moneymatters/ss/How-Much-US-Debt-Does-China-Own.htm

37 http://useconomy.about.com/od/monetarypolicy/f/Who-Owns-US-National-Debt.htm

Review Questions

Directions: *Answer the following questions based on the Lesson 28C reading.*

1. Why can the national government get away with deficit spending, while state and local governments must balance their budgets? *(2 points)*

2. Would raising taxes without reducing government spending resolve our economic difficulties? Why or why not? *(3 points)*

3. Do you believe Congress should ban special-interest groups from lobbying the federal government? Would this be a good idea or a bad change in policy? Explain your position on this issue and give examples to support your opinion. *(8 points)*

4. Are you encouraged or discouraged by the current economic climate of the United States? Why? *(5 points)*

NAME

DATE

Practical Application Activity: *Health Care Reform*

Grading: *See answer key for grading rubric.*

Background

In 2010, the U.S. Congress passed a health care reform bill popularly known as Obamacare. More than two decades before the passage of this legislation, Mr. Spickler and his economics students discussed and debated their own health care reform proposals. Below is the summary of their ongoing dialogue.

Directions: *Prepare for a discussion with your school supervisor by reading the proposed health care benefits system. Use a highlighter to mark those statements or sections of the document with which you disagree. Use a different-colored highlighter to distinguish those portions of the document that you like. Jot down reasons why you agree or disagree with specific statements or proposals in preparation for the discussion with your school supervisor.*

Proposal
Health Care Benefits System

The Need

The debate over health care reform in the United States illustrates both the need for reform and continuation of those institutions that have made our health care system the greatest in the world. The failed expectations of the Canadian and European nationalized health care systems should discourage us from implementing reforms that would grant the U.S. government greater control over health care or make it the major provider of health care services. A desire to grant complete health care coverage to every individual but the inability to fund such coverage using both private and public funds leads to unfulfilled expectations. Without tax increases or even more deficit spending, the federal government cannot provide universal health coverage. The only sustainable solution is to completely privatize health care and relegate the federal government to a regulatory role. Through radical reform of the existing system, we propose to make health care affordable for all Americans, even when it involves paying for it out of their own pockets.

The Plan

The first step in the process requires making health care a not-for-profit industry. This doesn't mean that doctors and nurses will be paid less than they deserve, or that we won't spend money on medical research to discover new medications or develop new medical equipment and treatments. We must remove all medical-related goods and services from the publically traded realm, including pharmaceutical companies and health insurance providers. By doing so, we will prove that the patient is more important than an investor's pocketbook. This will be a big step toward controlling health care costs that seem to increase faster than the rate of inflation.

At the same time, we must eliminate harmful chemicals from our agricultural practices and prepackaged foods—things that contribute to illness and disease. "An apple a day keeps the doctor away" is not true if the person eating apples consumes pesticide residue in the process. The human body thrives on unadulterated healthy foods. Ingredients found to have short-term or long-term harmful health effects must be immediately eliminated from food processing.

Next, we propose to eliminate the status quo monopoly of the existing system. Patients will be free to use naturopathic or other options. Cancer patients are currently denied or not informed about alternative treatments that have a proven track record of curing the disease rather than simply delaying the onset of death. Under this proposal, patients will be given even more options and control in selecting treatment options. Competition from herbal remedies and supplements will bring needed reform to pharmaceutical companies and lower prescription costs.

Having implemented the above-mentioned reforms vital to the success of the health care benefits system, we can then enact into law the actual proposal.

The Proposal

Congress will no longer be a health care provider. Medicare and Medicaid will be phased out as the new health care system takes effect.

All routine medical care (office visits, physicals, lab tests, optical and dental) will be paid for out of each family's health savings account. Employers and individuals can contribute unlimited monies each year tax-free to their health savings account. Health insurance will only be offered for catastrophic conditions (hospitalization, disease, or serious injuries).

Since individual health needs vary, consumers will be offered a choice of benefits rather than a "one-size-fits-all" package. Competing companies will offer the consumer five types of coverage with five different copayment amounts. These copayments only apply when using the health benefits coverage. Remember, all routine care must be paid out of pocket by the consumer using their health savings account. The consumer initiates the process of acquiring a health benefits package by completing a standardized application used by every company offering the health benefits insurance. Employers will no longer offer health insurance as part of a benefits package for their employees, but they may compensate their employees in whole or in part for the cost of the health benefits package. Consumers may use their health savings account monies to purchase their health benefits insurance. Upon receipt of the application and initial premium payment, the health insurer issues the insured a health benefits insurance photo-ID card. A combination of letters and numbers notifies the health care provider of the various benefits the cardholder selected. Letters on the consumer's health benefits card identify the copayment amounts for services rendered.

A: no copayments
B: 10% copayment
C: 20% copayment
D: 25% copayment
E: 50% copayment

Numbers on the card represent types of coverage provided.

1. Limited hospitalization and surgical benefits
2. Extended hospitalization and surgical benefits
3. Family plan/pregnancy
4. Catastrophic illness
5. Psychological or addiction treatment

Minimal insurance coverage will be available to all Americans based on its affordability. No one will be forced to purchase insurance until they can no longer afford to pay out-of-pocket for health care services. For instance, an individual breaks a leg and cannot pay for the emergency room visit and the follow-up care through their health savings account. At such a point in time, said individual must make payment arrangements for the care received plus purchase a level of insurance at least equal to the type of care they received and continue to carry that coverage until that level of coverage is no longer able to cover their medical expenses. An individual with #1 (limited hospitalization and surgical benefits) that is diagnosed with cancer must upgrade their policy to #4 (catastrophic illness). Individuals who cannot afford coverage are encouraged to seek out private charity to assist them in obtaining initial coverage or maintaining existing coverage. Coverage may be rescinded for non-payment of premium for three (3) consecutive months, at which time the patient forfeits the right to use U.S. health care providers or facilities except in cases where an emergency responder deems the patient's life is in jeopardy due to an automobile accident, house fire, etc. In these situations, the patient must re-obtain coverage equal to or greater than the care provided and is responsible for the medical expenses incurred; in other words, health care providers will no longer "write off" monies owed for services rendered. Recipients of emergency health care due to cancelation of insurance coverage for non-payment of premium are still responsible for the costs of their emergency care.

Self-rationing of health services would be encouraged by offering health benefit package discounts to consumers who did not utilize their health care benefits insurance the previous year. Discounts do not cease once a patient uses the health care benefits insurance. If you're hospitalized in 2012, your insurer will not offer you a discount on your 2013 health care benefits premium. However, if you don't submit any claims for 2013, your insurer must offer you a discounted premium for 2014.

The Cost

To make this proposal work, it's obvious that a multi-week cancer treatment cannot cost $50,000 per treatment. Health care costs must decrease dramatically with annual increases below the rate of inflation. This plan contains health care costs in several ways—by making health care a not-for-profit commodity, using standardized forms and payments for services rendered, requiring less paperwork and fewer employees needed to process it, and providing discounted premiums for those who practice good health habits that eliminate their need to use health care services. Additional savings will be obtained by limits on malpractice awards. Actual premiums and costs for various services rendered are beyond the scope of this proposal. In reality, these costs cannot be ascertained until implementation of the policies discussed in the plan (making health care a not-for-profit industry, providing healthier food, and making health care more competitive by including legitimate alternatives). Only after these reforms, can we truly determine the amount of health care needed in this country and accurately calculate the price for a routine doctor visit, the cost of various medications, or a fair charge for open-heart surgery.

Additional Thoughts to Stimulate Discussion

1. Making health care a not-for-profit industry and forcing food providers to eliminate unhealthy ingredients in food are anti-capitalist measures. Could we reform the current health care system without this kind of government legislation?
2. Why haven't free-market forces been able to control health care costs?
3. Would you be in favor of allowing consumers to spend excess funds in their health savings accounts on non-medical expenses? If so, would they be required to keep a minimum amount in the health savings account? What, if any, restrictions would you put on the use of health savings account monies?
4. If you benefit financially from the current health care system, would you be willing to accept less compensation in order to save the system?

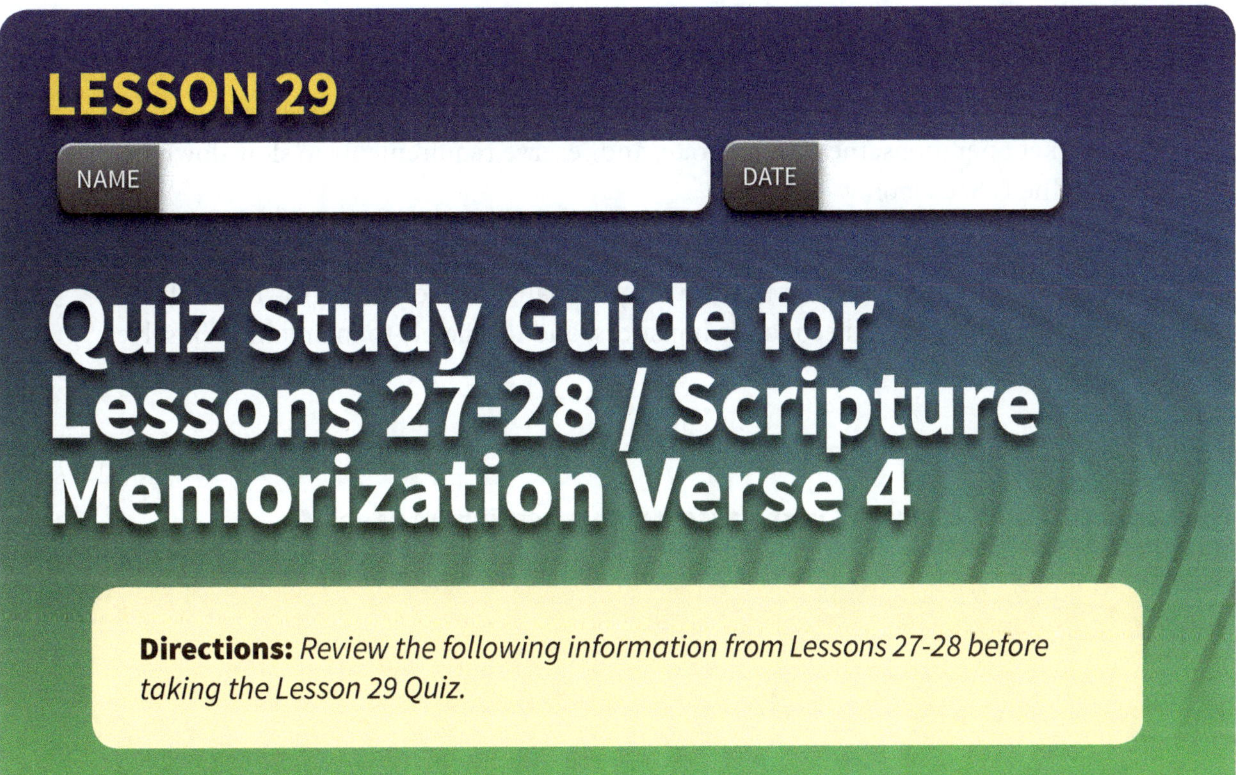

Scripture Memory

- **Psalm 37:25**—I have been young, and now am old; yet have I not seen the righteous forsaken, nor his seed begging bread.

Concepts to Review

- Individual proprietorships, partnerships, and corporations are the three main types of business organizations. Each type has specific advantages and disadvantages compared to the other two.
- Gross National Product (GNP) includes U.S. firms operating in foreign countries. Gross Domestic Product (GDP) excludes U.S. firms operating in foreign countries but does include foreign firms manufacturing in the United States.
- Profits are the rewards for meeting consumer wants and needs. Losses signal a failure to meet consumer wants and needs at a price consumers are willing to pay.
- Of the three ways of measuring profits, percentage of invested capital assures the most efficient allocation of capital resources.
- Profits that are the result of government intervention in the marketplace have no place in a free-market economy.
- Government intervention to prevent business losses hurts the economy in the long run by prolonging the life of a business that is failing to meet consumer wants and needs.
- Individual businesses and national economies go through the four stages of the business cycle—expansion, peak, recession, and trough. This expansion and decline occurs in fits and starts continuously.

- Governments use fiscal (taxing and spending) policies and monetary (manipulation of interest rates and the money supply) policies to control the economy.
- The Federal Reserve System (the central banking system of the United States) uses open market operations, the discount rate, and reserve requirements to slow down or speed up the U.S. economy.
- Monetizing the debt (printing more money) leads to hyperinflation.
- Government leaders interfere in the economy to maintain economic growth, control inflation, correct perceived economic injustices, and ultimately to maintain themselves in power.

The Lesson 29 Quiz is located in the assessments section on page 241.

NAME DATE

Imprimis Article #4

Dinner Table Discussion/Co-op Class Discussion

Directions: *Read the following article and prepare a list of five discussion questions based on the reading. Have your parents and any siblings old enough to engage in the conversation read the article, then schedule a mealtime to discuss the article as a family using your discussion questions. You will be graded on your understanding of the article (10 points), list of discussion questions (10 points), and participation in the discussion (30 points). If doing this assignment as part of a co-op class, your supervisor will ask you to write five discussion questions prior to the class discussion. Grading will be the same as if doing the assignment in a family setting.*

Imprimis article—Rolling Back Government: Lessons from New Zealand

Maurice P. McTigue (former New Zealand Cabinet Minister)

The following is adapted from a lecture delivered on February 11, 2004, on the Hillsdale campus, during a five-day seminar on "The Conditions of Free-Market Capitalism," co-sponsored by the Center for Constructive Alternatives and the Ludwig von Mises Lecture Series.

If we look back through history, growth in government has been a modern phenomenon. Beginning in the 1850s and lasting until the 1920s or '30s, the government's share of GDP in most of the world's industrialized economies was about six percent. From that period onwards—and particularly since the 1950s—we've seen a massive explosion in government share of GDP, in some places as much as 35-45 percent. (In the case of Sweden, of course, it reached 65 percent, and Sweden nearly self-destructed as a result. It is now starting to dismantle some of its social programs to remain economically viable.) Can this situation be halted or even rolled back? My view, based upon personal experience, is that the answer is "yes." But it requires high levels of transparency and significant consequences for bad decisions—and these are not easy things to bring about.

What we're seeing around the world at the moment is what I would call a silent revolution, reflected in a change in how people view government accountability. The old idea of accountability simply held that government should spend money in accordance with appropriations. The new accountability is based on asking, "What did we get in public benefits as a result of the expenditure of money?" This is a question that has always been asked in business, but has not been the norm for governments. And those governments today that are struggling valiantly with this question are showing quite extraordinary results. This was certainly the basis of the successful reforms in my own country of New Zealand.

New Zealand's per capita income in the period prior to the late 1950s was right around number three in the world, behind the United States and Canada. But by 1984, its per capita income had sunk to 27th in the world, alongside Portugal and Turkey. Not only that, but our unemployment rate was 11.6 percent, we'd had 23 successive years of deficits (sometimes ranging as high as 40 percent of GDP), our debt had grown to 65 percent of GDP, and our credit ratings were continually being downgraded. Government spending was a full 44 percent of GDP, investment capital was exiting in huge quantities, and government controls and micromanagement were pervasive at every level of the economy. We had foreign exchange controls that meant I couldn't buy a subscription to *The Economist* magazine without the permission of the Minister of Finance. I couldn't buy shares in a foreign company without surrendering my citizenship. There were price controls on all goods and services, on all shops and on all service industries. There were wage controls and wage freezes. I couldn't pay my employees more—or pay them bonuses—if I wanted to. There were import controls on the goods that I could bring into the country. There were massive levels of subsidies on industries in order to keep them viable. Young people were leaving in droves.

Spending and Taxes

When a reform government was elected in 1984, it identified three problems: too much spending, too much taxing and too much government. The question was how to cut spending and taxes and diminish government's role in the economy. Well, the first thing you have to do in this situation is to figure out what you're getting for dollars spent. Towards this end, we implemented a new policy whereby money wouldn't simply be allocated to government agencies; instead, there would be a purchase contract with the senior executives of those agencies that clearly delineated what was expected in return for the money. Those who headed up government agencies were now chosen on the basis of a worldwide search and received term contracts—five years with a possible extension of another three years. The only ground for their removal was non-performance, so a newly-elected government couldn't simply throw them out as had happened with civil servants under the old system. And of course, with those kinds of incentives, agency heads—like CEOs in the private sector—made certain that the next tier of people had very clear objectives that *they* were expected to achieve as well.

The first purchase that we made from every agency was policy advice. That policy advice was meant to produce a vigorous debate between the government and the agency heads about how to achieve goals like reducing hunger and homelessness. This didn't mean, by the way, how government could feed or house more people—that's not important. What's important is the extent to which hunger and homelessness are actually reduced. In other words, we made it clear that what's important is not how many people are on welfare, but how many people get off welfare and into independent living.

As we started to work through this process, we also asked some fundamental questions of the agencies. The first question was "What are you doing?" The second question was "What *should* you be doing?" Based on the answers, we then said, "Eliminate what you shouldn't be doing"—that is, if you are doing something that clearly is not a responsibility of the government, stop doing it. Then we asked the final question: "Who should be paying—the taxpayer, the user, the consumer, or the industry?" We asked this because, in many instances, the taxpayers were subsidizing things that did not benefit them. And if you take the cost of services away from actual consumers and users, you promote overuse and devalue whatever it is that you're doing.

When we started this process with the Department of Transportation, it had 5,600 employees. When we finished, it had 53. When we started with the Forest Service, it had 17,000 employees. When we finished, it had 17. When we applied it to the Ministry of Works, it had 28,000 employees. I used to be Minister of Works, and ended up being the *only* employee. In the latter case, most of what the department did was construction and engineering, and there are plenty of people who can do that without government involvement. And if you say to me, "But you killed all those jobs!" –well, that's just not true. The *government* stopped employing people in those jobs, but the need for the jobs didn't disappear. I visited some of the forestry workers some months after they'd lost their government jobs, and they were quite happy. They told me that they were now earning about three times what they used to earn—on top of which, they were surprised to learn that they could do about 60 percent more than they used to! The same lesson applies to the other jobs I mentioned.

Some of the things that government was doing simply didn't belong in the government. So we sold off telecommunications, airlines, irrigation schemes, computing services, government printing offices, insurance companies, banks, securities, mortgages, railways, bus services, hotels, shipping lines, agricultural advisory services, etc. In the main, when we sold those things off, their productivity went up and the cost of their services went down, translating into major gains for the economy. Furthermore, we decided that other agencies should be run as profit-making and tax-paying enterprises by government. For instance, the air traffic control system was made into a stand-alone company, given instructions that it had to make an acceptable rate of return and pay taxes, and told that it couldn't get any investment capital from its owner (the government). We did that with about 35 agencies. Together, these used to cost us about one billion dollars per year; now they produced about one billion dollars per year in revenues and taxes.

We achieved an overall reduction of 66 percent in the size of government, measured by the number of employees. The government's share of GDP dropped from 44 to 27 percent. We were now running surpluses, and we established a policy never to leave dollars on the table: We knew that if we didn't get rid of this money, some clown would spend it. So we used most of the surplus to pay off debt, and debt went from 63 percent down to 17 percent of GDP. We used the remainder of the surplus each year for tax relief. We reduced income tax rates by half and eliminated incidental taxes. As a result of these policies, revenue *increased* by 20 percent. Yes, Ronald Reagan was right: lower tax rates do produce more revenue.

Subsidies, Education, and Competitiveness

. . . What about invasive government in the form of subsidies? First, we need to recognize that the main problem with subsidies is that they make people dependent; and when you make people dependent, they lose their innovation and their creativity and become even *more* dependent.

Let me give you an example: By 1984, New Zealand sheep farming was receiving about 44 percent of its income from government subsidies. Its major product was lamb, and lamb in the international marketplace was selling for about $12.50 (with the government providing another $12.50) per carcass. Well, we did away with all sheep farming subsidies within one year. And of course the sheep farmers were unhappy. But once they accepted the fact that the subsidies weren't coming back, they put together a team of people charged with figuring out how they could get $30 per lamb carcass. The team reported back that this would be difficult, but not impossible. It required producing an entirely different product, processing it in a different way and selling it in different markets. And within two years, by 1989, they had succeeded in converting their $12.50 product into something worth $30. By 1991, it was worth $42; by 1994 it was worth $74; and by 1999 it was worth $115. In other words, the New Zealand sheep industry went out into the marketplace and found people who would pay higher prices for its product. You can now go into the best restaurants in the U.S. and buy New Zealand lamb, and you'll be paying somewhere between $35 and $60 per pound.

Needless to say, as we took government support away from industry, it was widely predicted that there would be a massive exodus of people. But that didn't happen. To give you one example, we lost only about three-quarters of one percent of the farming enterprises—and these were people who shouldn't have been farming in the first place. In addition, some predicted a major move towards corporate as opposed to family farming. But we've seen exactly the reverse. Corporate farming moved out and family farming expanded, probably because families are prepared to work for less than corporations. In the end, it was the best thing that possibly could have happened. And it demonstrated that if you give people no choice but to be creative and innovative, they will find solutions.

New Zealand had an education system that was failing as well. It was failing about 30 percent of its children—especially those in lower socio-economic areas. We had put more and more money into education for 20 years, and achieved worse and worse results. It cost us twice as much to get a poorer result than we did 20 years previously with much less money. So we decided to rethink what we were doing here as well.

The first thing we did was to identify where the dollars were going that we were pouring into education. We hired international consultants (because we didn't trust our own departments to do it), and they reported that for every dollar we were spending on education, 70 cents was being swallowed up by administration. Once we heard this, we immediately eliminated all of the Boards of Education in the country. Every single school came under the control of a board of trustees elected by the parents of the children at that school, and by nobody else. We gave schools a block of money based on the number of students that went to them, with no strings attached. At the same time, we told the parents that they had an absolute right to choose where their children would go to school. It is absolutely obnoxious to me that anybody would tell parents that they must send their children to a bad school. We converted 4,500 schools to this new system all on the same day.

But we went even further: We made it possible for privately owned schools to be funded in exactly the same way as publicly owned schools, giving parents the ability to spend their education dollars wherever they chose. Again, everybody predicted that there would be a major exodus of students from the public to the private schools, because the private schools showed an academic advantage of 14 to 15 percent. It didn't happen, however, because the differential between schools disappeared in about 18-24 months. Why? Because all of a sudden teachers realized that if they lost their students, they would lose their funding; and if they lost their funding, they would lose their jobs. Eighty-five percent of our students went to public schools at the beginning of this process. That fell to only about 84 percent over the first year or so of our reforms. But three years later, 87 percent of the students were going to public schools. More importantly, we moved from being about 14 or 15 percent *below* our international peers to being about 14 or 15 percent *above* our international peers in terms of educational attainment.

Now consider taxation and competitiveness: What many in the public sector today fail to recognize is that the challenge of competitiveness is worldwide. Capital and labor can move so freely and rapidly from place to place that the only way to stop business from leaving is to make certain that your business climate is better than anybody else's. Along these lines, there was a very interesting circumstance in Ireland just two years ago. The European Union, led by France, was highly critical of Irish tax policy—particularly on corporations—because the Irish had reduced their tax on corporations from 48 percent to 12 percent and business was flooding into Ireland. The European Union wanted to impose a penalty on Ireland in the form of a 17 percent corporate tax hike to bring them into line with other European countries. Needless to say, the Irish didn't buy that. The European community responded by saying that what the Irish were doing was unfair and uncompetitive. The Irish Minister of Finance agreed: He pointed out that Ireland was charging corporations 12 percent, while charging its citizens only 10 percent. So Ireland reduced the tax rate to 10 percent for corporations as well. There's another one the French lost!

When we in New Zealand looked at our revenue gathering process, we found the system extremely complicated in a way that distorted business as well as private decisions. So we asked ourselves some questions: Was our tax system concerned with collecting revenue? Was it concerned with collecting revenue and also delivering social services? Or was it concerned with collecting revenue, delivering social services and changing behavior, all three? We decided that the social services and behavioral components didn't have any place in a rational system of taxation. So we resolved that we would have only two mechanisms for gathering revenue—a tax on income and a tax on consumption—and that we would simplify those mechanisms and lower the rates as much as we possibly could. We lowered the high income tax rate from 66 to 33 percent, and set that flat rate for high-income earners. In addition, we brought the low end down from 38 to 19 percent, which became the flat rate for low-income earners. We then set a consumption tax rate of 10 percent and eliminated all other taxes—capital gains taxes, property taxes, etc. We carefully designed this system to produce exactly the same revenue as we were getting before and presented it to the public as a zero sum game. But what actually happened was that we received 20 percent more revenue than before. Why? We hadn't allowed for the increase in voluntary compliance. If tax rates are low, taxpayers won't employ high priced lawyers and accountants to find loopholes. Indeed, every country that I've looked at in the world that has dramatically simplified and lowered its tax rates has ended up with more revenue, not less.

What about regulations? The regulatory power is customarily delegated to non-elected officials who then constrain the people's liberties with little or no accountability. These regulations are extremely difficult to eliminate once they are in place. But we found a way: We simply rewrote the statutes on which they were based. For instance, we rewrote the environmental laws, transforming them into the Resource Management Act—reducing a law that was 25 inches thick to 348 pages. We rewrote the tax code, all of the farm acts, and the occupational safety and health acts. To do this, we brought our brightest brains together and told them to pretend that there was no pre-existing law and that they should create for us the best possible environment for industry to thrive. We then marketed it in terms of what it would save in taxes. These new laws, in effect, repealed the old, which meant that all existing regulations died—the whole lot, every single one.

Thinking Differently About Government

What I have been discussing is really just a new way of thinking about government. Let me tell you how we solved our deer problem: Our country had no large indigenous animals until the English imported deer for hunting. These deer proceeded to escape into the wild and become obnoxious pests. We then spent 120 years trying to eliminate them, until one day someone suggested that we just let people farm them. So we told the farming community that they could catch and farm the deer, as long as they would keep them inside eight-foot high fences. And we haven't spent a dollar on deer eradication from that day onwards. Not one. And New Zealand now supplies 40 percent of the world market in venison. By applying simple common sense, we turned a liability into an asset.

Let me share with you one last story: The Department of Transportation came to us one day and said they needed to increase the fees for driver's licenses. When we asked why, they said that the cost of relicensing wasn't being fully recovered at the current fee levels. Then we asked why we should be doing this sort of thing at all. The transportation people clearly thought that was a very stupid question: Everybody needs a driver's license, they said. I then pointed out that I received mine when I was fifteen and asked them: "What is it about relicensing that in any way tests driver competency?" We gave them ten days to think this over. At one point they suggested to us that the police need driver's licenses for identification purposes. We responded that this was the purpose of an identity card, not a driver's license. Finally they admitted that they could think of no good reason for what they were doing—so we abolished the whole process! Now a driver's license is good until a person is 74 years old, after which he must get an annual medical test to ensure he is still competent to drive. So not only did we not need new fees, we abolished a whole department. That's what I mean by thinking differently.

There are some great things happening along these lines in the United States today. You might not know it, but back in 1993 Congress passed a law called the Government Performance and Results Act. This law orders government departments to identify in a strategic plan what it is that they intend to achieve, and to report each year what they actually did achieve in terms of public benefits. Following on this, two years ago President Bush brought to the table something called the President's Management Agenda, which sifts through the information in these reports and decides how to respond. These mechanisms are promising if they are used properly.

Consider this: There are currently 178 federal programs designed to help people get back to work. They cost $8.4 billion, and 2.4 million people are employed as a result of them. But if we took the most effective three programs out of those 178 and put the $8.4 billion into them alone, the result would likely be that 14.7 million people would find jobs. The status quo costs America over 11 million jobs. The kind of new thinking I am talking about would build into the system a consequence for the administrator who is responsible for this failure of sound stewardship of taxpayer dollars. It is in this direction that the government needs to move.

"Reprinted by permission from *Imprimis*, the national speech digest of Hillsdale College, www.hillsdale.edu."

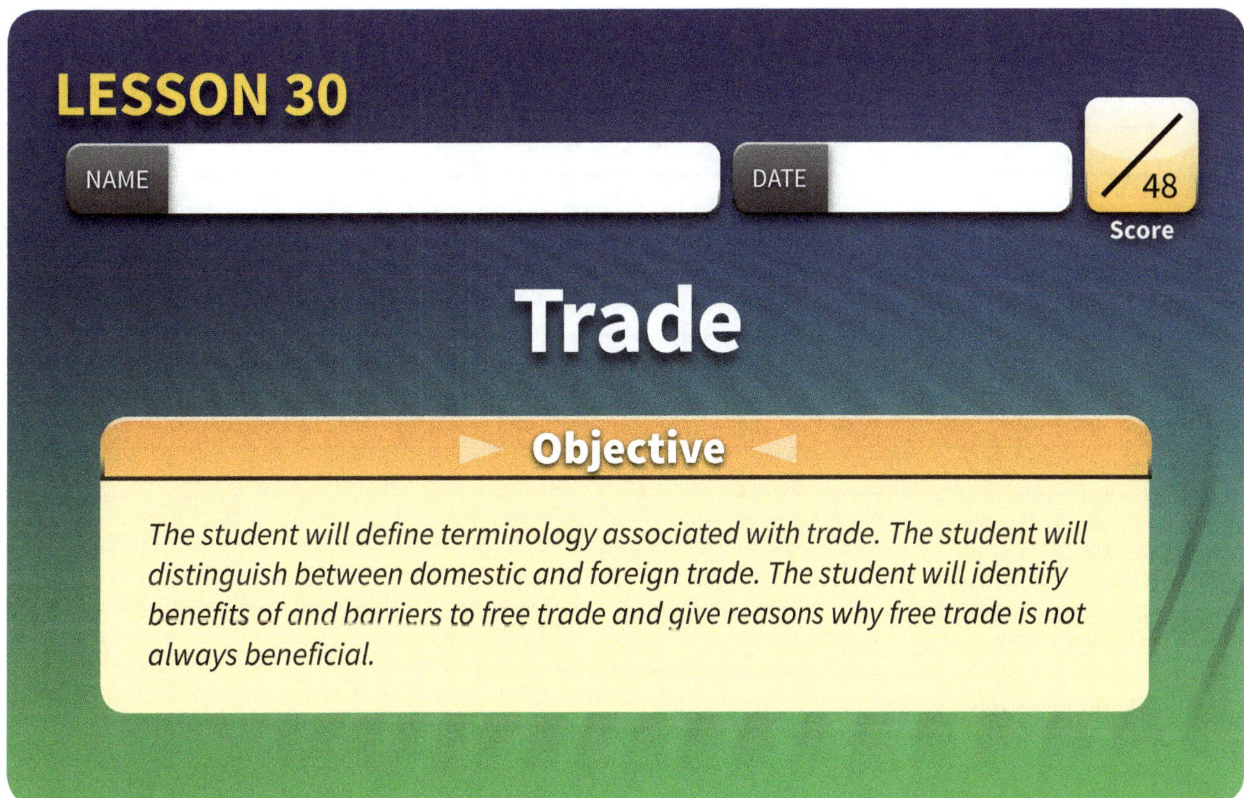

Lesson 30A Reading

The concept of **trade** has its own unique vocabulary. Before continuing with this lesson, define the following terms associated with international trade. You may wish to use an Internet website to make quick work of this assignment. *(2 points each)*

1. Autarky:
____
____

2. Customs Duties:
____
____

3. Export:
____
____

4. Import:
____
____

5. Quotas:

____

____

6. Subsidy:

____

____

7. Tariff:

____

____

8. Trade Deficit:

____

____

9. Trade Surplus:

____

____

Lesson 30B Reading

Trade is "the act or process of buying, selling, or exchanging commodities, at either wholesale or retail, within a country or between countries."[38] **Domestic trade** takes place within a country's borders (i.e., within a single U.S. state or between two or more states). Interstate trade disputes under the Articles of Confederation government contributed to the calling of the Constitutional Convention in 1787. Article I, Section 8, Clause 3 of the U.S. Constitution gives Congress authority "To regulate Commerce with foreign Nations, and among the several States, and with the Indian Tribes." **Foreign trade** takes place between two or more independent sovereign nations.

Free trade is "international trade that is free of such government interference as import quotas, export subsidies, protective tariffs, etc."[39] Notice that the definition of free trade does not exclude customs duties or eliminate tariffs altogether. Revenue from these fees pays for the cost of policing and inspecting imports. They might also supplement the nation's income. Free trade, however, eliminates protective tariffs designed to inflate the cost of imported goods so consumers will purchase domestic manufactures. Which begs the question: Is the North American Free Trade Agreement (NAFTA) truly "free trade"? Article 705 of the agreement deals with the con-

---

[38] trade. (n.d.). *Dictionary.com Unabridged*. Retrieved April 13, 2011, from Dictionary.com website: http://dictionary.reference.com/browse/trade

[39] free trade. (n.d.). *Collins English Dictionary - Complete & Unabridged 10th Edition*. Retrieved April 13, 2011, from Dictionary.com website: http://dictionary.reference.com/browse/free trade

troversial subject of export subsidies related to agricultural products. Paragraph 1 affirms the desire of the three nations to eliminate this type of government aid. "The Parties share the objective of the multilateral elimination of export subsidies for agricultural goods and shall cooperate in an effort to achieve an agreement under the GATT to eliminate those subsidies." Paragraphs 4 and 5 of the article provide exceptions to the goal of eliminating export subsidies. Paragraph 6 provides a framework for implementing the policy, but Paragraph 7 reads:

> "Notwithstanding any other provision of this Article:
>
> a) if the importing and exporting Parties agree to an export subsidy for an agricultural good exported to the territory of the importing Party, the exporting Party or Parties may adopt or maintain such subsidy; and
>
> b) each Party retains its rights to apply countervailing duties to subsidized imports of agricultural goods from the territory of a Party or non-Party."[40]

According to Paragraph 7, if Mexico and the United States agree to maintain an existing subsidy, then the export subsidy could remain in effect. This paragraph also allows unilateral implementation of higher tariffs to counteract the effects of export subsidies. Suppose, for example, that the Mexican government subsidizes Mexican lettuce farmers who sell lettuce to U.S. markets. With the subsidy, Mexican lettuce is 10 cents per head cheaper than U.S.-grown lettuce. The U.S. government could impose a 12 cents per head tariff on Mexican lettuce. Assuming that the quality of the lettuce is the same and that U.S. lettuce farmers can provide sufficient quantities of lettuce to meet domestic demand, wholesale lettuce buyers would purchase the cheaper U.S. lettuce. Mexico could file a complaint with the NAFTA Secretariat for dispute resolution under Chapter 19 (countervailing duties) or Chapter 20 (agricultural measures).[41] No wonder someone quipped that lawyers would be the chief beneficiaries of the North American Free Trade Agreement!

Free-trade advocates argue that the benefits of free trade outweigh the disadvantages. Free trade cultivates new markets and economic opportunities. There's an old story about two shoe salesmen who visited Africa. The pessimistic salesman told his superiors they were wasting their time in that part of the world because nobody wore shoes. The optimistic salesman wired his boss about the tremendous opportunities for their company because nobody wore shoes. Free trade is like the latter salesman because it provides new markets for opportunistic entrepreneurs and investors. It also encourages efficiency due to increased competition. Those businesses best able to arrange their factors of production to minimize production costs do well in the global marketplace. This can be both an economic blessing and a curse, as unemployed Americans displaced by cheaper foreign labor will loudly attest.

Nations that *export* more than they *import* have a **favorable balance of trade**. Nations that *import* more than they *export* have a **trade deficit**. According to the U.S. Census Bureau website, the United States trade deficit at the time of writing was

[40] http://www.nafta-sec-alena.org/en/view.aspx?conID=590&mtpiID=131#A705

[41] http://www.nafta-sec-alena.org/en/view.aspx?x=226

approaching $560 billion.[42] Of our nation's top 15 trading partners in July, 2012, only the Netherlands and Brazil purchased more from us than we imported from them. Is the enormous U.S. trade deficit a cause for alarm? In an article on the Cato Institute website, Daniel Griswold argues that trade deficits are actually a sign of a healthy economy. "America's annual trade deficits are sustainable as long as the United States remains a safe and profitable destination for the world's savings. The accumulating net foreign ownership of U.S. assets, America's so-called foreign debt, does not threaten our sovereignty, our ability to finance that investment, or continued economic expansion."[43] On the other side of the issue, then-Federal Reserve Chairman Alan Greenspan warned that ongoing U.S. trade deficits pose a major threat to the U.S. economy. Foreign nations no longer wishing to finance our trade imbalance, Greenspan argued, would rush to "unload investments in U.S. stocks and bonds, sending prices of the stocks and bonds plunging and interest rates soaring."[44] Greenspan believes that the trade deficit and federal government budget deficits put the United States in a precarious financial position. In a speech at Hillsdale College on January 29, 2006, Steve Forbes, Editor-in-Chief of *Forbes* magazine, gave his view on trade deficits.

> "But trade is not a transaction between countries. It takes place between parties. For example, *Forbes* magazine buys paper. For all of the 88 years that we've been in existence, we've run a trade deficit with our paper suppliers. If you look just at that trade deficit, you might think we are doing poorly. But if you look at the two parties involved, that turns out to be an illusion. The paper supplier thinks he's going to make money selling his paper. We think we're going to make money by taking the paper and putting print on it, with value added. So it's a mutually profitable transaction, even if it looks like a trade deficit. Or consider a book printed in Taiwan. Looking at the trade number alone, it appears there is a two dollar trade deficit with Taiwan. Yet the book comes back here and retails for $24.95. The value added is in the U.S. The author gets a cut, the publisher gets a cut, booksellers get a cut, distributors get a cut, and remainder stores get a cut. Something similar happened with iPods: A lot of its parts are made overseas, but where is most of the value added? Here in the United States. North America has had a merchandise trade deficit 350 out of the last 400 years, and we have done very well, thank you."[45]

Will uncertainty over the long-term consequences of trade deficits cause the U.S. government to curtail its free-trade policies in the quest for a more favorable balance of trade? Only time will tell.

---

[42] http://www.census.gov/foreign-trade/statistics/highlights/topcurmon.html

[43] http://www.cato.org/pub_display.php?pub_id=3645 February 9, 2001

[44] http://www.spokesman.com/stories/2004/nov/20/greenspan-warns-of-trade-deficit-dangers November 20, 2004

[45] Forbes, Steve. "The Great (and Continuing) Economic Debate of the 20th Century." (Reprinted by permission from *Imprimis*, the national speech digest of Hillsdale College, www.hillsdale.edu.)

Governments also regulate free trade to protect their citizens. In the spring of 2011, Germany banned the importation of cucumbers grown in Spain, claiming a connection between the cucumbers and an *e coli* outbreak responsible for dozens of fatalities throughout Europe. Free-trade nations could block the importation of invasive plants harmful to their native vegetation or prohibit entry of illegal substances such as narcotics. Free trade sometimes leads to a situation known as "dumping." A nation with excess inventory tries to "dump" its surplus onto its trading partners. Once the receiving nations recognize the dumping, the recipients retaliate with import quotas or higher tariffs to stop this practice harmful to their economic health. Of course, the offending nation might respond with quotas or increased duties on its imports.

Review Questions

Directions: *Answer the following questions based on the Lesson 30B reading.*

1. Define trade. *(1 point)*

____

____

____

2. Explain the difference between domestic trade and foreign trade. *(1 point)*

____

____

3. Is free trade a misnomer? Why or why not? *(3 points)*

____

____

____

____

____

____

4. Which nation (the United States, Canada, or Mexico) benefits the most from the North American Free Trade Agreement? Why? *(3 points)*

____

____

____

____

____

5. Do you agree with Mr. Griswold or Mr. Greenspan concerning the U.S. trade deficit? Why? *(3 points)*

6. The Hawley-Smoot protective tariff, enacted in 1930, raised duties on over 20,000 items to near-record levels. Why did the Hawley-Smoot tariff fail to revive the U.S. economy in the early years of the Great Depression? Can broad-based protective tariffs (tariffs on thousands of imported items) bring recovery to a nation's economy? Why or why not? *(7 points)*

Lesson 30C Reading

Why do nations trade with other countries? The obvious answer is to *obtain goods or services not available or easily obtainable in that nation.* Nations also trade to *obtain needed natural resources for their industries.* During the Age of Imperialism, European nations colonized much of Africa and Asia for that very reason—to control the resources of their colonies and provide additional markets for their manufactured goods. After World War II, however, as these former colonies gained their independence, the mother countries had to work out trade agreements with their newly independent colonies or find new trading partners in order to keep the factory machinery humming.

In the 1850s, Great Britain imported U.S.-grown cotton to supply the British textile industry. The phrase "Cotton is King" described the importance of this U.S. export in the years leading up to the Civil War. The cotton-growing southern states that joined the Confederate States of America believed that Great Britain would form an alliance with the secessionists because of its need for cotton. This Confederate strategy backfired when the British discovered they could grow cotton (better-quality cotton, too) in Egypt.

Nations that must import raw materials for manufacturing are at a disadvantage during wartime. Japan's situation in the 1930s illustrates this dilemma. Wanting to dominate the Pacific region, Japan invaded Manchuria in 1931. As the conflict with China escalated and eventually became a part of the Second World War, the Japanese needed more resources for the war effort, especially oil. Out of military necessity, Japan attacked the Philippines and Southeast Asia in pursuit of these resources, achieving great success in the early years of the war, but in the process bringing the United States into the conflict. Once the Allies halted Japan's expansion, however, the Japanese military could not defend their far-flung empire with its vital resources. A vicious cycle destroyed Japan's ability to wage war. Allied military forces decimated the Japanese merchant marine, depriving Japanese war industries of raw materials from the conquered territories. Without adequate arms and equipment due to a lack of resources, the Japanese military could not stop Allied forces from recapturing those nations overrun by Japan earlier in the war, in spite of determined efforts by kamikaze pilots and Japanese soldiers who would rather die fighting than surrender. Japanese dreams of a Greater East Asia Co-Prosperity Sphere died with their defeat. With U.S. aid, Japan rebounded quickly after the war thanks to the new threat of communist expansion in Asia, but this industrialized island nation remains vulnerable because of its need to import natural resources.

Some nations that could produce certain goods might choose to obtain these items through trade rather than manufacture the items domestically. If a nation specializes in producing a good, it might be to that country's advantage to focus on its specialty instead of trying to meet all of its needs by expanding its domestic manufacturing. A Central American nation with a climate conducive to growing coffee can trade this agricultural resource for any number of manufactured items from other nations. Specialization, however, can be dangerous, especially for agricultural-based economies. Crop failure due to natural disasters or unfavorable weather conditions leaves them with nothing to export. One-crop economies in particular need to diversify to prevent recurring problems associated with poor harvests.

The term **autarky** refers to a nation that is economically self-sufficient. It does not need to import goods from other countries or rely on foreign aid. When the League of Nations imposed sanctions on Italy in 1935 following the Italian invasion of Ethiopia, Mussolini tried to make Italy into an autarky. He achieved some measure of success toward this goal until the outbreak of the Second World War. Italian reversals on the battlefields of North Africa and Sicily enabled the Allies to invade Italy in 1943. German forces occupied northern Italy to delay the Allied advance up the Italian peninsula, but they could not stop the conquest of Italy. Mussolini's dream of empire and economic self-sufficiency came to an end with his violent death at the hands of Italian partisans on April 28, 1945. Other fascist states like Franco's Spain and Hitler's Germany pursued autarky, but technological advances and lack of sufficient fuel resources hindered their economic plans. No modern nation can totally meet consumer wants and needs on its own. Even the United States, with its abundant natural resources, cannot meet all of its economic needs alone or domestically consume its entire industrial output. Global trade is here to stay.

Review Questions

Directions: *Answer the following questions based on the Lesson 30C reading.*

1. Why do nations trade? *(1 point)*

2. Besides the examples given in the reading, use outside resources to find two historical examples of how trade contributed to or impacted a nation's war effort. *(4 points)*

3. How does specialization influence a nation's trade decisions? *(2 points)*

4. What are some risks associated with specialization? *(2 points)*

5. Is autarky a viable option in the 21st century? Why or why not? *(3 points)*

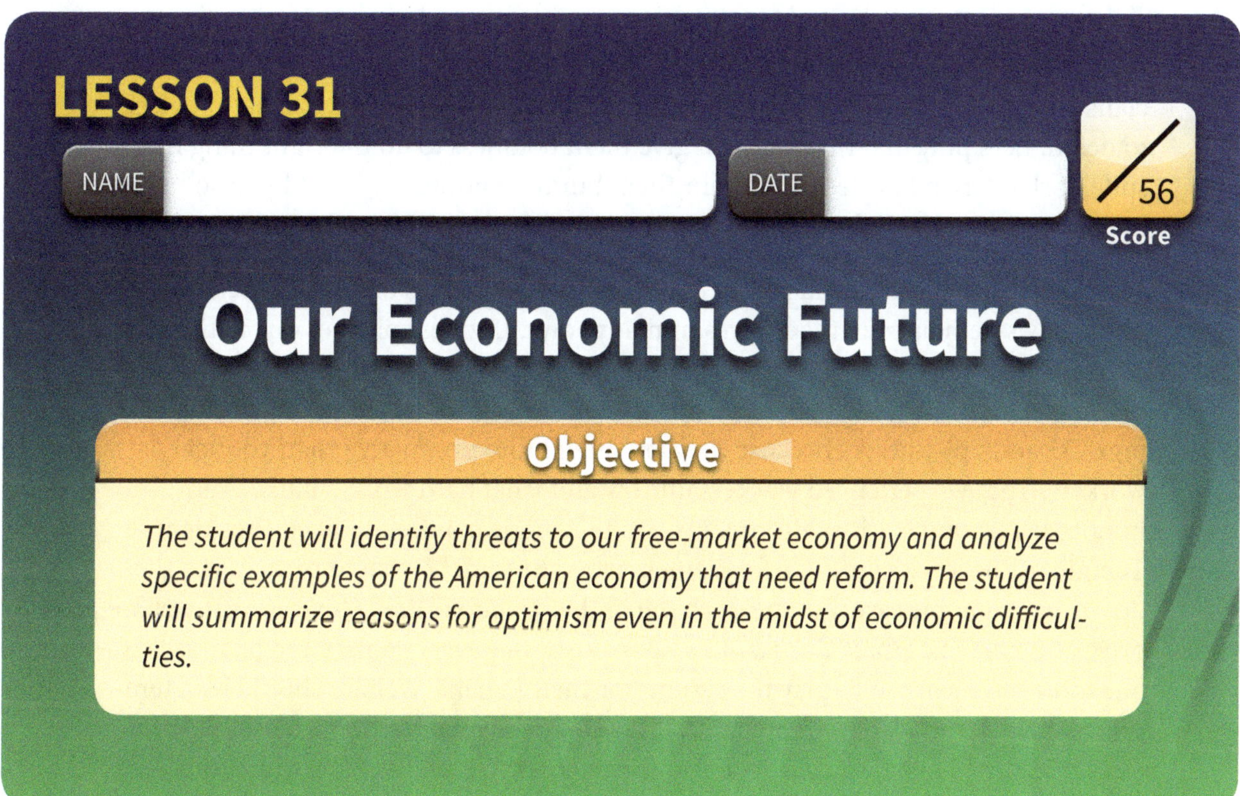

Lesson 31A Reading

Have you ever gone spotting for deer? Hunters in the region of Pennsylvania where the author grew up drive the back roads at night with powerful spotlights searching for these graceful but elusive creatures. They pan tree lines, farm fields and meadows where the deer love to forage. The hunters jabber excitedly every time the spotlight's beam illuminates a group of these creatures feeding or instinctively moving about their territory. For these men (and some women), spotting serves a useful purpose. They take mental notes on the prime deer locations and, unless the land is posted by the owner prohibiting hunting on that property, you'll find these hunters on the opening day of deer season stalking the land in search of a buck worthy of their boastful exploits. Like the hunters searching for deer, the author wants to shine a warning spotlight on three dangerous trends in the American economy: the budget deficit contributing to our growing national debt, the economic character flaws of many Americans, and the growth of the public sector.

The federal government must balance the budget and start reducing our national debt. Why do we think our national government can live beyond its means without dire consequences? For far too long we've been like ostriches with our heads in the sand hoping the situation will improve, but ignoring the problem won't make it go away. Over 42 cents of every federal dollar goes to fund our national debt. Almost half the nation's income goes to our creditors. What an astonishing statistic! We've created a false bubble of prosperity through government deficit spending—an unsustainable situation that will eventually lead to our financial ruin. When will that occur? We can't know for certain—perhaps when our creditors refuse to loan us any more money or when Congress attempts to solve the problem with a massive tax increase. Thankfully, the Tea Party movement calling for fiscal restraint seems to be gaining strength throughout the country and in Congress. God bless those politicians who are trying to stop the financial hemorrhaging before we as a nation bleed to death. Let's pray that the Lord will give them boldness to do the right thing in spite of slander and protest, and grant them humility not to say "I told you so" when history proves them right.

The second dangerous trend is the economic character flaws of many Americans. These flaws demonstrate themselves in many ways. Laziness plagues our nation. We don't want to put forth the effort to start or finish a task. A CBS evening news story on June 20, 2011, highlighted this issue. It seems companies are seeking out older (ages 55 and up) workers because they are often more productive than younger workers. These experienced workers understand what hard work entails, even in not-so-pleasant work environments. Some Americans need to heed President Theodore Roosevelt's antidote for laziness when he said, "I wish to preach, not the doctrine of ignoble ease, but the doctrine of the strenuous life." Government welfare programs can exacerbate this laziness. Obviously, not every welfare recipient is lazy, but some have learned to play the system for their benefit. Welfare should be a temporary helping hand, not a way of life. "If we take the route of the permanent handout," President Nixon warned, "the American character will itself be impoverished."

Greed is another American economic character flaw. Avarice consumes some people. They will do most anything, including illegal activities, in the pursuit of wealth (study the Enron scandal). Even Christians who know the futility of "laying up treasures on earth" sometimes succumb to greed. Proverbs 15:27 warns us that "he that is greedy of gain troubleth his own house; but he that hateth gifts shall live." Proverbs 1:19 says that the ways of greedy people lead to death.

Misuse of credit and excessive debt are other examples of these character flaws. Proverbs 22:7 tells us that "the rich ruleth over the poor, and the borrower is servant to the lender." Credit cards are a big temptation to live beyond our means. Easy credit leads to unrealistic expectations. We want what we want NOW without the hard work and sacrifice. Bankruptcy provides an out if we cannot pay off our overwhelming debt. We cannot hope to solve our economic predicament unless we eradicate these and other cancerous cells that are destroying the economic character of the American citizen.

A third trend that threatens our economic future is a growing public sector. The main problem with public sector jobs is that they rely on tax revenues or deficit spending to pay for them. During economic hard times, municipalities, state governments, and the national government may have difficulty providing pay raises and benefits for public sector employees, especially if voters can reject tax increases needed to compensate those employees. Like their private sector counterparts, public sector employees can be laid off or lose their jobs during a recession or depression. Which begs the question: If the public sector can get along without those employees during economic hard times, why do we need them when the economy is doing well? Fewer public sector employees means government needs fewer tax dollars to make ends meet—in the author's mind, a good thing. Lower our taxes and let millions of consumers decide how to spend that money rather than government bureaucrats.

As the author frequently points out in Zeezok Publishing's *A Noble Experiment* high school government course, the U.S. government over the years has taken on many extra-biblical and extra-constitutional responsibilities. Welfare is a good example of inappropriate government activity. Private charities should temporarily assist those in need, because the donor can hold those receiving assistance accountable for their actions. Government-funded welfare programs cannot demand that a woman stop having children out of wedlock, but a faith-based organization could require a change in lifestyle in exchange for financial help. Eliminating government's extra-biblical and extra-constitutional responsibilities will significantly reduce government's need for revenue, putting more money in the pockets of taxpayers and economic decision-making power back where it belongs in a free-market economy—in the hands of consumers.

Review Questions

Directions: *Answer the following questions based on the Lesson 31A reading.*

1. In your opinion, can we realistically hope to balance the federal budget? Why or why not? *(2 points)*

____

____

____

____

____

____

____

2. Explain the following statement made by George Washington. *(3 points)*

   "Few men have virtue to withstand the highest bidder."

____

____

____

____

3. Identify two personal economic character flaws and a specific solution to eliminate the flaw. *(4 points)*

____

____

____

____

____

4. List five specific agencies, programs, or public sector jobs that could be eliminated without compromising government's biblical and constitutional obligations. *(5 points)*

5. State laws require all vehicle owners and operators to have car insurance or some other proof of financial responsibility, but your auto insurance policy has a premium for uninsured and underinsured drivers. How can we solve this problem that makes every driver pay more for car insurance? *(5 points)*

6. How can we eliminate absurd compensation for athletes, movie stars, and musicians? What do these excessive salaries and incomes reveal about our priorities as a nation? Could we rein in their compensation without further eroding our free-market economy that enables them to acquire such wealth? *(7 points)*

7. Following is a list of three proposals that the author believes would economically simplify our society. Put a *Y* on the blank if you agree with the author's statement and an *N* if you disagree with the statement. Prepare to verbally defend your choices if your home school supervisor asks you to do so. *(6 points)*
   - We can reduce crime and eliminate the need for more prison space by swiftly meting out more severe punishments. ________
   - We should simplify the tax code, eliminating all deductions, exemptions, and adjustments to income. Everyone should pay a flat 1 percent federal income tax rate regardless of their income. ________
   - We all need to downsize; i.e., learn to live with less "stuff." ________

8. In what way is collective bargaining by unions a socialistic measure? *(4 points)*

____
____
____
____
____

9. Is retirement a biblical concept? Explain your answer. *(6 points)*

____
____
____
____
____
____
____

10. How is a store owner extending temporary credit to a family in need and saying "pay me back when you can" better than a government-run welfare program? *(5 points)*

____
____
____
____
____
____
____
____
____
____

11. How does government financing of higher education drive up the cost of a college education? *(2 points)*

12. The Apostle Paul said, "I have learned, in whatsoever state I am, therewith to be content. I know both how to be abased, and I know how to abound: every where and in all things I am instructed both to be full and to be hungry, both to abound and to suffer need." (Philippians 4:11-12) What economic lessons can we learn from these verses? *(3 points)*

13. The verse 1 Timothy 6:8 admonishes us to be content with "food" and "raiment." What does this mean for us living in North America in the 21st century? *(4 points)*

Lesson 31B Reading

Are you discouraged after reading the first part of Lesson 31? Our economic future, from a human perspective, looks mighty bleak. However, our God doesn't need the government or the Federal Reserve System to take care of His children. Read the following story written by the author's wife.

Our Journey to a Home . . .

By Kirsten A. Spickler

In thirteen years of marriage, our needs were graciously met by God. But there was one possession we knew would never be ours apart from His miraculous working. That was a home of our own. As a Christian school teacher, my husband receives a relatively low income, although the school continually tries to increase salaries and supplement however they can. We feel God wants me to be home with the three kids, working outside of the home as little as possible, and, so far, He has provided. We also made a commitment to debt-free living, which means we count every penny and limit large purchases until the majority of funds are in hand. There were times when we struggled to reconcile our desire to minister in Christian education with our concern for our tightly stretched finances, not to mention the little green monster of envy that so easily arose as we observed others' monetary success. We battled bitterness—when we saw the new vehicles the high school students were driving in contrast to our sometimes rusty and always well-used cars. We're only human, and God is continually working in us to produce a spirit of contentment. Sometimes we fail, and other times, by His grace, we succeed.

Longing to be homeowners, every couple of years we would look at available houses, study our budget, and dismally decide that we could not manage it. At the same time, realtors, family, and friends were telling us that the wise thing to do was purchase so that we weren't throwing away money on rent. We finally concluded in our hearts that, if God wanted us to be homeowners, He would miraculously provide for us. Then we sat back and, not so patiently, waited. For thirteen years, the Lord met our needs as we rented from an elderly woman at an unbelievably low rate. During those years, we were privileged to serve her and grow to be her friend, since she was widowed and without family of any kind. Looking back, we praise the Lord for this unique relationship, one in which we ministered to her needs for companionship and property maintenance and she ministered to our needs financially and with her friendship. When she passed away in June of 2001, we were distraught. Our financial situation had not changed and our need for other housing was imminent. But God continually impressed upon us that He was in charge of all aspects of our lives and would provide in His own time and way. During the next year, as her estate was settled, we were allowed to rent and pay her executor that same low rent. Even in this way, we saw God's gracious provision. At the same time, we were combing the county for a house within our budget, but we were beginning to doubt that any existed! The houses we viewed were downright depressing—moldy basements, woeful fixer-uppers, questionable neighborhoods, etc. We went to bed every night feeling the human hopelessness and yet the sovereign care of God. Our realtor made us aware of a program open only to teachers and police officers, whereby HUD houses can be purchased at half price if minimal requirements are met. We decided to pursue this unusual Internet bidding to see what would happen, and we bid on three different houses. In June of 2002, only one month after the house we were renting was sold, we received an e-mail congratulating us on our accepted bid! Though we knew God would provide, we were flabbergasted. Suddenly we were the owners of a beautiful split-level in a neighborhood that we could not have considered previously. We have lived here for over four months now, and each day we wake unbelievably thankful for the wonderful way that God met our needs above all that we expected or hoped.

But that isn't the end of the story! This week, nearly a year and a half after our former landlady's death, we received a gift from her estate that enabled us to pay off our remodeling bills *and* mortgage. In essence, God gave us our home for free! For so long we feebly served our Lord, trusting that He could provide (while we prayed, "Help our unbelief!"). Now we know without a shadow of a doubt that He does provide! We are painfully aware that we are not worthy of this blessing; it is solely a gift of God's grace. But we humbly thank Him for supplying our needs and for honoring our desire to live debt-free. Our prayer is that we will continue to love and follow Him in appreciation of Who He is and not just for the blessings that He pours out upon us.

The author's family is still enjoying the blessing of this home. It's not where he'd like to end his life on this earth, but he's thankful for God's provision even as he longingly prays for a place in the country (eight acres with some woods, large garden space, free-range chickens, pigs, a cow or two, bees for honey, and a simple shack for a home would be nice). Depending upon God's plan for our nation, this generation may not enjoy all of the material blessings that our grandparents and parents sometimes took for granted. However, the Christian has hope because Christ promised that He would "never leave us nor forsake us." He is with us through persecution or economic peril. Our Heavenly Father loves us so much, and He wants what is best for us. Perhaps our economic difficulties are His way of removing those idols that are keeping us from an intimate relationship with Him. Consider the testimony of Enoch. Genesis 5:24 says, "And Enoch walked with God: and he was not; for God took him." What an example to the self-sufficient citizens of the United States! Enoch recognized his complete dependence on God, and he had such a special relationship with his Creator that at the end of his life here on earth he entered God's presence without having to suffer physical death. Christians especially need to heed this testimony of a man who had the right priorities. "For what is your life? It is even a VAPOUR, that appeareth for a little time, and then vanisheth away."[46] We need to invest our time, effort, and resources in things with eternal value.

Someday this sin-cursed earth will come to an end. A glorious eternity awaits the believer. "But as it is written, Eye hath not seen, nor ear heard, neither have entered into the heart of man, the things which God hath prepared for them that love him."[47] One second in Christ's presence will make up for all the struggles of this life. It won't matter that you maybe never owned a high-definition, big-screen television or a brand-new automobile. All of the times we thought or verbalized that "life's not fair" will be forgotten as we begin to enjoy our new surroundings. The Apostle John got a glimpse of his (and every Christian's) future while in prison on the isle of Patmos. He wrote in Revelation 21:1-5:

> And I saw a new heaven and a new earth: for the first heaven and the first earth were passed away; and there was no more sea. And I John saw the holy city, new Jerusalem, coming down from God out of heaven, prepared as a bride adorned for her husband. And I heard a great voice out of heaven saying, Behold, the tabernacle of God is with men, and he will dwell with them, and they shall be his people, and God himself shall be with them, and be their God. And God shall wipe away all tears from their eyes; and there shall be no more death, neither sorrow, nor crying, neither shall there be any more pain: for the former things are passed away. And he that sat upon the throne said, Behold, I make all things new. And he said unto me, Write: for these words are true and faithful.

Even so, come quickly, Lord Jesus!

[46] James 4:14

[47] 1 Corinthians 2:9

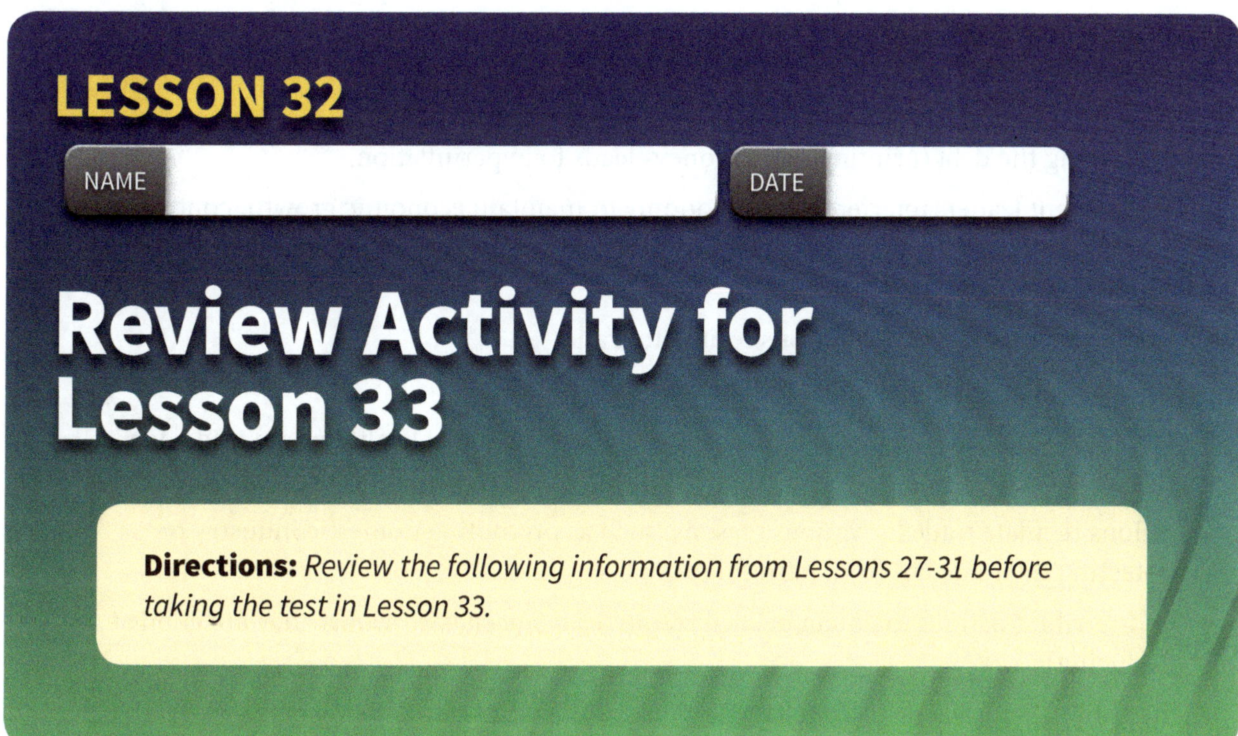

Review Activity for Lesson 33

Directions: *Review the following information from Lessons 27-31 before taking the test in Lesson 33.*

Scripture Memory

- **Psalm 37:25**—I have been young, and now am old; yet have I not seen the righteous forsaken, nor his seed begging bread.

Concepts to Review

- Individual proprietorships, partnerships, and corporations are the three main types of business organizations. Each type has specific advantages and disadvantages compared to the other two.
- Gross National Product (GNP) includes U.S. firms operating in foreign countries. Gross Domestic Product (GDP) excludes U.S. firms operating in foreign countries but does include foreign firms manufacturing in the United States.
- Profits are the rewards for meeting consumer wants and needs. Losses signal a failure to meet consumer wants and needs at a price consumers are willing to pay.
- Of the three ways of measuring profits, percentage of invested capital assures the most efficient allocation of capital resources.
- Profits that are the result of government intervention in the marketplace have no place in a free-market economy.
- Government intervention to prevent business losses hurts the economy in the long run by prolonging the life of a business that is failing to meet consumer wants and needs.
- Individual businesses and national economies go through the four stages of the business cycle—expansion, peak, recession, and trough. This expansion and decline occurs in fits and starts continuously.
- Governments use fiscal (taxing and spending) policies and monetary (manipulation of interest rates and the money supply) policies to control the economy.

- The Federal Reserve System (the central banking system of the United States) uses open market operations, the discount rate, and reserve requirements to slow down or speed up the U.S. economy.
- Monetizing the debt (printing more money) leads to hyperinflation.
- Government leaders interfere in the economy to maintain economic growth, control inflation, correct perceived economic injustices, and ultimately to maintain themselves in power
- Review the Lesson 30A definitions related to trade.
- Free trade is preferable to protective tariffs.
- Is a favorable balance of trade necessary to a nation's financial health, or are trade deficits okay?
- Nations regulate trade for various reasons, such as promoting domestic industry or protecting their citizens from harmful products.
- Trade enables nations to obtain needed resources or specialize in what they are good at producing.
- The United States faces a bleak financial future because of our growing national debt, the economic character flaws of many Americans, and a growing reliance on government.
- The Christian's hope is in God the Creator and Sustainer.

Practical Application

- Complete a personal trade deficit activity based on a fictitious chewing gum company.

The test for Lesson 33 is located in the assessments section on page 243.

LESSON 34

NAME | DATE

Review Activity for Final Exam

Note: *Since the final exam is a two-part exam, the student may prepare for the final exam by reviewing the Part I and Part II information separately.*

Part I—Scripture Memory

- Proverbs 14:34
- Psalm 33:12

Part I—Concepts to Review

- Explain the foundational economic concepts that are the result of God's creation of the earth and mankind.
- Give reasons why economics is not a "pure" science.
- Provide definitions of microeconomics and macroeconomics.
- Explain the difference between economic goods and services.
- Define the *post hoc* fallacy and the fallacy of composition problems of logic in economics.
- Define *ceteris paribus* and explain why it's an important economic principle.
- Match specific Bible references with their economic concepts.
- List advantages and disadvantages of traditional, command, and free market economies.
- Memorize the 10 principles of Marxism.
- Define value and explain the difference between subjective value and objective value.
- Summarize man's basic economic problem and its related consequences.
- Define opportunity cost.
- Show how supply and demand interact to establish prices in a free-market economy.
- Define elasticity and use the formula for elasticity to calculate elasticity measurements.

- List ways that economic competition benefits consumers.
- Explain the relationships between a good, substitute goods, and complementary goods.

Part II—Scripture Memory

- Matthew 6:33
- Psalm 37:25

Part II—Concepts to Review

- Define the four factors of production (land, labor, capital, entrepreneurship).
- Identify the difference between capital goods and consumer goods.
- Draw and explain a production possibility curve.
- Complete a cost schedule and give a reason for its use.
- Define transfer earnings and economic rent and discuss the reason for making a distinction between the two.
- Identify three ways to improve productivity.
- Explain how absolute advantage and comparative advantage can help increase productivity.
- Identify the three economic entities in every society and their interactions.
- Define utility and marginal utility.
- Discuss the advantages and disadvantages of individual proprietorships, partnerships, and corporations.
- Explain the difference between Gross National Product and Gross Domestic Product.
- Discuss the role of profits and losses in a free-market economy.
- Identify the various ways of measuring profit and explain why "percentage of invested capital" is the best way to measure profits.
- Discuss the pros and cons of government intervention in the economy.
- Draw, label, and explain a diagram of the business cycle.
- Explain how government uses fiscal and monetary policies to manipulate the economy.
- Discuss the Fed's methodology used to manipulate the U.S. economy.
- List reasons for government interference in the economy.
- Define trade-related terminology and explain why nations trade.
- Give reasons why nations might restrict trade.
- Summarize economic problems plaguing the United States.

Part I of the Final Exam (Lesson 35) is located in the assessments section on page 249.

Part II of the Final Exam (Lesson 36) is located in the assessments section on page 255.

Lesson 4—Quiz

NAME ____________________ DATE ____________

Score

Scripture Memory

Directions: *Write or recite Proverbs 14:34 from memory.* *(3 points)*

____

____

____

Content Questions

(1 point each unless otherwise indicated)

1. **True False** According to Psalm 24:1, God owns the earth and everything in it.
2. God gave man ____________________ (control) over His creation.
3. _____ Why should every human being take their "stewardship of the earth" responsibility seriously?
   A. If we don't take this responsibility seriously, man will destroy the environment.
   B. Every human being will someday stand before God and give an account of how they fulfilled this stewardship responsibility.
   C. We owe it to our children and grandchildren.
   D. Global warming must be stopped before it threatens mankind and the animal kingdom.
4. List three economic decisions non-Christians make that illustrate we are made in the image of God. *(3 points)*

   ____

   ____

   ____

5. What is the most important choice every man, woman, and child faces?

   ____

   ____

   ____

6. Economics is "the science that deals with the ____________________, ____________________, and consumption of goods and services." *(2 points)*
7. **True False** Economics is a "pure" science similar to the laboratory sciences.

8. What problems in isolating and controlling all the variables might you encounter if you attempt an economics experiment proving that a single person can live on an income of $10,000 per year? *(5 points)*

____

____

____

____

____

____

9. Explain the difference between microeconomics and macroeconomics. *(2 points)*

____

____

____

10. Economic goods are man-produced goods that have ____________________. Services are the product of man's labor with an associated ____________________. *(2 points)*

11. ______ What is the fallacy of composition?

    A. Using two few samples to prove your hypothesis.

    B. Stating a wrong cause in a cause-effect relationship.

    C. What is true of a part is true of the whole.

    D. Using unfamiliar vocabulary words to confuse the issue.

12. ______ Which of the following is an example of an economic decision NOT based on *ceteris paribus*?

    A. Putting money in the offering plate at church without claiming it as a deduction on your income tax return.

    B. After comparing your two favorite automobile models, buying the one with better quality and higher customer satisfaction ratings.

    C. If offered a job by two different companies, selecting the position with a higher salary and more benefits.

    D. Buying your fiancée a diamond engagement ring rather than a cubic zirconium ring.

13. Ecclesiastes 5:10 says, "He that loveth silver shall not be satisfied with silver; nor he that loveth abundance with increase: this is also vanity." How does this verse relate to Matthew 6:19-21? *(3 points)*

____

____

____

____

14. Suppose that tomorrow you face a dilemma. Your friends want you to spend the day with them at an amusement park, but your family had already made plans to work at an inner-city rescue mission. Would you back out on the family commitment for some fun with your friends? Would Matthew 6:33 assist you in making the right decision? *(3 points)*

____

____

____

____

____

____

Lesson 8—Test

NAME ____________________ DATE ____________

Score

Scripture Memory

Directions: *Write or recite Proverbs 14:34 from memory.* *(3 points)*

____

____

____

Content Questions

(1 point each unless otherwise indicated)

1. ______ Which of the following verses proclaims God's ownership of the earth?

   A. Genesis 3:17b **B.** Exodus 8:1 **C.** Psalm 24:1 **D.** 2 Peter 3:10

2. In Genesis 1:28, God gave man ____________________ (control) over His creation.

3. **True False** Man will answer to God for his stewardship of the earth.

4. According to Colossians 1:16-17, who sustains creation?

   ____

   ____

5. How does God demonstrate that He has not surrendered all of creation's stewardship to mankind? *(2 points)*

   ____

   ____

   ____

   ____

6. Every human being, having been made in the image of God, possesses a ____________________ mind and a free will that enables them to make economic decisions.

7. **True False** Only Christians receive creative abilities from God the Creator.

8. How should the reality of eternity impact our economic decisions? *(2 points)*

   ____

   ____

   ____

9. Write a brief paragraph (three to five sentences) based on your responses to the Lesson 1 Practical Application Activity "My Personal Stewardship Responsibility." Focus on lifestyle choices or changes made after completing the activity. *(10 points)*

____

____

____

____

____

____

____

____

10. **True False** The ancient Greeks and Romans used the word *economics* to refer to the interactions between consumers and businesses.

11. Economics is the science that deals with the ____________________, distribution, and ____________________ of goods and services. *(2 points)*

12. Explain the difference between microeconomics and macroeconomics. *(2 points)*

____

____

____

____

____

____

____

13. __________Which of the following statements is a problem faced by economists?

    A. Problem of objectivity.

    B. Problem of isolating and controlling all the variables.

    C. Problem of moral and ethical restraints because of dealing with people.

    D. All of the above.

14. Economic goods are ____________________ goods that have value.

15. How could you legally acquire an economic good without paying for it? *(2 points)*

____

____

____

____

____

____

Matching: *Match the problem of logic with its example. Answers may be used more than once or not at all. Some questions may have more than one correct answer.*

A. *Post hoc* fallacy
B. Fallacy of composition
C. Generalizing from small samples
D. Appeal to pity/appeal to fear

16. ______ We must raise the U.S. debt ceiling or the U.S. economy will collapse.

17. ______ Global warming is the result of extensive use of fossil fuels.

18. ______ We can reduce our reliance on foreign oil by investing in green technology.

19. ______ If Anytown, MO, can create jobs by cutting taxes, then so can Everytown, IA.

20. ______ Social Security reform will have an adverse effect on our senior citizens.

21. ______ Which of the following statements is an economic decision not based on *ceteris paribus*?

A. Giving 10 percent of your income to the Lord's work and not claiming it as a deduction on your income tax return.

B. Fast-food restaurants giving away free food samples in the food court at the mall.

C. Claiming a clothing contribution to the Salvation Army on your income tax return.

D. Making bimonthly payments on your home mortgage.

22. **True False** *Ceteris paribus* helps us understand consumers' motives behind their economic choices.

23. Based on the Hebrew words for "dress" (*a-vad'*) and "keep" (*sha-mar'*) in Genesis 2:15, what were Adam's two responsibilities in the Garden of Eden? *(2 points)*

____

____

24. How did Adam's work (and all work) change after the Fall (Genesis 3:17b, 18)? *(2 points)*

____

____

____

25. Deuteronomy 19:14 promotes the sanctity of ______________________.

26. ______ What economic principle is found in Ecclesiastes 5:10?

A. God put man in control of His creation.

B. God declares that the physical world He created is "good."

C. All land belongs to God.

D. Material wealth cannot satisfy.

27. "For where your ______________ is, there will your heart be also." (Matthew 6:21)

28. According to Matthew 6:24-33, why can Christians trust God to meet their needs? *(3 points)*

____

____

____

____

____

29. What situation in Acts, Chapters 4 and 5, demonstrated the failure of communism in the early church?

____

____

____

Matching: *Identify the following statements as illustrative of traditional, command, or free-market economies. Answers will be used more than once.*

A. Traditional **B.** Command **C.** Free Market

30. ______ Government or some other central planning agency decides what will be produced.

31. ______ This types of economy produces only what it needs.

32. ______ This type of economy tries to limit man's greed by keeping the majority of its people in poverty.

33. ______ Consumers determine what will be produced in this type of economy.

34. ______ This type of economy fosters family unity.

35. ______ This economy could use economic planning to accomplish economic goals.

36. ______ Natural or environmental disasters could have catastrophic consequences for this type of economy.

37. ______ Supply and demand determine the price levels at which exchanges take place in this type of economy.

38. ______ Periods of unprecedented economic growth are followed by prolonged recessions or severe depressions.

39. ______ This type of economy provides a greater variety of goods and services than the other two types of economies.

40. **True False** By removing the profit motive, command economies destroy man's incentive to work.

41. What's your favorite snack food item? ______________ How would you obtain this item in a traditional economy? *(2 points)*

____

____

____

____

____

42. How would you obtain your favorite snack food in a command economy? *(2 points)*

____

____

____

____

43. How would you obtain your favorite snack food in a free-market economy? *(2 points)*

____

____

____

44. **Principles of Marxism:** Write the missing word on the blank.

- Expropriation of landed ______________, with land rents used for public purposes
- A ______________ or progressive income tax
- State control of ______________ via a national bank and a monopoly on credit
- Centralized ______________ and transportation controlled by the state
- Free public ______________

45. Based on what you learned in this unit, can you really own a home? *(3 points)*

____

____

____

____

____

____

Lesson 12—Quiz

NAME ______ DATE ______

Score

Scripture Memory

Directions: *Write or recite Psalm 33:12 from memory.* *(3 points)*

Content Questions

(1 point each unless otherwise indicated)

1. Where does value exist? ______

2. Value changes with ______, place, and circumstances.

3. Explain the difference between subjective value and objective value. Give an example of each. *(2 points)*

4. **True False** Man's basic economic problem is a lack of good-paying jobs.

5. ______ Why must human beings make economic choices?
   - **A.** It's a prerequisite in a free-market economy.
   - **B.** Earth's limited resources force us to make choices.
   - **C.** Government refuses to make all our decisions.
   - **D.** Choices help businesses sell goods and services to customers.

6. **True False** Opportunity cost is the next best alternate choice.

Cape Cod

Colonial

Bungalow

Victorian

A-frame

American Craftsman

American Foursquare

Gable Front

Directions: *Refer to the houses on page 222 before answering questions #7 and #8.*

7. Which house style is your favorite? ____________________

8. Which house style is opportunity cost?

____

____

____

9. Use the graph paper on page 222 to draw a floor plan for a kitchen or recreational room (including furnishings), demonstrating your unique sense of value. *(7 points)*

10. Suppliers must have both the ____________________ and ____________________ to produce goods and services for sale in a free-market economy. *(2 points)*

11. Draw a supply curve using the following information for Willie's Whirly-Gigs. *(3 points)*

Price Per Whirly-Gig	Quantity Supplied
$1	2
$3	5
$5	9
$7	15
$9	24

12. Why does a typical **supply** curve slope upward from left to right?

____

____

____

____

____

____

13. Why does a typical **demand** curve slope downward from left to right?

____

____

____

____

____

____

14. Write a three- to five-sentence paragraph answering the following question: Explain the economic impact of abortion. *(5 points)*

____

____

____

____

____

____

15. Besides a nation's population, list two other factors that influence demand. *(2 points)*

____

____

____

Lesson 17—Test

NAME ______________________ DATE ______________

Score

Scripture Memory

Directions: *Write or recite Psalm 33:12 from memory. (3 points)*

____

____

____

Content Questions

(1 point each unless otherwise indicated)

1. Value exists in the ________________, and it changes with time, ________________, and circumstances. *(2 points)*

2. If you spend $100,000 on a four-year college degree, does your decision demonstrate subjective profit or objective profit? Explain your answer. *(4 points)*

____

____

____

____

____

____

3. **True False** Scarcity (limited resources) is mankind's basic economic problem.

4. ______ Why must human beings make economic choices?
   - **A.** It's a prerequisite in a free-market economy.
   - **B.** Earth's limited resources force us to make choices.
   - **C.** Government refuses to make all our decisions.
   - **D.** Choices help businesses sell goods and services to customers.

5. ______ If you take your boyfriend/girlfriend to a basketball game, which of the following could be your opportunity cost in this situation?
   - **A.** Go car shopping and buy a new automobile.
   - **B.** Pull weeds in your parent's garden.
   - **C.** Go out to eat at a restaurant.
   - **D.** Purchase a stove, refrigerator, big-screen TV, and a washer/dryer combo for your home since you're getting married two years from now.

6. **True False** Individuals and nations experience opportunity costs.

7. Suppliers in a free-market economy must have both the ____________________ and the ________________ to produce goods and services for sale in the market. *(2 points)*

8. Using the information in the chart, draw a supply curve for Ed's Organic Eggs. *(5 points)*

Price Per Dozen	Amount Supplied (in dozens)
$1.00	0
$1.50	1
$2.00	2
$3.00	5
$4.00	7
$5.00	10
$6.00	14
$7.00	17

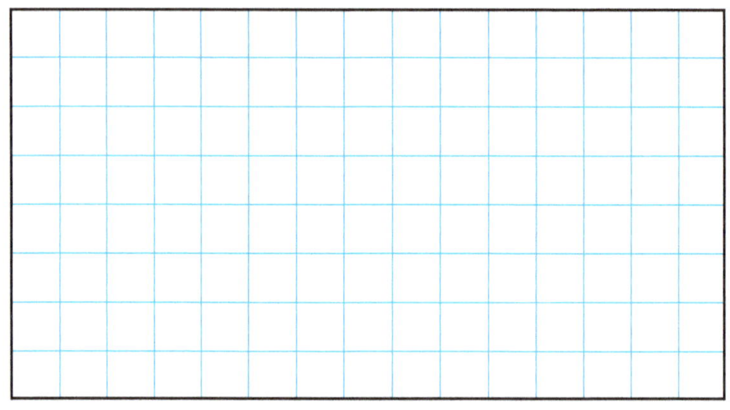

9. **True False** *Ceteris paribus*, buyers are willing to purchase more at lower prices than at higher prices.

10. Using the information in the chart, draw a demand curve for Ed's Organic Eggs. *(5 points)*

Price Per Dozen	Amount Demanded (in dozens)
$1.00	50
$1.50	46
$2.00	28
$3.00	12
$4.00	8
$5.00	5
$6.00	1
$7.00	0

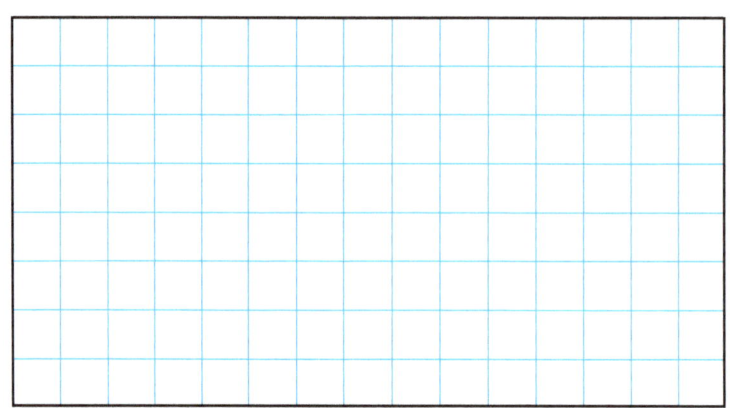

11. Demand is influenced by a nation's population, personal ______________________, consumer tastes, government policies, and the availability of ______________________ products. *(2 points)*

12. What is equilibrium price?

____

____

13. Using the supply and demand curves from questions #8 and #10, determine the equilibrium price for Ed's Organic Eggs. Draw a graph depicting the equilibrium price. *(5 points)*

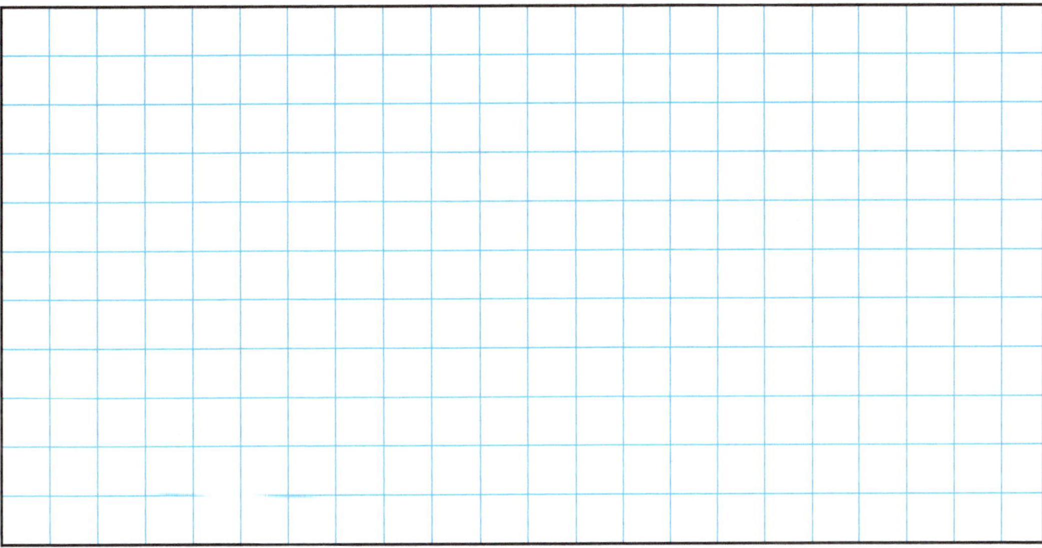

14. ______ Which of the following factors could cause a fluctuation of the equilibrium price for chicken wings?

    A. An avian flu epidemic wipes out 30 percent of the mature birds.

    B. Grain costs increase due to higher fuel prices.

    C. There are fewer consumers eating chicken wings.

    D. All of the above.

15. **True False** Elasticity measures people's response to changes in price.

16. Give the formula for calculating elasticity.

    ____

    ____

17. Calculate the following elasticity measurements for classic VW Beetle sales at Vicki's Used Volkswagens. *(5 points)*

Price	Quantity of VW Beetles Sold	Elasticity Measurement
$10,000	1	*******
$8,000	2	
$7,000	4	
$5,000	7	
$4,000	12	
$3,000	15	

18. From Vicki's perspective, did any of the sales "fail"? Why or why not? *(3 points)*

19. **True False** Necessity items and low-cost purchases tend to have elastic demand.

20. In what ways do business monopolies hurt consumers? *(2 points)*

21. Explain the difference between **perfect substitute goods** and **imperfect substitute goods.** Give an example of each. *(4 points)*

22. ______ If Product A and Product B are perfect complementary goods, what happens to sales of Product B when the price of Product A **increases**?

    A. The price of Product B increases.

    B. Demand for Product B increases.

    C. Demand for Product B decreases.

23. In the Washington Village subdivision, six young entrepreneurs (Bethanie, Mikayla, Alex, Freddy, Susan, and Peter) decide to set up lemonade stands to earn some summer spending money. Answer the following questions based on what you've learned in Lessons 2, 6 and 14. Assume that their parents are providing the needed ingredients free of charge.

    - In a free-market economy and *ceteris paribus*, which child would sell the most lemonade? *(2 points)*

    - What factors besides quality and price would impact the lemonade sales at each of these stands? *(2 points)*

- Freddy's location near the entrance of the subdivision gives him an advantage over the other children. Customers love his sweet-tart lemonade with floating lemon slices in the pitcher. When Freddy's mom goes on vacation, the quality of Freddy's lemonade declines significantly. What economic principle is at work if Freddy's sales drop due to offering customers awful-tasting cups of lemonade? *(1 point)*

- Susan's house is at the back of the development. Many potential customers don't have to drive past her house on their way to or from their homes. How can Susan get customers to drive out of their way to purchase her lemonade? *(2 points)*

- If all the children sold their lemonade for 50 cents per glass, what factor would cause the equilibrium price to change? *(1 point)*

- Theoretically, since the parents are paying for the ingredients, the children could sell their lemonade for one cent per glass and still make a profit. Would the equilibrium price ever drop that low? *(2 points)*

- Bethanie and Peter live next door to each other. If everybody buys Bethanie's lemonade, what is Peter's lemonade for Bethanie's customers? *(1 point)*

- Alex sold 10 glasses of lemonade at one dollar per glass on his first day. On the second day, he lowered the price to 75 cents per glass and sold 20 glasses of lemonade. What is the elasticity measurement of Alex's sales on Day Two? Did the sale result in elastic or inelastic demand for Alex's lemonade? *(2 points)*

Lesson 21—Quiz

NAME ______ DATE ______

Score

Scripture Memory

Directions: *Write or recite Matthew 6:33 from memory.* *(3 points)*

Content Questions

(1 point each unless otherwise indicated)

1. List and define the four basic factors of production. *(4 points)*

2. Which factor of production is the most important? Why? *(2 points)*

3. What determines if a good is a capital good or a consumer good? How can a baseball be both a capital good and a consumer good? *(2 points)*

4. **True False** A production possibility frontier is used to evaluate modern-day farming techniques.

5. Which type of production relies heavily on machinery and technology?

6. Why would an entrepreneur use a cost schedule?

7. List the formula for calculating average fixed cost (AFC).

8. List the formula for calculating marginal cost (MC).

9. Complete the following cost schedule for Willie's Whirly-Gigs. You may use a calculator for assistance. *(4 points)*

Hours	Q	TFC	TVC	TC	AFC	AVC	AC	MC
1	2	100	12					*******
2	5	100	30					
3	9	100	52					
4	13	100	70					
5	18	100	98					

10. **True False** Transfer earnings are what a factor of production must earn in order to keep it in its present use.

11. Transfer earnings and ____________________ rent help us determine the most efficient use of the factors of production.

12. Why is productivity an important economic concept? *(2 points)*

____

____

____

____

____

____

13. Division of labor, ____________________, and specialization help to increase productivity.

14. Explain the difference between **absolute** advantage and **comparative** advantage. *(2 points)*

____

____

____

____

____

____

____

15. **True False** Technology always helps productivity.

16. Why is multifactor productivity a better measure of productivity than labor productivity? *(2 points)*

____

____

____

____

____

____

Lesson 25—Test

NAME ____________________ DATE ____________

Score

Scripture Memory

Directions: *Write or recite Matthew 6:33 from memory.* *(3 points)*

____

____

____

Content Questions

(1 point each unless otherwise indicated)

1. ______________, labor, ______________, and entrepreneurship are the four factors of production. *(2 points)*

2. ______ Why is labor the most important factor of production?

   A. It's the one factor of production each person can control.

   B. It's the most expensive factor of production.

   C. Unlike the other factors of production, labor never diminishes in value.

   D. Adam Smith and Karl Marx said it's the most important factor of production; therefore, it must be true.

3. Why do economists make a distinction between land in its natural state and land with man-made improvements? *(2 points)*

   ____

   ____

   ____

4. **True False** Labor includes both physical and mental human effort.

5. Capital refers to the machines, tools, and buildings that help us produce ______________.

6. List the two roles of the entrepreneur in a free-market economy. *(2 points)*

   ____

   ____

   ____

7. What determines if a good is a capital good or a consumer good? *(1 point)* Give an example of an automobile being both a capital good and a consumer good. *(1 point)*

____

____

____

____

8. ______ Why do economists and entrepreneurs use production possibility frontiers?

   A. A PPF enables them to predict the health of the U.S. economy.

   B. Production possibility frontiers show all possible combinations for dual usage of a factor of production.

   C. A PPF is a useful tool for increasing labor productivity.

   D. Production possibility frontiers assess the potential value of previously unused land.

9. Your parents gave you a 20′ x 50′ section of the backyard to use to earn money for your college fund. You decide to install an inflatable bouncer on part of the land and grow a cash crop on the other portion. The bouncer takes up 200 square feet of the total 1,000-square-foot area. You grow red beets on the remaining 800 square feet. You charge $10/hour for playtime in the bouncer. Several neighborhood moms happily use your bouncer to entertain their children for an hour each day. Of course, they must sign a waiver releasing you from liability if their child gets hurt or injured while playing in the bouncer. The red beets take almost three months before you see any profit, but the fertile ground produces 30 bushels of red beets, which you sell for a profit of $20 per bushel. The following chart shows your income for the summer.

Profit from Inflatable Bouncer Patrons	Profit from Red Beets Cash Crop
$2,000	$600

Answer the following questions based on what you've learned in Lessons 18-20 and the information in question #9.

a. What factors might convince you to add another bouncer for next summer's fund-raising? *(2 points)*

____

____

____

____

b. Would growing a different legal cash crop bring you more income? *(2 points)*

____

____

____

____

c. Draw a production possibility frontier showing the land usage split between two bouncers and cash crop production. *(3 points)*

d. Can you assume that next year's profits would be $4,000 from bouncer patrons and $450 from red beet sales? Why or why not? *(2 points)*

e. For the following production processes on your backyard plot, specify if you would use labor-intensive production or capital-intensive production. List a reason for your choice. *(2 points each)*

A. Inflating the bouncers—

B. Helping patrons into the bouncer—

C. Preparing the soil—

D. Planting the red beet seed—

____

____

____

10. ______ Why would an entrepreneur use a cost schedule?

A. Cost schedules make it easier to give the employees a fair raise.

B. Cost schedules enable entrepreneurs to examine various inputs of a factor of production to determine the optimum level of production.

C. Cost schedules determine the price at which the product sells.

D. Cost schedules reveal areas where the business can save money.

11. Complete the cost schedule for Harry's Handsome Hats. Each variable input is another hour of labor. *(1/4 point for each blank, 6 points total)* Harry should make hats using five hours of labor. His average cost per hat is $39.23 (lowest average cost) and the marginal cost to produce at that level is the same as the other input levels.

Input	Q	TFC	TVC	TC	AFC	AVC	AC	MC
1	3	250	60					*****
2	7	250	140					
3	10	250	200					
4	12	250	240					
5	13	250	260					

12. ____________________ earnings are what a factor of production must earn in order to keep it in its current use.

13. Why is productivity important to a free-market economy? *(4 points)*

____

____

____

14. An assembly line is an example of which productivity technique—division of labor, use of technology, or specialization? *(2 points)*

____

____

____

____

____

____

15. Name an area in which you have an absolute advantage over your siblings. Name a different area in which you have a comparative advantage over them. *(2 points)*

____

____

____

____

____

____

16. If a Chinese company had an absolute advantage in computer technical support over companies from India and the United Kingdom, why might a U.S. computer producer choose to use the U.K. firm for its technical support rather than the Chinese company? *(3 points)*

____

____

____

____

17. **True False** If technology is your master rather than your servant, your productivity as a student will suffer.

18. Why can't productivity alone keep a nation competitive? *(3 points)*

____

____

____

____

19. ______ Why is multifactor productivity a better indicator of true productivity than labor productivity?

    A. Multifactor productivity takes into account those factors that affect labor productivity and over which the laborer has no control.

    B. Multifactor productivity examines the productivity of the entire nation.

    C. Illegal immigrant labor isn't included in labor productivity.

    D. Labor productivity statistics are prone to misrepresentation and inaccurate data.

20. Households, businesses, and ____________________ are the three economic entities found in every society.

21. In what ways is a farmer both a producer and a consumer? *(2 points)*

____

____

____

22. How do taxes interfere with the economic relationship between households and businesses? *(3 points)*

____

____

____

____

23. Why are public sector jobs vulnerable during economic recessions? *(2 points)*

____

____

____

____

24. Utility is the ____________________ derived from consuming a good or service.

25. Why is marginal utility an important concept in an economic society built upon consumption? List an example of how businesses in consumption-based economies try to increase consumption of their products. *(2 points)*

____

____

____

____

____

____

26. How could you objectively state the subjective satisfaction you feel from eating pizza? *(2 points)*

____

____

____

____

Lesson 29—Quiz

NAME ______________________ DATE ______________

Score

Scripture Memory

Directions: *Write or recite Psalm 37:25 from memory.* *(3 points)*

____

____

____

Content Questions

(1 point each unless otherwise indicated)

1. **True False** Unlike a sole proprietorship, corporations have unlimited liability for their actions.
2. "S" corporations avoid the problem of double taxation by allowing all profits or losses to be shown on the ______________ personal income tax return.
3. **True False** Members of a partnership are not responsible for actions of the other members.
4. Which type of business organization is the easiest to start?

   ____

   ____

5. Which type of business organization has an unlimited time span of existence?

   ____

   ____

6. **True False** Partnerships can acquire capital for business expansion by selling shares of stock.
7. Gross ______________ Product statistics exclude U.S. firms operating in foreign countries.
8. What do profits signal in a free-market economy?

   ____

   ____

9. _____ What method of measuring profits assures the most efficient allocation of capital resources?

   A. Percentage of sales

   B. Percentage of invested capital

   C. Percentage of ownership equity

10. List two ways government intervenes in the marketplace to guarantee profits. *(2 points)*

____

____

____

11. Why is government intervention to prevent business losses a problem for free-market economies? *(3 points)*

____

____

____

____

12. Draw and label a diagram of the business cycle. *(5 points)*

13. Explain the difference between **fiscal** policy and **monetary** policy. *(2 points)*

____

____

____

____

____

____

14. List and define the three tools used by the Federal Reserve to manipulate the economy. *(3 points)*

____

____

____

____

15. Monetizing the debt (printing more money) leads to ______________________.

16. List two reasons government leaders interfere in the economy. *(2 points)*

____

____

____

Lesson 33—Test

NAME ____________________ DATE ____________

Score

Scripture Memory

Directions: *Write or recite Psalm 37:25 from memory.* *(3 points)*

____

____

____

Content Questions

(1 point each unless otherwise indicated)

1. **True False** Individual proprietorships, cooperatives, and corporations are the three main types of business organizations.
2. The ____________________ is the easiest and simplest type of business to get started.
3. One of the main disadvantages of an individual proprietorship is ____________ liability (the owner is legally liable for all the actions of the company and any incidents related to company property).
4. **True False** Each member of a partnership is legally liable for the actions of the other partners.
5. The corporate ________ protects corporate management and stockholders from personal liability for the company's actions.

   A. lawyer **B.** shield **C.** liability policy
6. How are general corporations taxed differently than "S" corporations? *(2 points)*

   ____

   ____

   ____

   ____

   ____
7. Who owns a cooperative (co-op)?

   ____

   ____
8. Which type of business organization has the greatest financial resources to expand the business?

   ____

   ____

9. Which form of business organization (S corporation or Limited Liability Company) has fewer Internal Revenue Service regulations?

____

____

10. Explain the difference between Gross National Product and Gross Domestic Product. *(2 points)*

____

____

____

11. What is the basic assumption about a business firm?

____

12. **True False** In a free-market economy, profits are the rewards for meeting consumer wants and needs.

13. ______ Which method of measuring profits ensures the most efficient allocation of capital resources?

    A. Percentage of sales

    B. Percentage of ownership equity

    C. Percentage of invested capital

14. Why is government interference in the economy to guarantee profit or prevent business losses wrong? *(3 points)*

____

____

____

____

____

____

____

15. Businesses and national economies go through the four stages of the business cycle—expansion, ______________________, ______________________, and trough. *(2 points)*

16. ______ Which of the following is an example of the U.S. government using fiscal policy to stimulate the economy?

    A. Lowering interest rates on 30-year home mortgages

    B. Increasing the money supply by $10 billion

    C. Eliminating capital gains taxes

17. **True False** The Federal Reserve System is the central banking system of the United States.

18. What is the principal means by which the Fed regulates the U.S. economy?

____

____

____

19. The ____________________ rate is the interest rate the Federal Reserve charges for loans to commercial banks and other depository institutions.

20. If the Fed wants to decrease the money supply, what happens to the reserve ratio?

____

____

____

21. **True False** During periods of inflation, the Federal Reserve tries to slow down the U.S. economy.

22. Give a historical example of the consequences of monetizing the debt. *(2 points)*

____

____

____

____

____

23. Government leaders interfere in the economy to maintain economic ____________________, control ____________________, and correct economic ____________________. *(3 points)*

24. **True False** Excess demand without increased supply leads to inflation.

25. Why do nations trade?

____

____

26. A nation that practices *autarky* is trying to ________.

A. protect its citizens from harmful products

B. establish a favorable balance of trade

C. implement a free-trade policy

D. become economically self-sufficient

27. **True False** Nations that engage in free trade cannot collect customs duties.

28. If a nation wanted to limit the number of foreign-made automobiles coming into the country, it could do so by using ____________________ quotas.

29. Your friend Tom in the United Kingdom recently discovered a way to make chewing gum out of rubber bands. The neat thing about his invention is that the flavor lasts four times longer than ordinary gum and doesn't lose its intensity one iota until it's gone entirely. The suggested retail price for a pack of five sticks of gum is two dollars. Tom agrees to wholesale his invention to you at a 40 percent discount off the suggested retail price with terms of net 30 (you have 30 days from the date on the invoice to make payment on the product). Priority mail shipping from the U.K will cost you an additional $150 for 1,000 packs of gum.

a. What is the "per pack" wholesale price of the gum? ____________________

b. If you bought 1,000 packs of gum, how much would you pay for the gum?

____

c. What is the total amount of your invoice (including shipping)? ____________________

d. What is the "per pack" price for shipping?

____

e. How many packs of gum must you sell in 30 days to pay Tom's invoice?

____

f. If you sold all of the gum at the suggested retail price in the first 30 days, how much profit would you make? ____________________

g. What is your "trade deficit" with Tom when you place your first order?

____

h. After 10 days, you've only sold 10 packs of gum. What is your "trade deficit" after 10 days?

____

i. In order to pay Tom's invoice on time, you could try advertising and/or lowering the "per pack" price of the gum. Rather than spend more money on advertising, you decide to sell the remaining packs of gum for $1.50 per pack. This strategy enables you to sell 200 additional packs of gum before the invoice is due. What is your "trade deficit" at the end of 30 days?

____

____

j. What are your options for eliminating your "trade deficit" with Tom? *(3 points)*

____

____

____

____

____

k. Could you avoid a trade loss by selling the gum at "cost" ($1.35 per pack)?

____

____

____

l. If you sold all of the gum at $2.00 per pack within the 30 days, would having a temporary "trade deficit" with Tom be a good thing or a bad thing?

____

____

m. Would having an ongoing "trade deficit" with Tom be a good or a bad thing? *(3 points)*

____

____

____

____

____

n. Tom refuses to take back the unsold product but decides to extend you credit on the "past due" amount of the invoice. After six months, however, he changes his mind and demands immediate payment of the money you still owe him. Sales of the product are stagnant, and with the interest on the unpaid invoice balance, you still owe Tom $975.00. What are your options? *(3 points)*

____

____

____

____

____

30. How do export subsidies hinder international free trade? *(3 points)*

____

____

____

____

31. Why is free trade preferable to protective tariffs?

A. Protective tariffs could lead to retaliatory tariffs by other nations.

B. Protective tariffs lower the standard of living in underdeveloped countries.

C. Free trade cultivates new markets and economic opportunities.

D. Both A and B.

E. Both A and C.

F. Both B and C .

32. Nations regulate trade to promote ____________________ industry or protect their citizens from harmful products.

33. Why would a nation that could produce certain goods choose to obtain them through trade rather than domestic manufacturing? *(2 points)*

____

____

____

____

34. How might war interfere with a nation that practices trade specialization? Give a historical example to support your answer. *(4 points)*

____

____

____

____

____

____

35. According to the author, the United States faces a bleak financial future due to our growing national ____________________, the economic ____________________ flaws of many Americans, and our growing reliance on ____________________. *(3 points)*

Final Exam—Part I

NAME ______________________ DATE ______________

Score

Scripture Memory

Directions: *Write or recite Proverbs 14:34 and Psalm 33:12 from memory.* *(6 points)*

____

____

____

____

____

____

Content Questions

(1 point each unless otherwise indicated)

1. How is a belief in God as the Creator foundational to a proper understanding of economics? *(4 points)*

____

____

____

____

____

2. ______ Why is economics not a "pure" science?

   A. It cannot use the scientific method.

   B. Unlike laboratory scientists, economists cannot isolate and control all the variables.

   C. Pure science uses chemical compounds.

   D. Economists must get permission from the government to conduct experiments on human beings.

3. ______ deals with the "broad" and "general" aspects of an economy.

   A. microeconomics **B.** macroeconomics

4. What makes a good an "economic" good? *(2 points)*

____

____

5. **True False** "Services" have a cost because the consumer pays for the use of the labor to provide the service.

6. ______ Which of the following statements best explains the *post hoc* fallacy?

A. The *post hoc* fallacy plays on people's pity or fears.

B. This fallacy tries to make people believe what is true of a part is true of the whole.

C. The *post hoc* fallacy states a wrong cause in a cause-effect relationship.

D. This fallacy tries to make generalizations using small samples.

7. **True False** *Ceteris paribus* is a French term meaning "labor is the most important factor of production."

8. Why is *ceteris paribus* such an important concept for economics? *(3 points)*

____

____

____

9. **Matching:** Match the following Scripture verses with their correct economic principle. *(1 point each)*

A. Genesis 1:28

B. Genesis 2:15

C. Genesis 3:17-19

D. Deuteronomy 19:14

E. Matthew 6:19-21

F. Acts 4:32-Acts 5:5

a. ______ God gave Adam and Eve work to do in the Garden of Eden.
b. ______ Christians should lay up their treasures in heaven.
c. ______ God gave man dominion over creation.
d. ______ This Scripture records the early church's experiment with communism.
e. ______ Nature is stingy as a result of the Curse.
f. ______ God established the concept of private property.

10. **True False** All traditional economies totally reject the use of technology.

11. ______ How do command economies try to control man's greed?

A. They limit the salaries of government officials and corporate executives.

B. They make everyone's salaries equal.

C. They give everyone the same amount of material possessions.

D. They keep the vast majority of their citizens in perpetual poverty.

12. Which type of economy fosters family unity? ______________________

13. List two criticisms of free-market economies. *(2 points)*

____

____

____

14. How do traditional economies avoid the problem of overproduction?

____

____

15. Free-market economies try to control man's greed through ______________ exchange.

16. **True False** The key element of a command economy is some form of a central planning agency.

17. ______________ and ______________ determine price levels in a free-market economy. *(2 points)*

18. How do command economies destroy man's incentive to work?

____

____

____

19. **Marxism:** Use the word bank to complete the 10 tenets of Marxism.

Word Bank: factory, land, national, production, progressive, property, rural, urban

a. Expropriation of landed property with ______________ rents used for public purposes

b. A graduated or ______________ income tax

c. No inheritance rights

d. Confiscation of rebels' ______________

e. State control of finances: a ______________ bank and a monopoly on credit

f. Centralized communication and transportation controlled by the state

g. A planned economy—______________ factories, more cultivated land, and planned ______________ and agriculture

h. Universal and equal work using "industrial armies"

i. Elimination of ______________ and ______________ distinctions

j. Free public education, abolition of ______________ work for children, and combining education with material production

20. ______ Which of the following statements is NOT true concerning value?

A. Value changes with time, place, and circumstances.

B. Value exists in the mind.

C. Subjective value is measurable using dollars and cents.

21. What is man's basic economic problem? What does it cause him to do? *(2 points)*

____

____

22. Economists use the term ____________________ ____________________ to refer to the next best alternate choice.

23. Draw and label a **demand** curve given the following information. *(5 points)*

Price	Quantity
$78	5
$69	8
$53	15
$42	17
$35	21

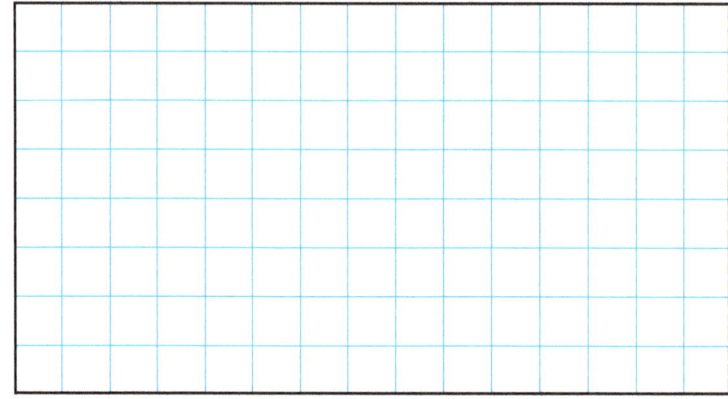

24. Draw and label a **supply** curve given the following information. *(5 points)*

Price	Quantity
$40	3
$50	11
$60	16
$70	19
$80	25

25. Using the graphs from questions #23 and #24, draw a graph showing the equilibrium price. *(5 points)*

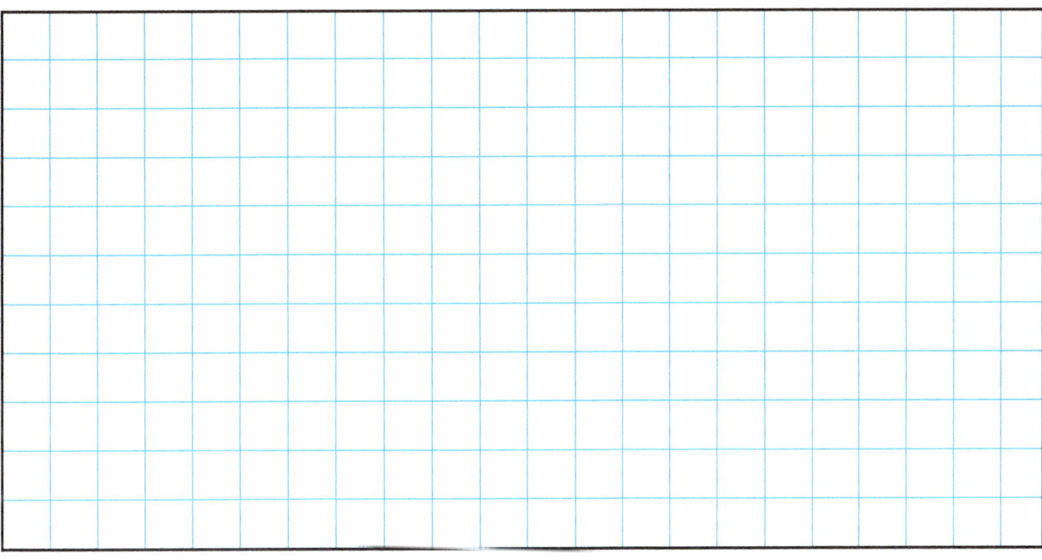

26. In question #25, at approximately what price does exchange take place?

____

____

____

27. **True False** Elasticity measures people's response to changes in price.

28. Elasticity: Calculate the following measurements of elasticity. *(1 point each)*

Price	Quantity	Elasticity Measurement
$100	1	*****
$75	4	
$50	8	
$25	12	

29. How does economic competition benefit consumers? *(2 points)*

____

____

____

____

____

____

____

____

____

30. Lettuce is an edible economic good. What would happen to the price of the salad bar at restaurants if a drought caused a shortage of lettuce?

31. Is there a close substitute good for lettuce?

32. List five complementary goods that would be affected by skyrocketing lettuce prices. *(5 points)*

Final Exam—Part II

NAME ____________________ DATE __________

Score

Scripture Memory

Directions: *Write or recite Matthew 6:33 and Psalm 37:25 from memory.* *(6 points)*

____

____

____

____

____

____

Content Questions

(1 point each unless otherwise indicated)

1. **True False** The economist's definition of land includes the man-made improvements to the land.

2. The definition of labor includes both ____________________ and ____________________ human effort. *(2 points)*

3. The factor of production called **capital** refers to anything used to create ____________________.

4. What is the entrepreneur's role in a free-market economy? *(2 points)*

   ____

   ____

   ____

   ____

   ____

5. **True False** A lathe used to make turnings for furniture is an example of a capital good.

6. Why do businesses use cost schedules? *(2 points)*

   ____

   ____

   ____

   ____

   ____

7. Complete the following cost schedule and circle the input level at which production should take place. *(10 points)*

Input	Q	TFC	TVC	TC	AFC	AVC	AC	MC
10	100	500	200					
15	130	500	300					
20	165	500	400					
25	199	500	500					
30	203	500	600					

8. What are transfer earnings? How do they differ from economic rent? *(2 points)*

____

____

____

____

____

____

9. Would a 1 percent interest rate on a six-month certificate of deposit (CD) be enough for you to leave your money in that investment? *(2 points)*

____

____

____

____

____

10. ______ Which of the following is NOT a method used to increase productivity?

A. Division of labor

B. Use of technology

C. Specialization

D. *Ceteris paribus*

11. How can absolute advantage and comparative advantage help a business increase its productivity? *(4 points)*

____

____

____

____

____

____

____

____

12. The three economic entities in every society are households, businesses, and ______________________. Each acts as both a producer and a ______________________ as it interacts with the other economic entities. *(2 points)*

13. How might households serve as producers for business?

____

____

____

____

____

____

____

____

14. Utility is the ______________________ derived from consuming a good or service.

15. ______ Which of the following individuals would be interested in your marginal utility for potato chips?

    A. Your local grocer
    B. A potato farmer in Idaho
    C. Employees at a potato chip factory
    D. Stockholders in a snack food company that produces potato chips
    E. B and C
    F. All of the above

16. Matching: Match the following statements with the appropriate type of business organization. *(1 point each)*

    A. Individual (Sole) Proprietorships
    B. Partnerships
    C. Corporations

- ________ All of its members are responsible for the actions of the other members.
- ________ This type has limited legal liability.
- ________ When one member leaves or dies, the business is dissolved.
- ________ This is the easiest and simplest type of business to start.
- ________ Certain types of this business pay double taxes.
- ________ This type has unlimited legal liability.
- ________ This type has access to a greater amount of capital than the two other types.

17. ______ excludes U.S. firms manufacturing in foreign countries.

    A. Gross National Product **B.** Gross Domestic Product

18. What do losses mean in a free-market economy?

____

____

____

____

19. Three methods of measuring profits are percentage of ________________, percentage of invested capital, and percentage of ownership ________________. *(2 points)*

20. Why is percentage of invested capital the best method for measuring profits? *(2 points)*

____

____

____

____

____

21. List three legitimate reasons for government interference in the economy. *(3 points)*

____

____

____

____

____

____

22. How do government bailouts to prevent business losses hurt a free-market economy? *(2 points)*

____

____

____

____

____

____

23. Draw and explain a diagram of the business cycle. *(5 points)*

____

____

____

____

____

____

24. Government uses ________________ policy (taxing and spending measures) as one means of controlling the economy.

25. What will be the result (inflation or deflation) if the Federal Reserve raises the reserve ratio?

______

______

______

______

26. If the Federal Reserve sells U.S. government securities, is it expanding or contracting the money supply?

______

______

______

______

27. List three reasons for government interference in the economy. *(3 points)*

______

______

______

28. Explain the difference between trade subsidies and trade quotas. *(2 points)*

______

______

______

______

______

29. Can any nation in the 21st century successfully practice autarky? *(2 points)*

______

______

______

______

30. In a global free-trade environment, why do nations restrict trade? *(2 points)*

______

______

______

31. ______ According to the author, which of the following is NOT a current economic problem plaguing the United States?

A. The growing U.S. national debt

B. The unfavorable balance of trade with other countries

C. A growing reliance on public sector jobs

D. Economic character flaws in the character of U.S. citizens

Glossary

Absolute advantage: a business situation in which a provider of goods or services is more profitable or efficient than all of its competitors.

Autarky: a nation that is economically self-sufficient.

Average cost (AC): cost schedule column found by adding the average fixed cost (AFC) column and the average variable cost (AVC) column.

Average fixed cost (AFC): column on a cost schedule found by dividing the total fixed cost (TFC) by the quantity resulting from the variable input.

Average variable cost (AVC): column on a cost schedule found by dividing the total variable cost (TFC) by the quantity resulting from the variable input.

Business firm: any organization or entity that arranges the various factors of production to provide a good or service.

Capital: economic factor of production referring to the machines, tools, and buildings used to create wealth.

Capital goods: economic goods that are used to create wealth.

Ceteris paribus (key-te-rees pah-ri-boo s)**:** a Latin phrase meaning "other things being equal." This concept applies to many areas of economics such as determining value, opportunity cost, and transactions between consumers and businesses.

Command economy: an economy in which the central government controls the means of production and decides what will be produced. This type of economy is sometimes referred to as a planned economy.

Comparative advantage: the ability of an individual or group to carry out an economic activity, such as production, at a lower cost and more efficiently than another entity.

Competition: economic situation in which multiple suppliers compete for customers.

Complementary goods: economic goods that go together and rely upon each other.

Consumer goods: "finished" economic goods intended for consumer use or consumption.

Contractionary monetary policy: economic policy used to slow down the rate of inflation by reducing the amount of money available in the economy.

Cooperative (co-op)**:** a business organization owned and controlled equally by the people who use its services or by the people who work there.

Corporation: a state-chartered business entity with legal rights as an entity separate from its owners.

Cost schedule: a chart used to examine a factor of production in isolation at various input levels to determine optimum output.

Customs duties: a tax or fee on imports to or exports from a country.

Demand: the willingness and ability of consumers to utilize goods and services.

Depression: a severe, prolonged downturn in a nation's economy.

Diminishing marginal utility: observable phenomenon in which each additional immediate use/consumption of a good or service provides decreased satisfaction.

Discount rate: the interest rate charged to commercial banks and other depository institutions on loans they receive from their regional Federal Reserve Bank's lending facility—the discount window. The Federal Reserve offers three different levels of credit to the financial institutions needing to use this monetary policy tool.

Division of labor: multiple employees performing specific steps in the process of making an economic good or providing a service.

Domestic trade: trade that takes place within a country's borders (i.e., within a single U.S. state or between two or more states).

Economic goods: man-made things that consumers value highly enough to purchase or acquire through other means.

Economic rent: income that a factor of production earns above transfer earnings.

Economics: the science that deals with the production, distribution, and consumption of goods and services, or the material welfare of humankind.

Elasticity: objective measurement of how people respond to changes in price. To calculate elasticity, divide the percentage of change in quantity by the percentage of change in price.

Entrepreneurship: economic factor of production referring to an individual's risk-taking mindset in an attempt to fulfill consumer wants and needs by providing a good or service in the marketplace.

Equilibrium price: in a free-market economy, the price at which exchanges take place; the intersection of the supply and demand curves for that good or service in which supply balances demand; also known as the market-clearing price.

Expansion: A period of time in which gross domestic product (GDP) increases.

Expansionary monetary policy: used to stimulate the economy during times of recession or depression.

Export: to ship a product out of a country or region.

Fiscal policy: the taxing and spending policies of the government.

Foreign trade: trade that takes place between two or more independent sovereign nations.

Free market: *see* Market economy.

Free trade: international trade that is free of such government interference as import quotas, export subsidies, protective tariffs, etc.

Global economics: the interdependent economies of the world's nations, regarded as a single economic system.

Goods: an economic term referring to items that have value.

Gross Domestic Product (GDP): measure of the total value of goods and services produced for final sale in a nation during a year; excludes U.S. firms manufacturing in foreign countries but does include foreign firms manufacturing in the United States.

Gross National Product (GNP): measure of the total value of goods and services produced for final sale in a nation during a year; includes U.S. firms operating outside the geographic boundaries of the United States.

Imperfect substitutes: economic goods or services that are similar; a close alternative.

Import: to have a product shipped into a country or region.

Individual proprietorship: type of business firm wholly owned by a single individual.

Labor: economic factor of production referring to physical and mental human effort.

Land: economic factor of production referring to the earth in its natural state exclusive of man-made objects.

Macroeconomics: the broad and general aspects of an economy, as the relationship between the income and investments of a country as a whole.

Marginal cost (MC): column on a cost schedule found by dividing the increase in total variable cost (TVC) by the increase in quantity resulting from the variable input.

Marginal utility: the additional usefulness or satisfaction derived from consuming a good or service.

Market-clearing price: *see* Equilibrium price.

Market economy: an economy that uses the interactions of individuals and businesses to determine production, distribution, and consumption, with little or no central government planning or intervention in the economy; also called a capitalist economy, a free- market economy, or the free-enterprise system.

Microeconomics: economic analysis of particular components of the economy, such as the growth of a single industry or demand for a single product.

Mixed economy: an economy that blends elements of the traditional, command, and market economies.

Monetary policy: the regulation of the money supply and interest rates by a central bank in order to control inflation and stabilize currency.

Monetizing the debt: when the government attempts to pay off its debts by printing more money.

Monopoly: economic situation in which one supplier controls the entire market for a good or service.

Objective value: value that can be measured in terms of dollars and cents.

Open market operations: monetary policy tool used by the Federal Reserve involving the purchases and sales of U.S. Treasury and federal agency securities.

Opportunity cost: the next best alternative based on the choice actually made.

Partnership: type of business firm owned by two or more individuals.

Peak: point at which a nation's economic expansion stops prior to an economic decline.

Percentage of invested capital: method of measuring profit found by dividing profit by the investment monies needed to start the business.

Percentage of ownership equity: method of measuring profit found by taking the profit minus interest payments on borrowed money and dividing it by the amount of money invested.

Percentage of sales: method of measuring profit defined as gross sales minus operating costs.

Perfect complementary goods: economic goods that must be consumed together; i.e., a battery-operated flashlight and batteries.

Perfect substitutes: economic goods or services that are exactly alike.

Production possibility frontier: an economic graph showing all possible combinations/uses of two factors of production.

Productivity: economic concept focusing on an individual worker's efficiency resulting in reduced production costs; effective use of human and physical resources resulting in economic expansion.

Profit: economic concept referring to making money.

Quotas: an allotment or limited amount. Nations not practicing free trade may place import quotas on products from other nations.

Recession: period of time when a nation's economy is in decline.

Reserve requirements: the amount of funds that a depository institution must hold in reserve against specified deposit liabilities.

Services: the product of human labor with an associated cost.

Specialization: productivity technique in which individuals, businesses, or nations concentrate on what they do best.

Speculation: engagement in business transactions involving considerable risk but offering the chance of large gains.

Subjective value: psychological value; value that exists in the mind and that cannot be measured monetarily.

Subsidy: financial aid given by the government to individuals or groups.

Substitute goods: economic goods that are interchangeable.

Supply: the side of an economy that deals with the willingness and the ability of individuals to produce a product or provide a service.

Tariff: a tax on imports.

Total cost (TC): column on a cost schedule found by adding the total fixed cost (TFC) and total variable cost (TVC) columns.

Total fixed cost (TFC): column on a cost schedule that does not change with each increasing variable input.

Total variable cost (TVC): column on a cost schedule that shows the increased costs associated with each new variable input.

Trade: the act or process of buying, selling, or exchanging commodities, at either wholesale or retail, within a country or between countries.

Trade deficit: a negative balance of trade (imports exceed exports).

Trade surplus: a positive balance of trade (exports exceed imports).

Traditional economy: an economic society consisting of a family, clan, or tribal unit preserving the cultural practices of their ancestors.

Transfer earnings: what a factor of production must earn in order to keep it in its present use.

Trend line: hypothetical static display of a nation's economy.

Trough: point at which a nation's economic decline "bottoms out" prior to a period of economic expansion.

Utility: the usefulness of a good or service to an individual; the satisfaction derived from consuming a good or service.

Value: economic concept referring to an individual's mental imputation of worth. Value changes with time, place, and circumstances.

Wealth: man-made goods that have value.

X-axis: the horizontal plane of an economic graph.

Y-axis: the vertical plane of an economic graph.

Answer Key

Lesson 1A

1. *Answers will vary. Genesis 1:1 and Psalm 24:1 tell us that God created the earth and He owns it. Like a patent protecting the rights of an inventor, God's Word confirms Him as the Creator and rightful Owner of His creation.*
2. *No. Since God owns it all anyway, I should gladly give back to Him a portion of what He has given to me.*
3. *Answers will vary. He intervenes to bring natural disasters (floods, earthquakes, volcanic eruptions, etc.) upon mankind. He uses carrion birds and microscopic organisms to dispose of dead animal skeletons. Decomposing natural matter nourishes and replenishes the soil. Volcanic eruptions produce fertile soil.*
4. *Answers will vary. Yes, it wastes electricity and hurts the family finances through higher utility bills.*
5. *Answers will vary. Environmentalists warn us that slash-and-burn agriculture permanently destroys the land's ability to grow vegetation. This photo proves otherwise. If vegetation can overrun an unused asphalt parking lot, then vegetation can certainly return to depleted rainforest soil once it is no longer being used to produce food crops.*
6. *Answers will vary. No, because God is in control of His creation. He may allow mankind to irreparably damage certain parts of the earth, but not enough to destroy the earth's ability to sustain life until He decides to allow it.*
7. *Answers will vary. Accept any carefully crafted answer that suggests a solution somewhere between the two extremes.*

Lesson 1B

1. *Man is creative like his Creator; man has a rational mind and a free will (the ability to make choices); as an eternal being, man must consider his future destiny.*
2. *Answers will vary. The student should honestly assess their talents and interests from an economic standpoint; i.e., my piano-playing abilities will allow me to give piano lessons or give paying concerts. Each student's answer should reflect all of their talents and interests—don't hesitate to have the student add to an incomplete answer.*
3. *Answers will vary. We voluntarily choose to accept His gift of salvation through Jesus Christ, thus desiring a relationship with our Creator. The Christian can also choose to accept His will, thereby trusting that God knows what is best for us. As we grow in our relationship with Him, we gain a greater appreciation for His mercy and grace toward us, and praise Him accordingly.*
4. *Answers will vary. I chose to study for my math test and got a 98 percent. I spent money on a new article of clothing. I said kind words to a sibling.*
5. *Answers will vary. Students may express the desire to put God first in their lives, to give a portion of their income to the Lord's work, or to go into vocational ministry. Responses should reflect an understanding that "only what's done for Christ will last."*

Lesson 2A

1. *Economics is a social science dealing with the production, distribution, and consumption of goods and services.*
2. *Answers will vary but should contain the following thoughts. Microeconomics deals with a specific industry or business, while macroeconomics focuses on the economy of a nation as a whole.*
3. *The three limitations involve objectivity, the impossibility of controlling all the variables, and moral and ethical issues in dealing with human beings.*
4. *Answers will vary. He could trade something else of value for it or work for the object's owner in exchange for the object. He could illegally obtain the item by stealing it from its owner.*
5. *Goods are man-made items that have value, while services are the product of human labor with an associated cost.*
6. *This person thinks it's wrong for government to help someone who's not willing to work.*
7. *Answers will vary. Many receiving government assistance are working, but their income is below the federal poverty level. Certain disabilities prevent some people from working to provide for themselves. Churches have neglected their responsibility to care for the poor, so government must step in to meet the need.*
8. *All of them. Fifty dollars a week, even back then, was not a large income. How can you objectively state that such an amount was adequate to meet your grandfather's needs? Would it cover unexpected medical expenses or allow his family to take a vacation every year? What might be adequate income in a rural region of the United States would not be sufficient income in a large city with a higher cost of living. An economist in the 1920s could not ethically force a family in New York City to live on the same income as, for instance, a family in a rural region of Pennsylvania.*

Lesson 2B

1. *The fallacy of composition is assuming that what is true of a part is true of the whole. Answers will vary. All professional basketball players can dunk the basketball. All pro hockey players like to fight.*
2. *The* post hoc *fallacy is ascribing a wrong cause in a cause-effect relationship.*
3. *Answers will vary. This statement may or may not be an example of the* post hoc *fallacy. Poor pitching or defensive errors may be the reason for the team's cur-*

rent losing streak. There's not enough information to definitively say that the statement is true or false.

4. Post hoc *fallacy. Answers will vary. Why are response times too slow? Could response times be reduced using the existing stations and equipment? How dramatically will the new fire station reduce response times? If the mayor closes an existing station upon completion of the new station, how will that affect response times in the city quadrant with the closed fire station?*

   Answers will vary (could be post hoc *fallacy, fallacy of composition, or generalizing from small samples). Will automobile emissions testing improve the air quality? Are factories rather than automobiles to blame for the poor air quality? How bad is the state's air quality?*

Lesson 2C

1. *It is a Latin phrase meaning "other things being equal."*
2. *Answers will vary. It helps us determine economic motives (why people choose Brand A over Brand B or why a business would invest in print advertising over radio advertisements) .*
3. *Answers will vary. The lesser-paying job might offer better benefits. Bob might be home more often or the over-the-road routes are more to his liking. Perhaps he likes the boss and other employees at the lesser-paying job. Maybe the 50-cents-per-mile company has better equipment, or his routes don't involve multiple stops and en route pickups of additional freight.*

Lesson 3A

Review Questions

1. *The Hebrew word* a-vad' *(translated* "*dress*"*) means* "*to work, labor, or till the ground.*"
2. Shamar *means to* "*keep, guard, protect, observe, or give heed.*"
3. *His work would be more strenuous (by the sweat of his brow) and the ground would be less productive (weeds would compete with the crops).*
4. *Deuteronomy 19:14 promotes the sanctity of private property.*
5. *No, Abram and Lot were very rich.*
6. *According to Ecclesiastes 5:10, wealth cannot satisfy. Those who think wealth can buy happiness will never be satisfied.*
7. *Wealth should be viewed as a gift from God.*

Proverbs Crossword Puzzle

Across

4. *Generosity—Proverbs 18:16*
7. *Honesty—Proverbs 16:8*
8. *Fraud—Proverbs 20:17*
9. *Liar—Proverbs 19:5 (NIV)*
10. *Hardwork—Proverbs 14:23*
13. *Understanding—Proverbs 4:7*
16. *Diligence—Proverbs 6:6-11*
17. *Happiness—Proverbs 15:6*
18. *Laziness—Proverbs 10:4*
19. *Wisdom—Proverbs 8:11*

Down

1. *Wealth—Proverbs 13:11*
2. *Greed—Proverbs 1:19*
3. *Abundance—Proverbs 12:11*
5. *Obedience—Proverbs 2:1-5*
6. *Righteousness—Proverbs 11:4*
8. *Fool—Proverbs 17:16 (NIV)*
11. *Avoidevil—Proverbs 7:25-26 (NIV)*
12. *Counsel—Proverbs 5:1*
14. *Labor—Proverbs 27:18*
15. *Giving—Proverbs 3:9-10*

Lesson 3B

1. *Answers will vary but should contain the following thoughts. Heavenly treasure does not decay (moth and rust damage earthly treasures), heavenly treasure is secure (thieves cannot steal it), and heavenly treasure reveals a heart focused on things of eternal value rather than temporary pleasure.*
2. *God promises in Matthew 6:24-33 that He will provide for our needs. Christians need to focus on serving Christ.*
3. *The believers had all things in common. Those with excess wealth sold it to help their fellow believers. Ananias and Sapphira sold a piece of property and kept part of the profits for themselves. This passage illustrates an inherent flaw in the communist philosophy. Man's sin nature and greed prevent human beings from doing everything for the benefit of others. Even Christians act selfishly at times.*
4. *Answers will vary. Apparently some Thessalonian believers were refusing to work, perhaps justifying a lack of secular employment by claiming they were "busy about the Lord's work." Paul refutes this position by pointing out that he sought gainful employment to provide for his physical needs while doing the work of the ministry at the same time.*

Lesson 4—Quiz

Scripture Memory

Proverbs 14:34 —Righteousness exalts a nation, but sin is a reproach to any people.

Content Questions

1. *True*
2. *dominion*
3. *B*
4. *Answers will vary. They place varying degrees of value on objects, they choose to get up and go to work, and they make rational decisions.*

5. *The most important choice is where they will spend eternity after this life is over.*
6. *production, distribution*
7. *False*
8. *Answers will vary. The cost of living varies throughout the United States. Some individuals participating in the experiment may have health care costs that consume most of their yearly allotment. Unexpected car repairs or rising gasoline prices could cause the experiment to fail. The control group individuals might have to share housing expenses or give up entertainment in order for the experiment to succeed.*
9. *Microeconomics focuses on a specific segment of the economy such as a single industry. Macroeconomics deals with a nation's economy as a whole.*
10. *value, cost*
11. *C*
12. *A*
13. *Answers will vary. Material possessions in this life cannot give us lasting happiness: therefore, Christians should obey Matthew 6:19 and lay up our treasures in heaven.*
14. *Answers will vary. Hopefully the student will honor the prior commitment. The amusement park will still be there another day. When we seek the kingdom of God and His righteousness, God promises to provide for our needs and even many of our wants. God will probably allow me to spend another day at the amusement park with my friends.*

Lesson 13

Award up to 50 points for the actual interview questions. The number of questions needed to successfully complete the project will vary based on the length of the responses to the questions.

Total Number of Questions: (1-10 points)

- *Are there a sufficient number of questions to produce a two - to three - page paper on the history of a business?*

Clarity of the Questions: (1-20 points)

- *Are the questions written in a question format?*
- *Are the questions concise and understandable? Will the interviewee be able to prepare for the interview without asking for clarification of multiple questions?*

Focus of the Questions: (1-20 points)

- *Are the questions related to the history of the selected business?*
- *Do the questions proceed logically from the inception of the business to the present?*
- *Will the questions enable the interviewer to produce a well-organized and well-written final paper?*

Lesson 6A

1. *Answers will vary. Family members depend on each other for survival. Each family member feels useful as they fulfill their role.*
2. *Traditional economies do not create surplus inventory; they have no unemployment due to overproduction or technological innovation; they foster family unity and are environmentally friendly.*
3. *Subsistence-level traditional economies are one bad harvest or natural disaster away from starvation and extinction.*
4. *Answers will vary. Perhaps. Although they continue to keep the traditions of their ancestors alive, some choose to leave the Amish community to live like the "English." Others have had to adopt and learn the use of technology in order to do business with the non-Amish community. The Amish are a traditional-leaning economy in the midst of a mixed economy tending toward capitalism.*

Lesson 6B

1. *Everyone works for the good of the state rather than personal gain. Without personal profit, individuals lack motivation to work hard and do their best.*
2. *The government determines what will be produced in a command economy.*
3. *Answers will vary. Entrepreneurs are innovators—a problem for the status quo mentality of the central planners of the command economy. An entrepreneur's willingness to question the existing economic order and propose a better way of doing things would directly threaten those in power who are profiting from their leadership positions. Unless the entrepreneur's proposals further the goals of the state, the entrepreneur is like a virus that must be stopped before it affects the entire nation.*
4. *Answers will vary. Traditional and market economies can engage in economic planning without resorting to a command economy. In economic planning, government and/or business leaders may identify an economic need and develop a plan of action to meet that need without undue government interference in the economy.*

Lesson 6C

1. *Answers will vary. Market economies by their nature experience periodic recessions and depressions. Market economies may also experience inflation (a period of rising prices). Greed can be a problem for market economies.*
2. *Answers will vary but may contain the following examples. The USPS has a monopoly on non-urgent mail. The government-run Tennessee Valley Authority competes with privately owned utility companies to provide electricity for that region. Progressive tax rates are an attempt to redistribute wealth. Amtrak*

has a monopoly on passenger rail transportation throughout the nation. The Federal Reserve System is our nation's centralized banking system.

3. *Answers will vary. In the sample answer, the X is just slightly right of center, tending toward a free market. Although still technically a capitalist economy, the United States is leaning more and more toward a command economy. As evidence, we cite the U.S. government bailout of General Motors and major financial firms, health care reform, the Federal Reserve System, government welfare programs creating a dependent class of people, and various government stimulus programs to jump-start a sluggish economy.*

Command Economy ▪▪▪▪▪▪▪▪▪**X**▪▪▪▪▪▪ **Free-Market Economy**

4. *No, because environmental regulations would be government interference with the business sector. In a truly free-market economy, the government does not regulate business in any way, shape, or form.*
5. *Answers will vary. The United States has never been a pure capitalist economy, but one could argue that under the Articles of Confederation (1781-1789) the nation came close to this ideal. The Articles Congress could not levy direct taxes, but it could collect customs duties on imports. The Constitution, which took effect in 1789, allowed Congress to regulate interstate commerce, stop the importation of slaves, and tax businesses directly and indirectly. Government regulation of business accelerated in the post-Civil War era. Due to unscrupulous businessmen the government was forced to pass regulatory legislation protecting the public from harmful or worthless patent medicine and unsanitary conditions in the meatpacking industry (the Pure Food & Drug Act).*

Lesson 6D

10 Tenets of Marxism

1. Expropriation of landed *property*, with land rents used for public purposes
2. A graduated or progressive *income* tax
3. No *inheritance* rights
4. *Confiscation* of rebels' property
5. State control of finances: a national *bank* and a monopoly on credit
6. Centralized communication and *transportation* controlled by the state
7. A planned *economy*—national factories, more cultivated land, and planned production and agriculture
8. Universal and equal work using "industrial armies"
9. Elimination of rural and *urban* distinctions
10. Free public education, abolition of factory work for children, and combining education with material production

Criticisms of Marxism

1. Advocates violent overthrow of the existing social order
2. Fails to recognize that *capitalism* could correct its problems
3. Goes against *God's* social order

Lesson 8 —Test

Scripture Memory

Proverbs 14:34 —Righteousness exalteth a nation, but sin is a reproach to any people.

Content Questions

1. *C*
2. *dominion*
3. *True*
4. *Jesus Christ sustains creation, according to Colossians 1:16-17.*
5. *Answers will vary. Suggested answers might include specific examples of natural disasters (floods, volcanoes, etc.) or use of microorganisms to decompose dead plants and animals.*
6. *rational*
7. *False*
8. *Answers will vary. We need to be ready to meet our Maker and we should invest in things of eternal value.*
9. *Answers will vary. Grader's Note: Don't hesitate to have the student rewrite their question #9 response to fix grammatical errors or improve the quality of the writing.*
10. *False*
11. *production, consumption*
12. *Answers will vary but should contain the following thoughts. Microeconomics deals with a specific industry or business, while macroeconomics focuses on the economy of a nation as a whole.*
13. *D*
14. *man-made*
15. *Answers will vary. You could trade something else of value for the economic good.*
16. *A or D*
17. *A*
18. *A, C, or D*
19. *B or C*
20. *D*
21. *A*
22. *True*
23. *Adam was to labor in and guard the Garden of Eden.*
24. *Adam's work would be more strenuous/less enjoyable (by the sweat of his brow) and the ground would be less productive (weeds would compete with the crops).*
25. *private property*
26. *D*
27. *treasure*
28. *Answers will vary. Because God takes care of the birds of the air and the flowers of the field, He can*

certainly provide for His children. Verse 32 tells us that He knows that we have need of food, clothing, and shelter to survive. Verse 33 tells us to pursue God's kingdom and His righteousness, and He will see that our earthly needs are met.

29. *Ananias and Sapphira lied about giving all the money from the sale of a parcel of land to the church.*
30. *B*
31. *A*
32. *B*
33. *C*
34. *A*
35. *A, B, or C*
36. *A*
37. *C*
38. *C*
39. *C*
40. *True*
41. *Answers will vary. Unless the snack is an agricultural-based item that can be produced by the traditional economy, the student may have to go without their favorite snack food or get it sent in from another country at great expense.*
42. *Answers will vary. The item may or may not be available in the command economy. If not, you could have it shipped in or, if the item is banned by the central planners, try to obtain it on the black market.*
43. *Answers will vary. The item is probably readily available in multiple locations for immediate purchase.*
44. Expropriation of landed *property*, with land rents used for public purposes

    A *graduated* or progressive income tax

    State control of *finances* via a national bank and a monopoly on credit

    Centralized *communication* and transportation controlled by the state

    Free public *education*
45. *Answers will vary. No, because even if you don't have a home mortgage, God owns everything. He allows you to have your house. If you fail to pay your property taxes, the government will foreclose and take away your home. Timely payment of property taxes is a prerequisite for the privilege of living in "your" home.*

Lesson 9A

1. *Value exists in the mind.*
2. *Value changes with* ***time***, ***place***, *and* ***circumstances***.
3. *She might never play it again, give it away to a friend, or trade it in for a different game.*
4. *If a player becomes a star athlete, his card will be worth a lot of money.*
5. *They don't need as large a home. They can save money on taxes and utilities by moving to a smaller residence. Health reasons might force them out of a two-story home into a single-level dwelling. Whatever the reason for downsizing, they mentally place a greater value on the new home than on their previous residence.*

Lesson 9B

1. *Subjective value consists of non-measurable variables, which are variables that cannot be quantified. Objective value is measurable in monetary terms.*
2. *You like long-sleeve dress shirts (subjective value), and on this particular occasion, you were willing to pay six dollars for a long-sleeve dress shirt (objective value).*
3. *Answers will vary. Your decision could be based on what you're in the mood for, which establishment is closest to your present location, other food items that will be a part of your meal, or what your friends will want if they'll be joining you for lunch.*

Lesson 9—Practical Application Activity: Value of a 1985 Mercury Grand Marquis

1. *Answers will vary.*
2. *Answers will vary.*
3. *Answers will vary.*
4. *Answers will vary.*
5. *Both. You must like the car enough to want to make an offer, and your offer is based on how much you're willing to spend before your money becomes more valuable than the vehicle.*
6. *D - Parents with teenage drivers*

    A - A classic car buff

    B - The owner of an auto salvage yard

    E - An auto mechanic

    C - A two-income family
7. *Answers will vary. Muscle cars, such as the Ford Mustang or Chevy Camaro, appeal to many individuals. Classic cars become collectibles. Well-maintained older vehicles with low mileage may be worth more now than when they were new.*

Lesson 10A

1. *Man's basic economic problem is limited resources.*
2. *This problem forces us to make choices.*
3. *Answers will vary but may contain the following thoughts: Gorgeous sunrises/sunsets, Beautiful location/views, Water sports (boating, snorkeling, water skiing, fishing, etc.), Relaxing sound of waves striking the beach, Prestige factor*
4. *Price—it's very expensive.*

5. *Answers will vary. Many municipalities provide public access to waterfront property via a city park or public marina. You could rent a beachfront condo for a family vacation.*
6. *Answers will vary but may contain the following thoughts: Give up free time because you would have to work longer hours to pay for the property, Both husband and wife working to afford the mortgage payment, Smaller or no car payments, No vacations*
7. *Answers will vary. Affirmative responses might include: "It's so romantic" or "I like the sound of waves crashing on the beach" or "Owning beachfront property is a status symbol." Students who believe the price tag isn't worth it might argue: "I have more important things to spend money on" or "I don't care for beachfront property" or "I don't want to deal with the possibility of hurricanes or tsunamis."*

Lesson 10B

1. *Opportunity cost is the value of the next best alternative compared to a choice actually made.*
2. *The bank has less money to lend out. Fewer loans mean less profit for the bank.*
3. *The geothermal heating system should be the opportunity cost. The homeowner should first increase his home's energy efficiency by adding adequate insulation. He'll save money on heating the home with the current furnace. When it's time to replace the current furnace, he can better evaluate the potential savings of the geothermal system over simply replacing the furnace.*
4. *Answers will vary. There may be cheaper alternatives, especially if you have to borrow money to replace a vehicle you already own. Will the fuel savings make the car payments? If not, finding a job closer to home, carpooling, eliminating use of the vehicle for a single errand, walking or biking at times to cut down on use of the vehicle, etc., might be more cost effective. You can buy a lot of gasoline with a $200-per-month car payment.*
5. *Answers will vary. Your presence in the building or food-court areas makes you a potential customer. Free samples are an attempt by the business to make you an actual customer rather than having their product or restaurant become your opportunity cost at that moment.*
6. *Answers will vary. Businesses use advertising to keep existing customers from choosing a competitor's product while luring opportunity cost into becoming new customers.*
7. *Answers will vary. Many of these sites contain questions related to a person's areas of interest. Mail-order companies send information to those who complete this section of the survey, giving these potential customers even more options from which to choose in the future.*
8. *Cruise lines. Answers will vary. Cruises are a luxury item, while food is a necessity. During downturns in the economy, people can give up taking a cruise, but they must eat in order to survive. An expensive cruise would have a greater impact on competing cruise lines than the more affordable menu options of a fast-food chain. With a much larger potential customer base than the cruise ship industry, the fast-food industry can absorb opportunity cost more easily.*
9. *Answers will vary. Possible answers include faster personal travel; increased need for automobiles; greater business development along the highways; ongoing construction and maintenance jobs; military transportation during times of war; easier visits to extended family; more tourism in the United States; increased demand for concrete, rebar, oil, asphalt, and road signs, as well as for tractors and mowers for the medians, bulldozers and other heavy construction equipment, etc.*
10. *Answers will vary, but students should provide only one alternative use (the option that seems most valuable to them). Possible answers might include less traffic noise, less roadkill, more commuters using trains and planes, fewer tax dollars needed to build roads, better maintenance of existing roads, more farmland, reduction of the federal budget, etc.*
11. *Answers will vary. Is the ground fertile enough to warrant growing food crops? Tall plants and trees could potentially restrict sight distances. Motorists might illegally stop to pick food items, causing a safety hazard. Accidents related to farming the medians could result in lawsuits against the state. Fences would be required to keep wildlife from consuming the crops. More wildlife going after the crops in the median means more roadkill. How would slow-moving farm equipment safely enter and exit the medians?*
12. *Answers will vary. No. Too many potential problems outweigh the benefits.*

Lesson 11A

1. *Suppliers must be **willing** and **able** to produce.*
2. *Suppliers are willing to supply more of a good or service at a higher price than at a lower price.*
3. 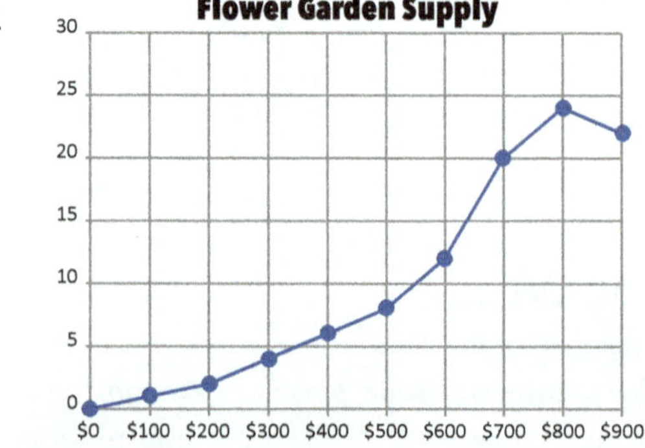

4. *Answers will vary. This phenomenon illustrates the backward-bending supply curve of labor. At a high enough wage, Tom is not willing to give up more leisure time in order to earn additional income. In other words, his subjective value of leisure is higher than the objective value of increased income from planting more flower beds.*

Lesson 11B

1. *Although her wealth makes it possible to purchase a small car, her distaste for such vehicles precludes her purchasing one. In other words, she has the ability but not the willingness to buy a compact car.*
2. *Answers will vary. Both parts result in actual purchases.*
3. *As the price decreases, buyers consume more.*
4. *Answers will vary. A newly discovered painting by a famous artist might have many bidders, even as the price increases. Demand for luxury items might increase, as more and more people want to own these status symbols.*
5. *Six factors that influence demand are population, people's tastes, income, government policies, availability of substitute products, and fads and crazes.*
6.

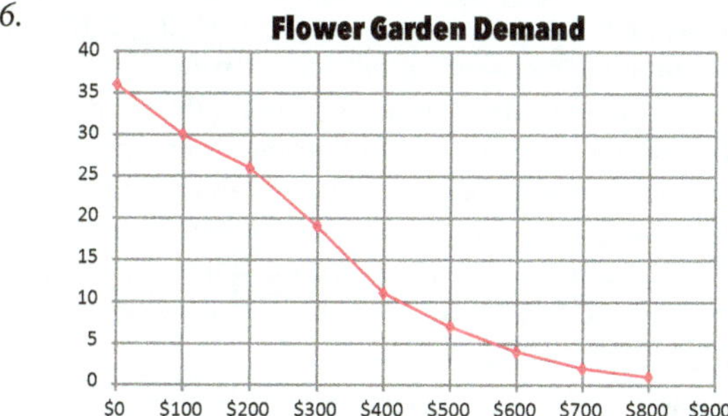

Lesson 12—Quiz

Scripture Memory

Psalm 33:12—Blessed is the nation whose God is the LORD; and the people whom He hath chosen for His own inheritance.

Content Questions

1. *Value exists in the mind.*
2. *time*
3. *Subjective value contains non-measurable variables. I like baseball but dislike golf. Objective value is measurable in monetary terms. I like baseball enough to pay $15 for a ticket to go see a game.*
4. *False*
5. *B*
6. *True*
7. *Answers will vary.*
8. *Answers will vary but the option chosen should be the student's second favorite choice.*

10. *willingness, ability*

11.

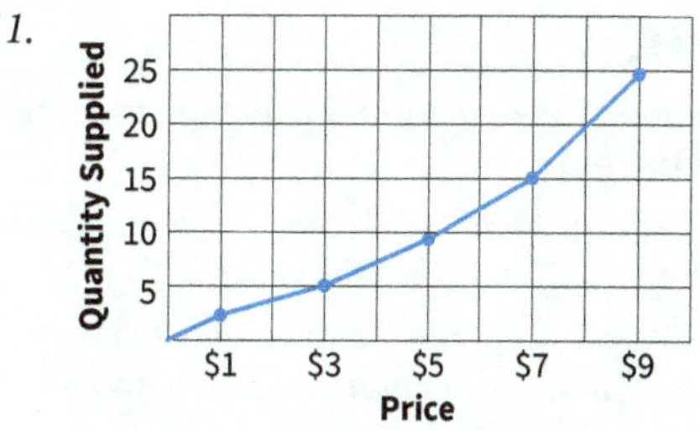

12. *Suppliers are willing to supply more at a higher price than at a lower price.*
13. *Buyers are willing to purchase more at a lower price than at a higher price.*
14. *Answers will vary. Look for the following thoughts in the student's response. Abortion reduces a nation's population. Less population means less demand for consumer goods and services. Abortion negatively impacts a nation's economy—fewer jobs and fewer tax dollars. Each aborted baby is one less consumer of clothing, food, automobiles, housing, education, etc.*
15. *Answers will vary but may include personal income, consumer tastes, government policies, and the availability of substitute or alternative products.*

Lesson 13

Award up to 100 points for the interview and completion of the written transcript of the interview.

Preparation for the Interview: (1-10 points)

- *Was the student prepared for the interview on the scheduled date?*
- *Did the student have all necessary items for the interview (recording device, extra copy of the questions for the interviewee) ready prior to the interview date?*

Conducting of the Interview: (1-40 points)

- *Did the student dress professionally and appropriately for the interview?* (5 points)
- *Did the student thank the interviewee for their time and willingness to help with the project?* (5 points)
- *Did the student ask the interviewee if any of the questions needed clarification prior to the interview?* (5 points)
- *Did the student check the recording device prior to starting the interview to make sure it was working and that the responses could be heard?* (5 points)
- *Did the student express genuine interest in the interviewee's responses with appropriate facial gestures and body language?* (1-10 points)
- *At the conclusion of the interview, did the student thank the interviewee for their time?* (5 points)
- *Did the student send the interviewee a thank-you note following the interview?* (5 points)

Completion of the Transcript: (1-50 points)

- *Did the student produce a word-for-word transcript of the entire interview?*

Lesson 14A

1. *The intersection of the supply and demand curves sets the equilibrium price.*
2. **Increase**—*Reason: More fans (greater demand) and limited seating result in higher ticket prices.*

   Increase—*Reason: The endorsement adds to the item's "coolness" and creates additional demand for the product.*

   Decrease—*Reason: Less demand puts these items on the clearance rack.*
3. The price and quantity will be a*pproximately seven to eight flower gardens at $500 each.*
4. *Prices will decrease to stimulate demand for the surplus.*

Lesson 14B

1. *The elasticity formula is* % Δ Quantity / % Δ Price. *(In words, it is the percentage of change in quantity divided by the percentage of change in price.)*
2. *Elastic. A 100 percent increase in the price of airline tickets prior to summer vacation season would cause many travelers to view airline travel as an opportunity cost. Vacation travelers could use alternative means of transportation or take a vacation closer to home to get more value out of their vacation bucks.*
3. *Inelastic. Answers will vary. Gasoline is a necessity. The percentage of increase would not be enough to cause gasoline users to cut back significantly on fuel consumption.*
4.

Price	Quantity	Elasticity
$237	2	*******
$209	4	100% / 12% = 8.33
$195	8	100% / 7% = 14.29
$189	12	50% / 3% = 16.67
$143	18	50% / 24% = 2.10
$125	30	67% / 13% = 5.77
$116	33	10% / 7% = 1.43
$109	40	21% / .06% = 3.50
$99	50	25% / 9% = 2.78
$78	43	14% / 21% = .67

5. *Answers will vary. Not likely. Consumers will probably not decrease their bread consumption over such a small price increase, and as a perishable food item, excess bread inventory would go to waste. Suppliers could not increase their profits through both the price increase and supplying the market with more loaves of bread.*

Lesson 15A

1. *Competition occurs when multiple suppliers compete for customers. In a monopoly, one supplier dominates the entire market for a product.*
2. *Answers will vary. It would be very boring because there's no real competition if the outcome is always the same. Attendance would decline along with revenues for the losing teams.*
3. *Food and beverages would cost less because the vendors would lower prices to attract the greatest possible number of customers.*

Lesson 15B

1. *Consumers pay lower prices due to competition between the suppliers. If something disrupts the supply from one supplier, other suppliers can provide additional product to meet consumer demand.*
2. *Perfect substitutes are exactly alike. You could go to a professional baseball game in Cleveland, Detroit, or Chicago—although the teams are different, it's still professional baseball. Imperfect substitutes are similar but not exactly the same. You could go to a Little League baseball game—it's the same game but the quality of play and the atmosphere are quite different from a game at the professional level. Another example of imperfect substitutes would be any professional sporting event—although the games played are different, they're all professional sports.*
3. *When the price of a product decreases, some consumers will abandon the perfect and imperfect substitutes and buy the lower-priced product. Answers will vary. If a fast-food chain runs a "two for a dollar" sale on cheeseburgers, consumers will probably buy fewer of the larger, more expensive, sandwiches during the cheeseburger sale period. This explains why competing fast-food restaurants try to run simultaneous sales on similar items, in order not to lose customers to the competition during the sale.*
4. *Answers will vary. Gasoline is a perfect complementary good to a lawn mower with an internal combustion engine that runs on gasoline.*
5. *Answers will vary but should contain the following idea(s). Since the items are dependent upon each other, a price increase for one component results in a corresponding decline in demand for the other component. As gasoline prices soar, sales of gasoline-powered lawn mowers will decrease in favor of human-powered reel mowers, electric-powered mowers, or sheep to trim the turf.*

Practical Application Activity: Competition

Award up to 10 points for completion of the chart. Award up to 10 points for student responses to the two discussion questions.

Completion of the Competition Chart: *(1-10 points)*

- *Did the student select a product produced by multiple suppliers?*

- *Did the student complete enough rows on the chart to prove that the product is produced by multiple suppliers?*
- *Did the student complete all of the appropriate columns for the product evaluated? For example, column #2 (package size/weight) would be necessary for jars of peanut butter but not applicable if the student was comparing athletic shoes.*
- *Was the information recorded in the chart accurate?*

Discussion Question #1: (1-5 points)

- *From the products listed on the chart, did the student select a favorite?*
- *Did the student provide two or more valid reasons to support their selection?*

Discussion Question #2: (1-5 points)

- *Did the student take a stand based on the first part of the question? In other words, did the student actually say "more competition would be beneficial" or "less competition would be beneficial" as a part of their response?*
- *Did the student provide one or more valid reasons for why more or less competition would be beneficial?*

Lesson 17—Test

Scripture Memory

Psalm 33:12—Blessed is the nation whose God is the LORD; and the people whom He hath chosen for His own inheritance.

Content Questions

1. *mind, place*
2. *Both. Answers will vary. From an objective standpoint, your degree is worth $100,000 because you were willing to spend that amount of money for it. Subjectively, you were willing to give up four years of your life and $100,000 dollars because you believe that the initial effort and expense will help you earn way more than that over your lifetime.*
3. *True*
4. *B*
5. *C*
6. *True*
7. *willingness, ability*
8. 

9. *True*
10. 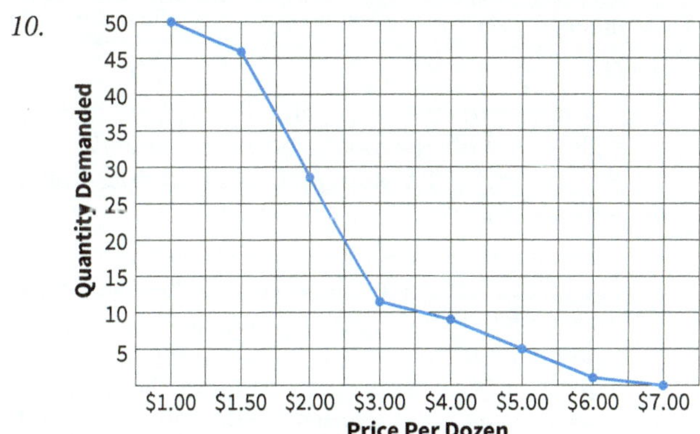

11. *income, alternative*
12. *It's the price at which sales take place in a free-market economy.*
13. 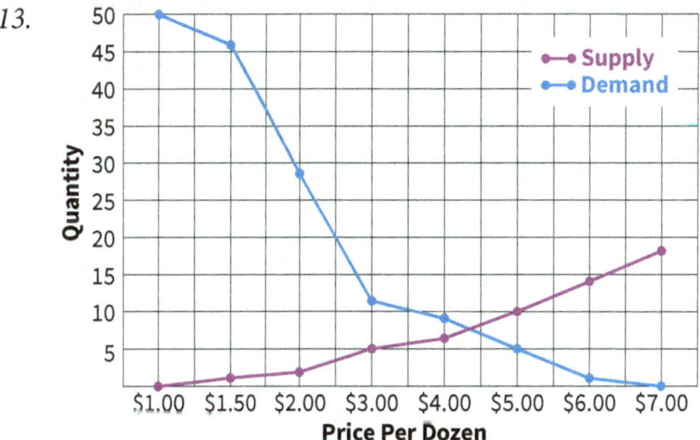

14. *D*
15. *True*
16. *The formula for elasticity is % Δ Quantity / % Δ Price.*
17.

Price	Quantity of VW Beetles Sold	Elasticity Measurement
$10,000	1	*******
$8,000	2	*5*
$7,000	4	*8*
$5,000	7	*2.62*
$4,000	12	*3.55*
$3,000	15	*1*

18. *Answers will vary. No, because none of the elasticity measurements were less than 1. The percentage of cars sold at each price level exceeded the "percent off" price at the new price level.*
19. *False*
20. *Answers will vary but should contain the following thought. Consumers pay higher prices for inferior quality products.*
21. *Answers will vary. Perfect substitute goods are exactly like the product they are replacing. A compact car built by Ford is a perfect substitute for a compact automobile built by GM. Imperfect substitute goods are a close alternative to the product they are replacing. Iced tea and lemonade are different types of beverages that could serve as imperfect substitutes for each other.*
22. *C*
23. In a free-market economy and *ceteris paribus*, which child would sell the most lemonade? *The child with the best-tasting lemonade at the cheapest price would sell the most.*

    What factors besides quality and price would impact the lemonade sales at each of these stands? *Answers will vary. Possible answers could include location of the lemonade stand in relationship to the amount of traffic, outdoor temperature, the number of friends and family patronizing the lemonade stand, amount of spare change potential customers have in their wallet, or locations of the competing lemonade stands.*

    Freddy's location near the entrance of the subdivision gives him an advantage over the other children. Customers love his sweet-tart lemonade with floating lemon slices in the pitcher. When Freddy's mom goes on vacation, the quality of Freddy's lemonade declines significantly. What economic principle is at work if Freddy's sales drop due to offering customers awful-tasting cups of lemonade? *Value changes with time, place, and circumstances. His former customers mentally devalued Freddy's lemonade after tasting the horrible concoctions he produced while his mother was on vacation.*

    Susan's house is at the back of the development. Many potential customers don't have to drive past her house on their way to or from their homes. How can Susan get customers to drive out of their way to purchase her lemonade? *Answers will vary. She could advertise, lower her price compared to her competitors, or sell an imperfect substitute good (iced tea) along with the lemonade. She could also offer additional incentives (buy a glass of lemonade and get a free ice cream cone).*

    If all the children sold their lemonade for 50 cents per glass, what factor would cause the equilibrium price to change? *If one child lowered the price of their lemonade to attract more customers and the other children followed suit, the new lower price would become the equilibrium price.*

    Theoretically, since the parents are paying for the ingredients, the children could sell their lemonade for one cent per glass and still make a profit. Would the equilibrium price ever drop that low? *Answers will vary. Probably not. The children would not likely put forth so much effort for so little profit.*

    Bethanie and Peter live next door to each other. If everybody buys Bethanie's lemonade, what is Peter's lemonade for Bethanie's customers? *Peter's lemonade is opportunity cost for all of Bethanie's customers.*

    Alex sold 10 glasses of lemonade at one dollar per glass on his first day. On the second day, he lowered the price to 75 cents per glass and sold 20 glasses of lemonade. What is the elasticity measurement of Alex's sales on Day Two? Did the sale result in elastic or inelastic demand for Alex's lemonade? *The elasticity measurement is 4. A 100 percent increase in sales divided by a 25 percent reduction in price equals 4. The sale created elastic demand (demand >1).*

Lesson 18A

1. *The four basic factors of production are:*

   Land—the earth in its natural state without man-made improvements.

   Labor—mankind's physical and mental human effort.

   Capital—the machines, tools, and buildings used to create things of value.

   Entrepreneurship—the risk-taking mindset and ability to project consumers' needs in the future.
2. *Answers will vary. It depends on the developer's expenses in preparing the property for building lots, but the amount of return per acre does seem exorbitant.*

Lesson 18B

1. *The PPF shows all possible combinations of two uses of a factor of production.*
2. 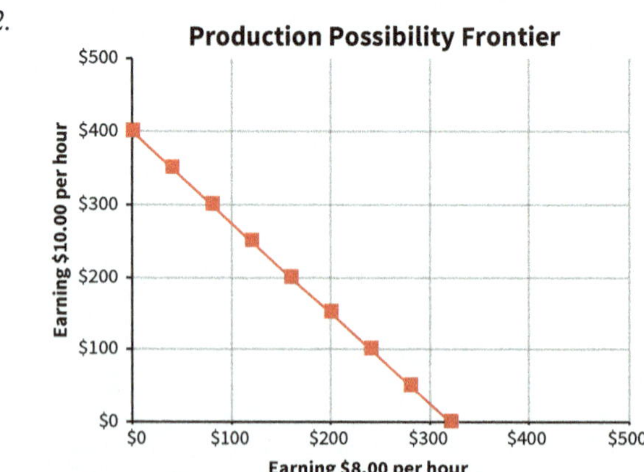

Lesson 18C

1. *Cost schedules help entrepreneurs examine production possibilities using varying input levels of a factor of production.*
2. *The nine columns of a cost schedule are:*

   Column 1—input

   Column 2—quantity produced

Column 3—total fixed cost

Column 4—total variable cost

Column 5—total cost

Column 6—average fixed cost

Column 7—average variable cost

Column 8—average cost

Column 9—marginal cost

3. *The formulas are:*

   TC (add TFC and TVC)

   AFC (divide TFC by Q)

   AVC (divide TVC by Q)

   AC (add AFC and AVC)

   *MC (divide the **increase** in TVC by the **increase** in Q)*

Lesson 18—Practical Application Activity: Cost Schedule

Input	Q	TFC	TVC	TC	AFC	AVC	AC	MC
1	22	200,000	35,000	235,000	9,090.91	1,590.91	10,681.22	****
2	36	200,000	70,000	270,000	5,555.56	1,944.44	7,500.00	2,500
3	45	200,000	105,000	305,000	4,444.44	2,333.33	6,777.77	3,889
4	58	200,000	140,000	340,000	3,448.28	2,413.79	5,862.07	2,692
5	67	200,000	175,000	375,000	2,985.07	2,611.94	5,597.01	3,889
6	79	200,000	210,000	410,000	2,531.65	2,658.23	5,189.88	2.917
7	81	200,000	245,000	445,000	2,469.13	3,024.69	5,493.82	17,500
8	80	200,000	280,000	480,000	2,500.00	3,500.00	6,000.00	****
9	78	200,000	315,000	515,000	2,564.10	4,038.46	6,602.56	****
10	71	200,000	350,000	550,000	2,816.90	4,929.58	7,746.48	****

1. *Possible answers might include: Dan has to do paperwork, which takes him away from the production floor; his factory layout could hinder the second worker's productivity; Dan might have to spend production time training his new employee; his employee might take some sick days and/or vacation days; the new employee is still learning the job, or he is lazy.*
2. *Answers will vary but may contain the following thoughts. There's not enough room in the existing workshop to keep eight employees gainfully employed; too much socializing and not enough work; not enough tools for everyone to achieve maximum productivity.*
3. *Dan should have five employees. At that level, he more than tripled his yearly production and lowered the average cost of each doghouse from $10,681.22 to $4,549.27. He can meet demand for the doghouses more quickly and increase his profit margin significantly.*

Lesson 19A

1. *Transfer earnings are what a factor of production must earn in its present use to avoid transferring it to another use.*
2. *Economic rent is the income that a factor of production earns above its transfer earnings.*
3. *Answers will vary but may contain the following thoughts. You don't want to move, more travel time, fewer benefits, farther away from family and relatives, etc.*
4. *Answers will vary but should contain the following thoughts. No, because food is a necessity. Dwindling acreage devoted to farming is currently being offset by greater productivity from the land under cultivation. If increased yields from existing farmland fail to provide enough food for a growing population, then food shortages will drive up the cost of food. Higher food prices mean greater profits for food producers. More land will be diverted to farming until supply balances demand at a new equilibrium price.*
5. *Answers will vary. No. Sometimes factors other than transfer earnings and economic rent influence the rental decision. If the highest bidder is engaged in illegal activities, you wouldn't want to rent to them and become an accessory to their crimes. If a family member or friend wanted to rent the space, you probably wouldn't charge them top dollar for the real estate. If the highest bidder demands expensive renovations to the space, you might rent to another tenant willing to use the space "as is."*

Lesson 19—Practical Application Activity: Transfer Earnings Case Study

Answers will vary but may contain the following thoughts.

What are Mrs. Smith's and the children's attitudes toward moving? What about the health of Mrs. Smith's parents? What if Mr. Smith's parents needed their son's help due to their declining health? How do the grandparents feel about their grandchildren moving away? Where do the Smith children plan to go to college? Is Mrs. Smith willing to go to work to make up for lost income? Is Mr. Smith willing to find a different job in the Columbus, Ohio, area after he returns from Mexico?

When does Mr. Smith plan to retire? Where do the Smiths want to live after he retires? WHAT DOES GOD WANT THEM TO DO?

Lesson 20A

1. *Answers will vary. Productivity is not an issue when communicating with someone you love. You're not trying to crank out as many love letters as possible in an hour. A handwritten note is more personal and meaningful than a typewritten love letter.*

2. *Microeconomic productivity focuses on the individual worker, while macroeconomic productivity deals with a nation's effective use of its human and physical resources.*
3. *Answers will vary. Without increased productivity, nations with population increases will experience a decline in the overall standard of living.*
4. *Answers will vary. Increased productivity results in a great supply of a good at a lower cost. The decreased cost of the good stimulates demand. Consumers pay less for the item, giving them more spending power.*
5. *Answers will vary. Workers get paid more, businesses make more money, investors receive more dividends, consumers pay less, and government gets more tax money as a result of increased productivity.*

Lesson 20B

1. *Three factors affecting productivity are: division of labor, technology, and specialization.*
2. *Answers will vary. Student responses may reflect a personal relationship with this phenomenon (for example, if a parent lost a job for this reason). Although it does create a hardship in the short run for those who find themselves out of work, it also redirects labor resources into more realistic employment fields for the future.*
3. *Drivers would be needed to transport requested and returned items between the libraries in the network.*
4. *Specialization. Electricians who wire houses every day are more efficient at wiring than a general contractor who may know how to wire a house but doesn't specialize in wiring.*
5. *Answers will vary. Not necessarily. You might have trained for a dying industry or field. You could expand your skill set into other areas to make you more attractive to potential employers.*
6. *Most students will probably choose da Vinci because of his multiple talents. It's not an argument against specialization, but a rationale for developing as many skills as possible to improve your employment possibilities.*

Lesson 20C

1. *Absolute advantage is more efficient production than your immediate competitors, while comparative advantage is more efficient production than at least one other competitor.*
2. *Answers will vary. Most likely, Mom has the absolute advantage. The student taking this course may have a comparative advantage over Dad or another sibling with less experience in washing dishes. Student's response should include a reason for or against their comparative advantage related to dishwashing.*
3. *Answers will vary. Perhaps there is a less-expensive alternative (i.e., paving over the existing concrete). If the finished concrete driveway you install is of inferior quality, you have no way of knowing if it's your fault as an amateur concrete finisher or a problem with the concrete mix. By using a professional concrete contractor, you have options if the end result is substandard.*

Lesson 20D

1. *Answers will vary. Yes. Although it cannot improve her typing speed, the computer's ability to store and retrieve information could make her more productive. For instance, she could store a template of the church bulletin and simply update the information each week rather than retype the entire bulletin.*
2. *Answers will vary. Two examples might be playing solitaire on the computer rather than doing your science project research; surfing the Internet instead of completing your English research paper.*
3. *A yes response might focus on the speed of communication, ease of completing schoolwork, or a computer's ability to control machinery. A no response might list the temptation to waste time surfing the Internet, eyestrain from staring at a computer screen for long periods of time, or the health risks from electrical and electronic radiation.*

Lesson 20E

1. *Answers will vary. Attractive factors might be fewer government and environmental regulations, lower taxes, proximity to natural resources, and locations closer to potential foreign markets for the finished product.*
2. *Labor productivity compares the value of output to the input of labor. Multifactor productivity looks at factors affecting labor's productivity, such as working conditions or the use of capital and technology.*
3. *Answers will vary. Part-time employees may skew the productivity numbers. Full-time employees may be diverted to other tasks (cleaning or maintenance) if there aren't enough raw materials to maintain full production. In these scenarios, hours actually involved in production give a more accurate measure of productivity than number of employees.*

Lesson 21—Quiz

Scripture Memory

Matthew 6:33—But seek ye first the kingdom of God, and His righteousness; and all these things shall be added unto you.

Content Questions

1. *The four basic factors of production are:*
   Land—the earth in its natural state without man-made improvements.
   Labor—mankind's physical and mental human effort.
   Capital—the machines, tools, and buildings used to create things of value.

Entrepreneurship—the risk-taking mindset and ability to project consumers' needs in the future.

2. *Labor is the most important factor of production. It's the one factor of production every human being can control.*
3. *Its intended use determines if a good is a capital good or a consumer good. When professional baseball teams play an opponent, the ball is a capital good—it's being used by the players to make a living. When you and your relatives play a pickup game of baseball during the family reunion, the ball is a consumer good—it makes for an entertaining afternoon of fun during the reunion.*
4. *True*
5. *Capital-intensive production relies heavily on machinery and technology.*
6. *The cost schedule enables the entrepreneur to determine the optimum level of production for the business.*
7. *The formula for average fixed cost is total fixed cost (TFC) divided by quantity (Q).*
8. *To calculate marginal cost, divide the* ***increase*** *in total variable cost by the* ***increase*** *in quantity.*
9.

Hours	Q	TFC	TVC	TC	AFC	AVC	AC	MC
1	2	100	12	112.00	50.00	6.00	56.00	****
2	5	100	30	130.00	20.00	6.00	26.00	6.00
3	9	100	52	152.00	11.00	5.78	16.78	5.50
4	13	100	70	170.00	7.69	5.31	13.00	4.50
5	18	100	98	198.00	5.56	5.44	11.00	5.60

10. *True*
11. *economic*
12. *Productivity helps a nation maintain its standard of living and compete in a global economic environment.*
13. *technology*
14. *Answers will vary. Absolute advantage is more efficient production than your immediate competitors, while comparative advantage is more efficient production than at least one other competitor.*
15. *False*
16. *Answers will vary but may contain the following thought. Multifactor productivity takes into account those areas that affect labor productivity, such as poor working conditions and the use of machinery.*

Lesson 22A

1. *The three economic entities are individual households, businesses, and government.*
2. *Answers will vary. The student's diagram should illustrate the specific interactions between the two based on details provided in the reading segment. Farmer Brown's family provides vegetables, labor, and income for the store. It receives income and pig feed from the store.*

Lesson 22B

1. *Answers will vary. The student could repeat the information from question #2 in the previous review questions section and add the government's interactions with the previous two entities.*

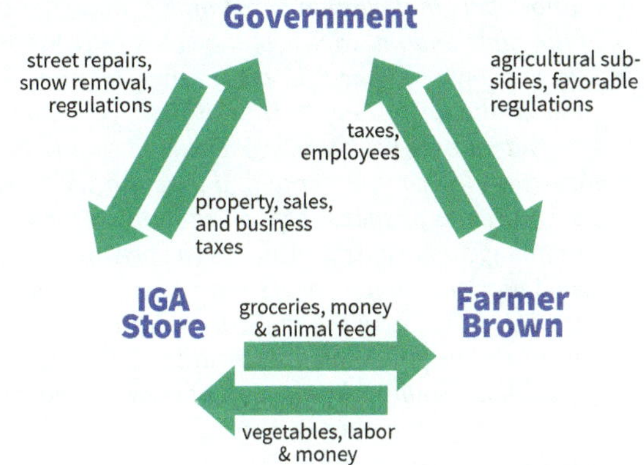

2. *Answers will vary but should contain the following thought. U.S. meat processors were producing an unhealthy product.*
3. *Answers will vary. Unfunded mandates are "regulations or conditions for receiving grants that impose costs on state or local governments or private entities for which they are not reimbursed by the federal government." Yes, these two laws fit into this category. Business expenses related to compliance with the two laws would be passed on to consumers via higher prices for the products.*
4. *Answers will vary but should contain the following thought. Man's sin nature causes him to act greedy and selfish at the expense of others.*

Lesson 22C

1. *The government's two biblical responsibilities are to punish evildoers and praise those who do well.*
2. *Government policies create a favorable business climate. The government also directly or indirectly aids certain businesses through subsidies, tax advantages, or bailouts.*
3. *Government collects taxes from individuals and businesses.*
4. *Answers will vary but may contain the following thoughts. Deficit spending enables the government to spend money it doesn't have. It allows Congress to live beyond its means. Programs and personnel funded by deficit spending will fight tooth and nail to prevent cuts needed to balance the federal budget. Deficit spending, like a smoke screen, merely disguises reality. There will come a time when the smoke clears, revealing the real economic danger the United States is in.*

5. *Answers will vary. As a recipient of one of these homes, the author of this course acknowledges his bias in favor of this program. As a teacher in a Christian school, he would not have been able to buy a home without its assistance. However, he understands the "slippery slope" of depending upon the national government. Beneficiaries are beholden to their benefactors. Government assistance in any form fosters a spirit of dependence rather than independence.*
6. *Note to Teacher: Answers in Columns 1 and 2 are the author's personal opinion based on his understanding of the Bible and knowledge of the U.S. Constitution. Use your own judgment in evaluating student responses and defenses of their positions. For example, the student may believe the government should fund medical research in order to find cures for life-threatening diseases or sponsor space exploration for the technological benefits it brings to the private sector. Don't mark down a student's response just because the student agrees with the extra-biblical or extra-constitutional government expenditure. The student's grade should reflect the strength of their arguments in support of or against government spending in each particular category.*

Government Expenditure	Column 1	Column 2 Y or N	Points Awarded 1-Weak 2-Adequate 3-Excellent
Space exploration		N	
Art projects		N	
Scientific research		N	
Military defense	X**	Y	
ATF (Bureau of Alcohol, Tobacco, and Firearms	X*	Y	
Medical research		N	
Education		N	
Welfare		N	
Family planning		N	
TSA (Transportation Security Administration)	X*	Y	

**Based on government's biblical responsibility to punish evildoers*
***Based on government's constitutional authority*

Lesson 23A

1. *Utility is the satisfaction derived from consuming a good or service.*
2. *Answers will vary (ice cream, cherry pie, chips, popcorn, etc.).*
3. *Answers will vary.*

Lesson 23B

1. *Marginal utility is the additional satisfaction from consuming an additional unit of a good or service, while total utility is the sum total of all utility for a particular good or service.*

Lesson 23C

1. *Answers will vary but may contain the following ideas. They know that people's appetites and hunger levels vary. Not everyone is going to consume six plates of food. Certain foods such as breads and casseroles fill you up quickly, so the restaurant includes a good variety of these on the buffet along with the more expensive meats or seafood. They charge exorbitant amounts for cheaply produced drinks in order to keep the per-person food charge reasonable and competitive.*
2. *They want to know the point at which you will stop consuming their good or service in order to "push" you toward maximum consumption. For instance, if you could eat three bowls of ice cream, but limit yourself to just one bowl, ice cream manufacturers are currently selling you only one-third of the ice cream you could consume. If the potential ice cream consumption is opportunity cost rather than health-related (afraid of becoming overweight or harming your body with all that sugar), suppliers could lower their costs to induce you to buy more ice cream.*

Lesson 23D

1. *Answers will vary. The felt satisfaction from the previous consumption of the good or service diminishes over time, forcing the consumer to reindulge in the good or service to experience renewed satisfaction.*
2. *Answers will vary. When the satisfaction level of your current job declines, you begin looking for a new employment venue.*

Lesson 25—Test

Scripture Memory

Matthew 6:33—But seek ye first the kingdom of God, and His righteousness; and all these things shall be added unto you.

Content Questions

1. *Land, capital*
2. *A*
3. *Answers will vary but should contain the following idea. Land in its natural state is not as valuable as land with man-made improvements.*
4. *True*
5. *wealth*
6. *An entrepreneur is a risk-taker (hoping that the business will succeed) and must also try to accurately predict consumer wants and needs.*
7. *Its intended use determines whether a good is a capital or consumer good. Using your car to get to work makes it a capital good—it's being used to make money. Your car is a consumer good when you take your girlfriend on a date.*
8. *B*

9. **a.** *Answers will vary. If children had to wait to use the bouncer because it was filled to capacity, adding another bouncer would be a good idea. Bouncers are much less physical work than planting, tending, and harvesting red beets.*

   b. *Not likely. Other cash crops would need more space to produce sufficient quantities for the same profit level as the red beets.*

   c. *Grader's Note: The student response should show 400 square feet used for bouncers and 600 square feet for growing red beets.*

   d. *Answers will vary. You cannot assume those profit levels. The second bouncer could be underutilized if bouncer patronage does not double from this year. Lack of rainfall or red beet pests could reduce red beet yields. Some of this year's bouncer patrons might move out of the neighborhood. Parents might decide not to spend $10 per hour for their child to use the bouncer. This year's red beet customers may decide to spend their money on a different vegetable next year. Any number of factors could influence next year's profit levels.*

   e. Inflating the bouncers—*Capital-intensive. Bouncers need a constant source of air to keep them inflated. I could not initially inflate them and keep them inflated by blowing air out of my lungs into the bouncer, so I'll use an air pump.*

   Helping patrons into the bouncer—*Labor-intensive. I have to sit near the opening to supervise the children who are playing, so it doesn't make sense to use a machine to boost them into or assist them out of the bouncer.*

   Preparing the soil—*Capital-intensive. I could dig a 600-square-foot garden by hand, but a rototiller would make it so much easier.*

   Planting the red beet seed—*Labor-intensive or capital-intensive. I could plant the seeds by hand or use a broadcast spreader to distribute the seed over the entire area. My choice probably depends on whether I'm planting in straight rows or wide rows.*

10. *B*

11. *Harry should make hats using four hours of labor. His average cost per hat is $39.58 and his marginal cost to manufacture hats at that level is only $10.00.*

Input	Q	TFC	TVC	TC	AFC	AVC	AC	MC
1	3	250	60	*310*	*83.33*	*20.00*	*103.33*	*xxxxx*
2	7	250	140	*390*	*35.71*	*20.00*	*55.71*	*20.00*
3	10	250	200	*450*	*25.00*	*20.00*	*45.00*	*20.00*
4	12	250	240	*490*	*20.83*	*20.00*	*40.83*	*20.00*
5	13	250	260	*510*	*19.23*	*20.00*	*39.23*	*20.00*

12. *Transfer*

13. *Answers will vary but should contain the following thoughts. Productivity helps a nation maintain or improve its standard of living and be competitive in the global economy.*

14. *Answers will vary. An assembly line uses all three techniques. Production of the various parts and assembly of the finished product are broken down into less-complex steps (division of labor). Technology such as computers and machines makes the process easier. Specialization occurs when workers doing repetitive tasks become proficient at their jobs or become highly skilled at utilizing machinery to maximize production.*

15. *Answers will vary. Grader's Note: Student responses for absolute advantage should be something they can always do better than their siblings (play the piano, catch a touchdown pass, mow the grass, etc.). Their responses for comparative advantage should be something they are good at but not better at than a brother or sister (playing a specific sport, cleaning their room, etc.).*

16. *Answers will vary. The U.S. computer manufacturer may not wish to support companies based in communist China. U.S. computer users may have an easier time understanding technical support personnel with a British accent rather than the Asian accents of Chinese technical support personnel.*

17. *True*

18. *Answers will vary. Productivity cannot totally compensate for cheap foreign labor, excessive government regulations, or unfair trade practices such as protective tariffs or government subsidies to domestic manufacturing.*

19. *A*

20. *government*

21. *Answers will vary. He produces agricultural products. He consumes seed, feed, and fuel to produce his products.*

22. *Answers will vary but should contain the following thoughts. Taxes remove economic decision-making power from households and businesses and give it to the taxing authority. Taxes give households and businesses less money to spend.*

23. *Answers will vary. Their salaries and benefits are dependent on tax revenue. When government revenue declines, public sector employees at the state and local levels face layoffs or elimination of their jobs.*

24. *satisfaction*

25. *Answers will vary. Marginal utility is the satisfaction derived from consuming more of a good or service. Businesses in an economy built upon consumption will want to maximize consumption in order to maximize their profits. They will use advertising and other gimmicks such as "buy one, get one free" to get consumers to buy things "on the margin" to achieve this goal.*

26. *Answers will vary. You could tell someone how many pieces of pizza you ate or how much you paid for the entire pizza. This quantifies the psychological satisfaction you experience from eating pizza.*

Lesson 26

Award up to 100 points for completion of the finished paper.

Paper's Structure: (1-20 points)

- *Did the student use complete sentences?*
- *Did the student use correct punctuation and grammar?*
- *Is the student's paper organized (paragraphs, logical and historical progression of thoughts)?*

Paper's Creativity: (1-20 points)

- *Did the student attempt to improve their writing skills as a result of this project?*
- *Did they work on varying sentence structure and demonstrate increased use of vocabulary?*

Paper's Content: (1-60 points)

- *Did the student utilize the vast majority of the information from the interview?*
- *Did the student accurately present the history of the business based on the information from the interview and the written transcript of the interview?*

Lesson 27A

1. *A business firm is an organization that arranges the factors of production to produce a good or service.*
2. *Business firms exist to meet consumer wants and needs.*
3. *An individual (sole) proprietorship is the easiest business to start.*
4. *Unlimited liability and limited resources for growing the business are disadvantages of the sole proprietorship.*
5. *All of the doctors in the partnership are liable for the actions of the other partners. A medical malpractice lawsuit against one of the doctors could name all of the doctors as defendants.*
6. *The corporate shield insulates investors from corporate actions.*
7. *The general corporation is taxed twice: the corporation is taxed on its business earnings and its shareholders must report corporate dividends on their personal income tax returns. The S corporation avoids this disadvantage because the shareholder can report all business profits (or losses) on a personal income tax return.*
8. *A cooperative is a business organization owned and controlled equally by the people who use its services or by the people who work there.*
9. *The LLC has fewer IRS regulations.*

Lesson 27B

1. *Gross National Product includes U.S. firms operating in foreign countries. Gross Domestic Product excludes U.S. firms operating in foreign countries but includes foreign firms manufacturing in the United States.*
2. *GDP in constant dollars is adjusted for inflation. This enables economists to more accurately evaluate economic growth over time.*
3. *Unemployment and inflation measurements also help to evaluate the nation's economic health.*

Lesson 27C

1. *They are in business to make a profit.*
2. *The business is successfully meeting consumer wants and needs.*
3. *The three methods of measuring profits are: Method #1: percentage of sales (gross sales minus operating expenses), Method #2: percentage of invested capital (profit divided by capital invested), Method #3: percentage of ownership equity (profit minus interest payments on borrowed money divided by capital invested).*
4. *Answers will vary. The student's response should reflect the concept that subjective profit exists in the mind and therefore is not measurable in terms of dollars and cents. A business owner might plant flowers to beautify her downtown retail establishment. The flowers don't qualify as a deductible business expense, but they do make her feel better about the business in her mind.*
5. *Losses tell entrepreneurs that they need to change what they're doing because they are not currently meeting consumers' wants and needs.*
6. *A true capitalist must disagree with the government's action in this situation. Penn Central's financial difficulties boiled down to operating expenses that exceeded revenue. To become profitable, Penn Central needed to attract more business, reduce costs, or some combination of both. In this case, government intervention prevented free-market forces from eliminating several losing business ventures. Conrail's competitors didn't appreciate this U.S. government policy that deprived them of future business once Penn Central went out of business. We'll never know if the temporary economic ramifications of Penn Central's bankruptcy would have been more damaging to the U.S. economy than the bailout precedent has been for U.S. taxpayers.*
7. *Answers will vary. Yes, from a denotative reading of the text but not a connotative understanding of the reasoning behind the policy. If businesses could indiscriminately develop our national parks, they would pursue construction until they oversaturated the market. The failed businesses would pull out, leaving deteriorating buildings behind to destroy the beauty of the natural environment.*

   Answers will vary. Probably not—in fact, the trade agreement might have the opposite effect. Fear of lawsuits brought by U.S. companies might deter diversification of service providers in our national parks.

Lesson 27—Practical Application Activity: An Unprofitable Restaurant

1. *Answers will vary but may include the following. The building is very small for a restaurant—it doesn't have a lot of seating, the parking lot is very small and hard to access for westbound drivers, the building isn't very attractive, it's too far away for employees at the county administration building to walk there for lunch, too many additional restaurants in the immediate vicinity.*
2. *Answers will vary. With few non-restaurant businesses in the immediate vicinity open after 5 p.m., people don't have additional reasons to come into downtown. If they're going to eat out, they would probably prefer doing so near the mall or stores that are open.*
3. *Answers will vary: easier access for eastbound and westbound traffic, a larger parking lot, the video rental store, consumer tastes.*
4. *We cannot know for sure. More people passing through the downtown area means more potential customers, but with eight other restaurants vying for business within a four-block area, the unprofitable location faces an uphill battle.*
5. *Answers will vary: exorbitant rent; undependable appliances requiring frequent maintenance; owner not willing to remodel the interior; owner not wanting the property to succeed because he reports it as a loss on his income tax return to offset profits from other ventures.*
6. *income, expenses*

Lesson 28A

1. *See Figure 28:1.*
2. *Both are a period of decline in a nation's economy. Depressions last longer, with more severe consequences.*
3. *Fiscal policy refers to the government's taxing and spending policies.*
4. *Answers will vary but should contain the following thought. No, because consumers and businesses might decide to save the money rather than spend it.*
5. *The Federal Reserve is the central banking system of the United States.*
6. *Answers should include the following information: a seven-member Board of Governors, a 12-member Federal Open Market Committee made up of the Board of Governors and five presidents of the Federal Reserve Banks, and 12 districts serviced by 12 Federal Reserve Banks.*
7. *The Fed regulates the economy primarily through open market operations (buying and selling U.S. government securities).*
8. *The reserve ratio decreases, giving banks more money to lend.*
9. *Answers will vary. Yes, because at some point in time the debt must be repaid in order to maintain confidence in the U.S. economy and the U.S. government's ability to pay its creditors. Out-of-control government spending puts the United States in a precarious position, exponentially increasing the yearly size of the deficits and the overall U.S. public debt. According to the website http://www.brillig.com/debt_clock/, the U.S. debt as of mid-September2012 was $16,030,916,638,735.00—over $51,000.00 for every person in the United States.*

Lesson 28B

1. *Government leaders meddle with the economy to maintain economic growth, minimize the impact of recessions or depressions, control inflation, "fix" economic problems, help political leaders get re-elected, etc.*
2. *Excess demand without increased supply causes shortages. Prices will rise to force some consumers out of the market.*
3. *Answers will vary but should contain the following idea. Businesses, unable to absorb rising production costs, must pass these costs on to consumers by charging more for their product or service.*
4. *Every business providing a good or service needs fuel for production or distribution.*

Lesson 28C

1. *Answers will vary. The Constitution does not require Congress to balance the budget. Most state and local governments are required by law to balance their budgets.*
2. *Answers will vary but should contain the following thought. No, because without a balanced federal budget, Congress lacks the willpower to use the additional revenue to pay down the national debt. Uncontrolled spending, not insufficient revenue, is our primary problem.*
3. *Answers will vary based on the student's worldview and beliefs about the role of the federal government in the lives of its citizens. A Christian deplores actions of our government that are contrary to God's Word. Any individual or organization that lobbies the federal government to promote unbiblical activities (abortion, homosexuals demanding extra-constitutional privileges, or artists seeking government funding for offensive artwork, to name just a few) is a problem for those who believe in God and the principles upon which our nation was founded. Of course, we enjoy the same lobbying rights to defend a biblical view of marriage and the family. We cannot deny others their First Amendment rights to free speech and to "petition the government for a redress of grievances." This question illustrates the difficulties of maintaining a democratic government in a society with widely differing moral and philosophical beliefs. Without God's Word as the absolute standard of right and*

wrong, today's lobbyists can convince our government to pursue policies that will ultimately result in God's judgment on our nation. Stopping all lobbying would not solve the problem. Those with a vested interest in congressional legislation would find other legal or illegal means to influence Congress.

4. *Answers will vary based on the student's worldview. Those with a biblical worldview recognize that one of the characteristics of the end times will be worldwide economic difficulties. Others with marketable skills for our high-tech workforce may not worry about finding employment after high school and college. Some may express concern about paying for college, marriage and raising a family in these uncertain times. Christian students should express optimism based on their confidence in the eternal God who provides for His children.*

Lesson 28—Practical Application Activity: Health Care Reform

Award up to 50 points for preparation for and participation in the discussion related to the proposed health care benefits system.

Preparation for the Discussion: (1-20 points)

- *Did the student read the assigned proposal?*
- *Did the student mark the statements with which they agree or disagree? Did the student write down reasons they agree or disagree with various parts of the proposal?*

Participation in the Discussion: (1-30 points)

- *Did the student share their thoughts and opinions in a respectful manner?*
- *Did the student give valid reasons in support of or against the parts of the proposal?*

Lesson 29—Quiz

Scripture Memory

Psalm 37:25—I have been young, and now am old; yet have I not seen the righteous forsaken, nor his seed begging bread.

Content Questions

1. *False*
2. *shareholder's*
3. *False*
4. *An individual (sole) proprietorship is the easiest to start.*
5. *The corporation has an unlimited time span of existence.*
6. *False*
7. *Domestic*
8. *The business firm is meeting consumer wants and needs.*
9. *B*
10. *Answers will vary but may include protective tariffs, subsidies, government purchases, or government grants.*
11. *Answers will vary but should include the following concepts. Losses in a free-market economy are a signal that the business is failing to meet consumer wants and needs at prices consumers are willing to pay. Government bailouts prevent market mechanisms from eliminating unprofitable businesses.*
12. *The student's graph should show expansion, peak, recession, trough and a trend line.*
13. *Fiscal policy refers to the government's taxing and spending policies. For example, a tax decrease gives consumers more money to spend to stimulate the economy. The government can also use monetary policy to impact the economy through manipulation of interest rates and controlling the amount of money in circulation. For example, if the government wants to slow the rate of inflation, it can raise interest rates. Higher interest rates will discourage some consumers from borrowing money until the rates decrease. Decreased demand due to higher interest rates helps to control inflation.*
14. *The Federal Reserve can manipulate the economy through open market operations (buying and selling U.S. government securities), the discount rate (interest rate charged to other banks by the Federal Reserve banks), and the reserve requirement (amount of cash banks must have available to meet the withdrawal needs of their depositors).*
15. *hyperinflation*
16. *Answers will vary. It helps their re-election chances. It convinces citizens they are serious about solving the nation's economic problems.*

Lesson 30A

Definitions provided are from http://www.investorwords.com.

1. *a nation that is economically self-sufficient*
2. *a tax or fee on imports to or exports from a country*
3. *to ship a product out of a country or region*
4. *to have a product shipped into a country or region*
5. *an allotment or limited amount*
6. *financial aid given by the government to individuals or groups*
7. *a tax on imports*
8. *a negative balance of trade where imports exceed exports*
9. *a positive balance of trade where exports exceed imports*

Lesson 30B

1. *Trade is "the act or process of buying, selling, or exchanging commodities, at either wholesale or retail, within a country or between countries.*

2. *Domestic trade occurs* ***within*** *a country, and foreign trade occurs* ***between*** *countries.*
3. *Answers will vary. In a technical sense, totally free trade between nations does not exist. If a nation charges customs duties on just one imported item, then the trade is not truly "free." The term* ***free trade*** *is best understood in a comparative sense. Next to import quotas, export subsidies, and protective tariffs, trade with minimal customs duties seems like free trade.*
4. *Answers will vary. Probably Mexico. With a population of 112.5 million people and per capita income of $14,200, Mexico lags behind its more prosperous neighbors to the north. Jobs provided by NAFTA could mean a significant decline in poverty rates and an elevated standard of living for many Mexicans.*
5. *Answers will vary. The author sides with Mr. Greenspan on this issue. He wouldn't trust foreign nations facing their own economic difficulties to put U.S. interests above their own. Cash-strapped nations holding U.S. debt could demand immediate payment, putting the U.S. and other nations' economies in jeopardy.*
6. *Answers will vary but may contain the following thoughts. Protective tariff advocates fail to consider retaliatory policies that will hurt U.S. exports. Legislators who enact protective tariffs cannot predict how other nations will respond to the increased tariff rates. Tariffs designed to assist U.S. steelmakers might hurt foreign sales of U.S. automobiles. Without perfect knowledge of global markets, governments cannot design protective tariffs that would help but not hinder all domestic businesses.*

Lesson 30C

1. *They trade to obtain desired goods, services, or resources.*
2. *Answers will vary. The War of 1812 came about partly because of British attempts to halt American commerce with France. Before Hitler invaded the Soviet Union in World War II, Stalin and the Soviets supplied the Nazis with food, fuel, and other resources, which the Germans lost after the start of Operation Barbarossa.*
3. *Nations that specialize in producing certain items can concentrate on their specialty and trade for other items their people want or need.*
4. *Wars, depletion of domestic sources of natural resources needed for manufacturing, or crop failures (if the specialization is an agricultural product) may disrupt or destroy the specialty item needed to maintain trade with other nations.*
5. *Answers will vary. Although the idea of not needing to depend on other nations sounds like a great idea, it's not practical in the modern world. Nations without large supplies of fossil fuels must trade to obtain needed fuel resources. An economic self-sufficient mentality stifles potential markets in other nations. A shoe manufacturer in a nation that practices autarky, for instance, can only sell so many shoes to its own people. With adequate manufacturing capability, it could export shoes to billions of potential customers in other countries.*

Lesson 31A

1. *Answers will vary. Not likely without wholesale changes in public perceptions. Americans view Congress as the farmer putting pig feed into the trough. We grunt, snort, and shoulder our way in to get what we perceive to be our fair share of the slop. Congress, however, has nothing in and of itself to give. It must take from some in order to redistribute to others. If Americans once again buy into this thought—"that government governs best which governs least"—then maybe we can salvage our financial future.*
2. *Answers will vary but may contain the following thought. Our first president believed that money is a powerful motivator. Men will sacrifice their principles in pursuit of wealth.*
3. *Answers will vary. For instance, the student could state she doesn't know how to handle money wisely. The proposed solution could be to develop a budget and have the student's parents hold her accountable for sticking to the new budget. Another student might state that he struggles with laziness, and he wants to take on more chore responsibilities around the house. Grader's Note: Give full credit for two economic character flaws and a reasonable solution for each flaw.*
4. *Answers will vary. Possible answers may include the National Aeronautics and Space Administration (NASA), spending for education, medical research, funding for the arts, employees of Health and Human Services, or agricultural subsidies.*
5. *Answers will vary but may contain the following thoughts. We could raise the state minimum coverage amounts to a level high enough to cover 99.9 percent of all accidents. Those caught driving without insurance and who are involved in an at-fault accident should go to debtor's prison until they pay up.*
6. *It's almost impossible because a free-market economy is built around the principle of "charging what the market will bear." If a star player asks for $40 million per year and a team owner wants to pay that amount for the player's services, then the athlete will be paid that amount in a free-market economy. Absurd salaries are the result of misplaced priorities. We value entertainment more than those who protect us, teach our children, or grow our food. The only way to put a stop to these exorbitant salaries is for consumers to collectively stop financing these entertainment venues or for employers to negotiate contracts that tie compensation to performance. If a star baseball player gets injured, his salary could be reduced to the league's minimum salary for 2011 ($414,000) until he returns to the active roster. Every professional athlete's contract could have 20 percent of the negotiated amount held in escrow and given back if the team fails to win the championship. Otherwise, I don't*

see how we can rein in their compensation without resorting to socialist measures such as salary caps.

8. *Collective bargaining is a socialist technique that destroys individual initiative to work harder than those in the same classification. Why should a union member excel above their peers if they cannot profit from their motivation?*
9. *Answers will vary but may contain the following thoughts. Although voluntary retirement or retirement due to physical decline is not specifically mentioned in Scripture, the principle of the ant in Proverbs 6 provides some insight into this concept. The ant works hard to provide food for the winter months. Those anticipating retirement should plan for and lay aside resources to sustain them during their retirement years in order not to be a burden to others.*
10. *Answers will vary. The store owner gets to fulfill his biblical responsibility to help those in need. Christ said that when we provide for our destitute brothers and sisters in Christ we are actually serving Him. The aid recipients get to gratefully acknowledge God's provision for their need and thank the one who helped them in their time of difficulty. They repay their creditor as quickly as possible in order to fulfill their biblical responsibility to "pay thy vows." This kind of charity is better than government welfare because it doesn't foster a spirit of dependency (long-term reliance on charity) or an attitude of "others owe me something because of my circumstances."*
11. *Answers will vary but should contain the following thought. Government financing actually drives up the cost of a college education by creating demand that otherwise wouldn't exist. In addition to the monies actually spent on grants or scholarships, tax revenues are needed to fund the jobs necessary to administer the educational aid program.*
12. *Answers will vary. Paul's happiness didn't depend on the number of his material possessions or on his physical comfort. He had learned to trust God to meet his needs. When his needs weren't met, he still had faith to believe that God would help him through the difficult circumstances.*
13. *Answers will vary but may contain the following thoughts. Food and clothing were the two essentials for survival in the mild Middle Eastern climate. Material possessions cannot make us happy. The Greek word translated "content" is* arkeō (är-ke'-ō). *It means to be possessed of unfailing strength or to be satisfied. As long as our needs are met, we can be satisfied. The problem many Christians have is distinguishing between wants and needs. Food, clothing, and shelter would probably be a correct interpretation of this verse for modern-day Americans.*

Lesson 33—Test

Scripture Memory

Psalm 37:25—I have been young, and now am old; yet have I not seen the righteous forsaken, nor his seed begging bread.

Content Questions

1. *False*
2. *individual proprietorship*
3. *unlimited*
4. *True*
5. *B*
6. *Answers will vary but should contain the following thoughts. General corporations pay business taxes and shareholders pay taxes on dividends received from the corporation. "S" corporations allow business income or losses to be reported on the shareholder's personal income tax return. In other words, "S" corporations avoid double taxation.*
7. *Its members—the people who use its services or work there own the co-op.*
8. *Corporations have the greatest financial resources for expansion.*
9. *The Limited Liability Company (LLC) has fewer IRS regulations.*
10. *GNP includes U.S. firms operating in foreign countries. GDP excludes U.S. firms operating in foreign countries but includes foreign firms manufacturing in the United States.*
11. *It is in business to make a profit.*
12. *True*
13. *C*
14. *Answers will vary. The free market works best without any government interference in the economy. Providing government subsidies or tax advantages to prop up profits favors some businesses over others. It also makes the business less responsive to market forces that would otherwise impact the business. Government interference to prevent business losses lets government dictate company policies in exchange for the bailout. Government should provide a good climate for business without subsidizing profits or preventing losses.*
15. *peak, recession*
16. *C*
17. *True*
18. *The Fed's principal means to regulate the economy is through open market operations (buying and selling U.S. government securities).*
19. *discount*
20. *The reserve ratio increases, meaning banks have less money to lend, thereby tightening the money supply.*
21. *True*
22. *Answers will vary. The two examples given in the text were the United States during the American Revolution and post-World War I Germany. In both cases, the government printed huge amounts of money to pay its obligations, causing hyperinflation and worthless currency.*
23. *growth, inflation, inequalities*
24. *True*
25. *They trade to obtain desired goods, services, or resources.*

26. *D*
27. *False*
28. *import*
29. **a.** *$1.20*

    b. *With your 40 percent discount, you would pay $1,200 dollars (1,000 x $1.20 = $1,200)*

    c. *$1,350.00*

    d. *15 cents per pack (150.00/1,000 = .15)*

    e. *675 packs ($1,350.00/$2.00 = 675)*

    f. *$650 ($2,000.00 - $1,350.00 = $650.00)*

    g. *$1,350.00 (the cost of the product plus shipping)*

    h. *$1,330.00 ($1,350.00 - $20.00 in sales = $1,330.00)*

    i. *$1,030.00 (200 packs x $1.50 = $300 + the $20.00 in previous sales makes $320.00 in total sales; $1,350.00 - $320.00 = $1,030.00*

    j. *Answers will vary. If Tom will let you, you could ship back the remaining product at your expense. You could ask Tom to grant you more time to pay the invoice, but he will probably charge you interest on the unpaid balance (typically 1 to 1½ percent per month on the unpaid balance). You could take $1,030 from your savings and pay Tom the remaining outstanding balance.*

    k. *Only if you could do so within the 30 days. If Tom charges you interest on the unpaid invoice balance, you would lose money selling the gum at $1.35 per pack.*

    l. *A good thing. You would make $650.00 profit in 30 days.*

    m. *Answers will vary. If Tom is willing to extend you credit and you're still making a profit after paying the additional interest on the outstanding invoice balance, then it's probably a good thing. If you lose money because of having to sell the product at a lower cost and/or paying additional interest on the "past due" amount of the invoice, it's a bad thing.*

    n. *Answers will vary. You could take $975.00 from your savings and pay back Tom. If you don't have $975.00 in savings, you could borrow the money to pay back Tom. If no one will loan you $975.00, you must default on the payment. It is at this point that trade deficits become a problem (when the debtor cannot repay the creditor).*
30. *Answers will vary. Government-subsidized exports allow businesses to sell at or below their costs on the world market. This gives them an unfair advantage when competing with businesses that don't receive subsidies from their governments.*
31. *E*
32. *domestic*
33. *Answers will vary. It might be cheaper to obtain the item through trade. The nation could also choose to specialize in certain items and acquire other desired goods via trade.*
34. *Answers will vary but should contain the following thought. War might disrupt the nation's trade, preventing or hindering the exportation and importation of goods. Due to the Union blockade of southern ports, the Confederacy had difficulty exporting its cotton to Great Britain during the Civil War. Japan had difficulty importing raw materials for its war industries during the latter years of World War II.*
35. *debt, character, government*

Final Exam—Part I

Scripture Memory

Proverbs 14:34—Righteousness exalteth a nation, but sin is a reproach to any people.

Psalm 33:12—Blessed is the nation whose God is the LORD; and the people whom He hath chosen for His own inheritance.

Content Questions

1. *Answers will vary but should contain the following thoughts. God as the Creator owns everything. He made mankind and endowed us with creative abilities, a rational mind, the ability to make choices, and gave us dominion (control) over His creation. We will stand before Him someday and give an account of our stewardship.*
2. *B*
3. *macroeconomics*
4. *It must be man-made and have value.*
5. *True*
6. *C*
7. *False*
8. *Answers will vary. This phrase meaning "all else being equal" helps us understand the motives behind people's economic choices.*
9. **a.** *B*

    b. *E*

    c. *A*

    d. *F*

    e. *C*

    f. *D*
10. *False*
11. *D*
12. *Traditional*
13. *Answers will vary. Free-market economies experience periodic recessions and depressions. They promote greed. The interactions of suppliers and consumers sometimes lead to shortages or surpluses.*
14. *They produce only what they need when they need it.*
15. *voluntary*
16. *True*
17. *Supply, demand*
18. *They remove the profit motivation. Why should I work hard to get ahead if I cannot profit from my efforts?*

19. **a.** *land*
    b. *progressive*
    d. *property*
    e. *national*
    g. *national* and *production*
    i. *rural* and *urban*
    j. *factory*
20. *C*
21. *Limited resources; make choices*
22. *opportunity cost*
23.

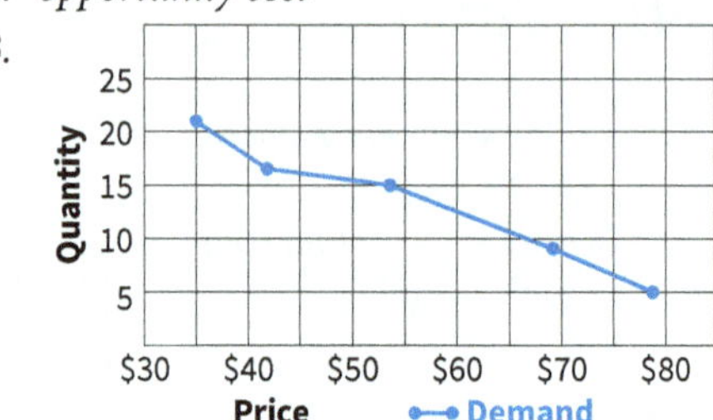

24.

25.

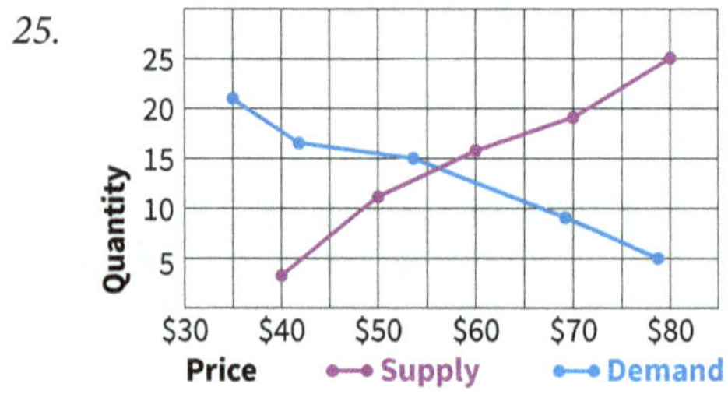

26. *Fifteen units would sell at approximately $55.*
27. *True*
28.

Price	Quantity	Elasticity Measurement
$100	1	xxxxxx
$75	4	*16*
$50	8	*3*
$25	12	*1*

29. *Answers will vary. Consumers pay lower prices for goods. Competition results in higher quality and a greater variety of goods.*
30. *Salad bar prices would increase, reflecting the shortage of lettuce.*
31. *Answers will vary. No. You could try cabbage as the main ingredient in a salad, but it wouldn't be the same.*
32. *Answers will vary but could include salad dressings, tomatoes, carrots, cucumbers, onions, or any other food item that people put in their salads.*

Final Exam—Part II

Scripture Memory

Matthew 6:33—But seek ye first the kingdom of God, and His righteousness; and all these things shall be added unto you.

Psalm 37:25—I have been young, and now am old; yet have I not seen the righteous forsaken, nor his seed begging bread.

Content Questions

1. *False*
2. *physical, mental*
3. *wealth*
4. *Answers will vary but should contain the following thoughts. He tries to predict consumer wants and needs, then minimize his production costs to supply the good or service at a price consumers are willing to pay.*
5. *True*
6. *Answers will vary but should contain the following thought. Cost schedules help them determine the optimum level of production with a specific factor of production.*
7. *The firm should produce at input level 25 with the average cost of each product 5.02.*

Input	Q	TFC	TVC	TC	AFC	AVC	AC	MC
10	100	500	200	700	5.00	2.00	7.00	****
15	130	500	300	800	3.85	2.31	6.16	3.33
20	165	500	400	900	3.03	2.42	5.45	2.86
25	199	500	500	1,000	2.51	2.51	5.02	2.94
30	203	500	600	1,100	2.46	2.96	5.42	25.00

8. *Transfer earnings are what a factor of production must earn in its present use in order not to transfer it to another use. Economic rent is earnings over and above transfer earnings.*
9. *Answers will vary but should reflect the student's understanding of transfer earnings. If the student is not satisfied with the 1 percent interest rate, they will express a desire to find a more lucrative investment.*
10. *D*
11. *Answers will vary. Absolute advantage refers to a provider of goods and services that is more efficient than all its competitors. Comparative advantage is when the provider of the good or service is more efficient than one other competitor. If the business can hire employees with absolute or comparative advantage, its productivity will increase.*
12. *government, consumer*
13. *Answers will vary. Households provide labor and in some cases, goods (for instance, farm produce or handcrafted quilts) for businesses.*

14. *satisfaction*
15. *F*
16. All of its members are responsible for the actions of the other members. *B*

    This type has limited legal liability. *C*

    When one member leaves or dies, the business is dissolved. *B*

    This is the easiest and simplest type of business to start. *A*

    Certain types of this business pay double taxes. *C*

    This type has unlimited legal liability. *A*

    This type has access to a greater amount of capital than the two other types. *C*
17. *B*
18. *The entrepreneur failed to meet consumer wants and needs.*
19. *sales, equity*
20. *It leads to the most efficient utilization of capital resources.*
21. *Answers will vary depending upon the student's belief about the role of government in the economy. If the student believes in a biblical and constitutional role of government, then government's involvement in the economy will be minimal, mainly to prevent wrongdoing (protecting consumers from unsafe products, preventing illegal trading on the stock market, preserving a business climate that fosters competition, etc.).*
22. *Answers will vary but should include the following thoughts. Government bailouts of failing businesses prop up businesses that are not meeting consumer wants and needs. Bailouts encourage corporate leaders to make unwise business decisions knowing that the government will cover for them.*
23. *The student's diagram should show a period of expansion culminating at the peak, followed by a decline (a recession) that bottoms out at a point known as the trough, at which time the process begins all over again.*
24. *fiscal*
25. *Deflation will occur as a result of less money in circulation in the economy.*
26. *It is contracting the economy.*
27. *Answers will vary but may include that the government interferes to help politicians get re-elected, to "fix" economic problems, and to maintain economic growth.*
28. *A trade subsidy is government financial aid to domestic producers that helps them compete in the global marketplace. Trade quotas are allotments or limits on a country's imports.*
29. *No. Every nation needs to trade to acquire resources or manufactured goods it cannot produce domestically.*
30. *Answers will vary. Nations might restrict trade to keep out harmful products or protect themselves from "dumping" by other nations.*
31. *B*

Photo Credits

Unless otherwise noted, the following photos are used and released under the Creative Commons License: Front cover & title page—bank teller copyright istockphoto.com contributor Juanmonino, p.2—bison courtesy flickr.com user usfwsmtnprairie, p.4—courtesy flickr.com user dandeluca, p.9—car factory copyright Rainer Plendl, p.13—old truck courtesy flickr.com user imlsdcc, p.15—firehouse courtesy Jennifer Mansfield-Jones, p.18—open bible courtesy David Ball, p.27—Chicago skyline courtesy Daniel Schwen, p.32—Morgan body structures courtesy flickr.com user exfordy, p.33—horse and plow courtesy flickr.com user exfordy, p.36—factory courtesy Mikko J. Putkonen, p.38—shopping mall courtesy commons.wikimedia.org user Jarcje, p.52—beach sunset courtesy Tony Hisgett, p.53—greenhouse courtesy commons.wikimedia.org user Zuzu, p.53—forklift courtesy Ildar Sagdejev, p.55—house in snow courtesy flickr.com user roger4336, p.56—interstate highway courtesy Allan Ferguson, p.79—kids on a seesaw courtesy flickr.com user jimjarmo, p.82—washer/drier courtesy commons.wikimedia.org user BrokenSphere, p.84—bread courtesy flickr.com user katiebordner, p.85—Safeco field courtesy commons.wikimedia.org user Cacophony, p.87—supermarket isle copyright Vasiliy Danillin, p.96—robot welder courtesy commons.wikimedia.org user Robotworx, p.104—courtesy flickr.com user nicadlr, p.113—woman using computer courtesy Brian Kerrigan, p.121—garment manufacturing courtesy flickr.com user kheelcenter, p.150—wooden barrel courtesy pixabay.com user Hans, p.154—comic shop courtesy flickr.com user roughgroove, p.159—courtesy flickr.com user petrick, p.161—car factory courtesy flickr.com user that_chrysler_guy, p.172—White House courtesy Matt H. Wade, p.222—Colonial courtesy Thomas Kelley, p.222—bungalow courtesy commons.wikimedia.org user W.Marsh, p.222—American Craftsman courtesy Allan Ferguson, p.222—American Foursquare courtesy Jeffrey Beall.

All other photographs are original works or are in the public domain.

www.ingramcontent.com/pod-product-compliance
Lightning Source LLC
LaVergne TN
LVHW082019270125
802301LV00005B/536
9781610061056